THE NEW

Taste *of* Home

Bakeshop Classics

TASTE OF HOME BOOKS • RDA ENTHUSIAST BRANDS, LLC • MILWAUKEE, WI

© 2024 RDA Enthusiast Brands, LLC.
1610 N. 2nd St., Suite 102,
Milwaukee WI 53212-3906

Visit us at **tasteofhome.com** for other Taste of
Home books and products.

International Standard Book Numbers
HC: 979-8-88977-014-5
PB: 979-8-88977-024-4

Content Director: Mark Hagen
Creative Director: Raeann Thompson
Senior Editor: Christine Rukavena
Senior Art Director: Courtney Lovetere
Assistant Art Director: Jazmin Delgado
Deputy Editor, Copy Desk: Ann Walter
Copy Editor: Elizabeth Pollock Bruch
Contributing Copy Editor: Pam Grandy

Cover Photography:
Photographer: Dan Roberts
Set Stylist: Melissa Franco
Food Stylist: Sue Draheim

Pictured on front cover:
Yellow Cupcakes, p. 253; Pretty Petits Fours, p. 63;
Contest-Winning White Chocolate Cheesecake,
p. 140; Chocolate Eclairs, p. 117

Pictured on back cover:
Fresh Cherry Pie, p. 93; Pistachio Meringue
Sandwich Cookies, p. 40; Chocolate Babka, p. 164;
Surprise Cake, p. 265, Chocolate Coffee, p. 233;
Peanut Caramel Brownie Bites, p. 28

Printed in China

1 3 5 7 9 10 8 6 4 2

Contents

MASTER THE CLASSICS.
MAKE SWEET-SHOP MAGIC!

Create the classic bakeshop repertoire at home! Whether you're a beginning baker or an ace, you'll find step-by-step instructions, helpful how-to's and creative ideas for adding your own unique touch to these 200+ favorite recipes for fruit tarts, French macarons, custard eclairs, cinnamon rolls and more.

This cookbook offers a delightful array of on-trend treats you can easily make in your own kitchen. From adorable cake pops and a piñata-inspired surprise cake to homemade Irish cream and decadent Frappuccino sippers, you will love bringing these Instagram-worthy delights to the table.

So grab an apron and get ready to make your own bakeshop classics right at home. Here's how to get started.

CREATE YOUR INGREDIENT PANTRY

Keep staples on hand and you'll be ready to bake when the fancy strikes. Here are the building blocks for cookies, breads, cakes and more.

ESSENTIALS

- Baking powder
- Baking soda
- Chocolate (bars, chips, mini chips)
- Cinnamon
- Cocoa powder
- Cornstarch
- Extracts (almond, vanilla)
- Flour
- Oil (canola or vegetable)
- Old-fashioned oats
- Salt
- Sugar (brown, confectioners', granulated)
- Yeast

EXTRAS

- Applesauce
- Cake mix
- Canned pumpkin
- Decorative sugars and sprinkles
- Honey
- Marshmallows
- Maple syrup
- Molasses
- Nuts
- Orange extract
- Peanut butter
- Pie filling
- Raisins, other dried fruits
- Shortening
- Shredded coconut
- Specialty flours (cake, gluten-free, whole wheat, rye)
- Spices

Here's how to maximize your ingredients' shelf life:

INGREDIENT	SHELF LIFE	IDEAL STORAGE
Baking powder	1 year	Original sealed container
Baking soda	3 years	Airtight container
Chocolate	2 years	Original sealed bag; after opening, in an airtight container
Cocoa powder	3 years	Airtight container away from light and heat
Cornstarch	Forever	Original container in a cool, dark place away from moisture
Extracts	Forever	Dark bottle in a cool, dark place
Flour	2 years	Airtight container (refrigerate whole wheat flour)
Oats	2 years	Original cardboard container up to 1 year; airtight container if longer
Oil	2 years	Dark, cool spot in the pantry
Salt	Forever	Cool, dark, dry place where temperatures remain consistent
Shortening	2 years	Pantry; fridge in warmer climates
Spices	4 years	Airtight jars in a cool, dark place
Sugar (brown or confectioners')	2 years after opening	Airtight container
Sugar (granulated)	Forever	Airtight container in a cool, dark place
Yeast	2 years	Cool, dark, dry place

BUILD YOUR BAKEWARE COLLECTION

Choose bakeware based on what you want to make most frequently. A 13x9-in. pan, a loaf pan, and a muffin tin make a good starter collection.

IF YOU DON'T HAVE THIS ...	USE THIS INSTEAD
One 9x5-in. loaf pan	Three 5¾x3-in. mini loaf pans or one 9-in. round
One 8x4-in. loaf pan	Two 5¾x3x2-in. mini loaf pans or one 8-in. round
One 9-in. round baking pan	One 8-in. square baking pan
Two 9-in. round baking pans	One 13x9-in. baking pan
One 10-in. fluted tube pan	One 10-in. tube pan or two 9x5-in. loaf pans
One 11x7-in. baking pan	10-in. cast-iron skillet
One 13x9-in. baking pan	Two 9-in. round baking pans, two 8-in. square baking pans or one 12-in. skillet
24 muffin cups	48 mini muffin cups or 12 jumbo muffin cups
8-oz. ramekins	Stoneware bowls or coffee cups
Oven-safe Dutch oven	Large baking pan and a cookie sheet as a lid

When using a glass baking dish instead of a pan, reduce the baking temperature by 25°.

When using disposable foil pans, reduce the baking temperature by 25°, decrease baking time if necessary, and bake with a cookie sheet under the pans for added support.

For shallower pans, reduce baking time by about 25%. For deeper pans, increase baking time by about 25%.

Be careful not to overfill. Here are some guidelines.

Unless the recipe instructs otherwise:

- Fill deep pans (tube pans) half full.
- Fill round, square and rectangular cake pans half to two-thirds full.
- Fill loaf pans and muffin tins two-thirds full.
- Fill souffle dishes and steamed pudding molds to within 1 in. of the rim.
- Fill jelly-roll pans at least half full or to within ¼ in. of the rim.

FRENCH MACARONS,
PAGE 19

Cookies, Brownies & Bars

Reach for the ultimate in handheld snacking and easy sharing. Grandma's cookie jar has nothing on these.

HOMEMADE MOON PIES

My husband loved moon pies when he was a child, and he definitely loves this grown-up version. You can add jam or dulce de leche to the cookie sandwich before adding the marshmallow creme if desired.
—*Shawn Barto, Palmetto, FL*

- -

Prep: 1 hour + chilling
Bake: 10 min./batch + cooling
Makes: about 3½ dozen

- 1 cup butter, softened
- ¾ cup packed brown sugar
- 1 large egg, room temperature
- 3 Tbsp. honey
- 1 Tbsp. molasses
- 1 tsp. vanilla extract
- 1½ cups all-purpose flour
- 1½ cups whole wheat flour
- 1 tsp. baking soda
- 1 tsp. ground cinnamon
- ½ tsp. salt
- 1 jar (7½ oz.) plus ½ cup marshmallow creme
- 3 pkg. (10 oz. each) dark chocolate candy coating, such as Ghirardelli

1. In a large bowl, cream butter and brown sugar until light and fluffy, 5-7 minutes. Beat in egg, honey, molasses and vanilla. In another bowl, whisk flours, baking soda, cinnamon and salt; gradually beat into creamed mixture.
2. Divide the dough in half. Shape each into a disk; wrap. Refrigerate until firm enough to roll, about 1 hour.
3. Preheat oven to 350°. On a lightly floured surface, roll each portion of dough to ⅛-in. thickness. Cut with a floured 2-in. round cookie cutter. Place 2 in. apart on parchment-lined baking sheets.
4. Bake until just set, 9-11 minutes. Cool on pans 2 minutes. Remove to wire racks to cool completely.
5. Spread 1 Tbsp. marshmallow fluff on bottoms of half the cookies; cover with remaining cookies. Freeze until filling is set, about 1 hour. In a microwave, melt chocolate candy coating; stir until smooth.
6. Dip each cookie into coating; allow excess to drip off. Place on parchment-lined baking sheets and refrigerate until set.

1 SANDWICH COOKIE: 217 cal., 11g fat (7g sat. fat), 15mg chol., 105mg sod., 28g carb. (19g sugars, 1g fiber), 2g pro.

THICK SUGAR COOKIES

Thicker than the norm, this sugar cookie is like one you might find at a good bakery. My children often request these treats for their birthdays and are always happy to help decorate.
—*Heather Biedler, Martinsburg, WV*

- -

Prep: 25 min. + chilling
Bake: 10 min./batch + cooling
Makes: about 3 dozen

- 1 cup butter, softened
- 1 cup sugar
- 2 large eggs, room temperature
- 3 large egg yolks, room temperature
- 1½ tsp. vanilla extract
- ¾ tsp. almond extract
- 3½ cups all-purpose flour
- 1½ tsp. baking powder
- ¼ tsp. salt

FROSTING
- 4 cups confectioners' sugar
- ½ cup butter, softened
- ½ cup shortening
- 1 tsp. vanilla extract
- ½ tsp. almond extract
- 2 to 3 Tbsp. 2% milk
  Assorted colored sprinkles, optional

1. In a large bowl, cream butter and sugar until light and fluffy, 5-7 minutes. Beat in eggs, egg yolks and extracts. In another bowl, whisk flour, baking powder and salt; gradually beat into creamed mixture. Shape into a disk; wrap and refrigerate 1 hour or until firm enough to roll.
2. Preheat oven to 375°. On a lightly floured surface, roll dough to ½-in. thickness. Cut with a floured 2-in. cookie cutter. Place cutouts 1 in. apart on ungreased baking sheets.
3. Bake until edges begin to brown, 10-12 minutes. Cool on pans for 5 minutes. Remove to wire racks to cool completely.
4. For frosting, in a large bowl, beat confectioners' sugar, butter, shortening, extracts and enough milk to reach desired consistency. Spread over the cookies. If desired, decorate with sprinkles.

1 FROSTED COOKIE : 219 cal., 11g fat (6g sat. fat), 49mg chol., 92mg sod., 28g carb. (18g sugars, 0 fiber), 2g pro.

LEMON ANISE BISCOTTI

With the growing popularity of gourmet coffees, cappuccino and espresso, I'm finding lots of people enjoy these classic Sicilian dipping cookies.
—*Carrie Sherrill, Forestville, WI*

Prep: 25 min. • **Bake:** 40 min. + cooling
Makes: 3 dozen

2 large eggs
1 cup sugar
¼ cup canola oil
½ tsp. lemon extract
¼ tsp. vanilla extract
2 cups all-purpose flour
1 tsp. baking powder
½ tsp. salt
4 tsp. grated lemon zest
2 tsp. aniseed, crushed

OPTIONAL GLAZE:
2 cups confectioners' sugar
3 to 4 Tbsp. lemon juice
Grated lemon zest

1. Preheat oven to 350°. In a small bowl, beat eggs and sugar until thickened, about 2 minutes. Add oil and extracts; mix well. Combine flour, baking powder and salt; beat into egg mixture. Beat in the lemon zest and aniseed.

2. Divide dough in half. On a lightly floured surface, shape each portion into a 12x2-in. rectangle. Transfer to a baking sheet lined with parchment. Flatten to ½-in. thickness.

3. Bake until golden and tops begin to crack, 30-35 minutes. Carefully remove to wire racks; cool for 5 minutes.

4. Transfer to a cutting board; cut with a serrated knife into scant ¾-in. slices. Place cut side down on ungreased baking sheets. Bake 5 minutes. Turn and bake until firm and golden brown, 5-7 minutes. Remove to wire racks to cool completely. If using glaze, whisk confectioners' sugar and lemon juice in a small bowl. Drizzle over biscotti; sprinkle with lemon zest. Store in an airtight container.

1 COOKIE: 65 cal., 2g fat (0 sat. fat), 10mg chol., 50mg sod., 11g carb. (6g sugars, 0 fiber), 1g pro.

LEMON BISCOTTI TIPS

• **Can you use lemon extract instead of grated lemon zest?** If you're out of fresh lemons, you may use lemon extract instead. Our rule of thumb is to substitute ½ tsp. of lemon extract for every 1 tsp. of lemon zest. Or you could substitute an equal amount of lime zest.

• **How do you serve lemon biscotti?** Lemon biscotti are the perfect thing to serve with a cup of coffee or tea.

• **How should you store lemon biscotti?** You can store cooled lemon biscotti in an airtight container for up to 2 weeks, but you'll probably polish them off before then!

OATMEAL S'MORE COOKIES

I can't count how many times I have made these cookies—they are our favorites. I love to bake all kinds of goodies with my two daughters, and my husband loves to sample the treats.
—*Carmen Rae, New Haven, IN*

Prep: 20 min. + chilling
Bake: 10 min./batch + cooling
Makes: about 5½ dozen

- ½ cup butter, softened
- ½ cup shortening
- 1 cup packed brown sugar
- ½ cup sugar
- 2 large eggs, room temperature
- 1½ tsp. vanilla extract
- 3 cups all-purpose flour
- 1 tsp. baking soda
- ¼ tsp. salt
- 1½ cups old-fashioned oats
- 1 cup semisweet chocolate chips
- 1 cup miniature marshmallows

1. In a large bowl, cream the butter, shortening and sugars until light and fluffy, 5-7 minutes. Add eggs, 1 at a time, beating well after each addition. Beat in vanilla. Combine the flour, baking soda and salt; gradually add to creamed mixture and mix well. Stir in the oats, chocolate chips and marshmallows; refrigerate until dough is chilled, about 30 minutes.

2. Roll tablespoons of dough into balls; place 2 in. apart onto greased baking sheets. Bake at 350° for 8-10 minutes or until golden brown. Cool cookies for 1-2 minutes before removing from pans to wire racks to cool completely.

1 COOKIE: 89 cal., 4g fat (2g sat. fat), 9mg chol., 43mg sod., 13g carb. (7g sugars, 0 fiber), 1g pro.

WHITE CHOCOLATE RASPBERRY THUMBPRINTS

When I pass around the cookie tray, all eyes land on these fancy thumbprints. The white chocolate filling and dab of jewel-toned jam will satisfy the most discriminating sweet tooth.
—*Agnes Ward, Stratford, ON*

Prep: 25 min. + chilling
Bake: 10 min./batch + cooling
Makes: about 3 dozen

- ¾ cup butter, softened
- ½ cup packed brown sugar
- 2 large eggs, separated, room temperature, divided use
- 1¼ cups all-purpose flour
- ¼ cup baking cocoa
- 1¼ cups finely chopped pecans or walnuts

FILLING
- 4 oz. white baking chocolate, coarsely chopped
- 2 Tbsp. butter
- ¼ cup seedless raspberry jam

1. In a large bowl, cream butter and brown sugar until light and fluffy, 5-7 minutes. Beat in the egg yolks. Combine flour and cocoa; gradually add to creamed mixture and mix well. Cover and refrigerate for 1-2 hours or until easy to handle.

2. In a shallow bowl, whisk egg whites until foamy. Place nuts in another shallow bowl. Shape dough into 1-in. balls. Dip into egg whites, then roll in nuts.

3. Using a wooden spoon handle, make an indentation in center of each cookie. Place 1 in. apart on greased baking sheets. Bake cookies at 350° until set, 8-10 minutes. Remove to wire racks to cool completely.

4. In a microwave, melt white chocolate and butter; stir until smooth. Spoon about ½ tsp. into each cookie. Top each with about ¼ tsp. jam. Store in an airtight container.

1 COOKIE: 120 cal., 8g fat (4g sat. fat), 22mg chol., 43mg sod., 11g carb. (7g sugars, 1g fiber), 2g pro.

CHOCOLATE-CHERRY SANDWICH COOKIES

I make these often at Christmastime, but they're great for summer parties, too. Chilling the cookies before you dip them in chocolate is important because it firms up the filling.
—*Amy Sauerwalt, Columbia, MD*

Prep: 35 min. + chilling
Makes: 3½ dozen

- 4   oz. cream cheese, softened
- ½   cup confectioners' sugar
- ½   cup finely chopped maraschino cherries, drained
- ¼   tsp. almond extract
- 1   pkg. (12 oz.) vanilla wafers
- 18 oz. milk chocolate candy coating, melted
      Red and white sprinkles or colored sugar

1. In a small bowl, beat cream cheese and confectioners' sugar until smooth; stir in cherries and extract. Spread 1 tsp. cream cheese mixture on bottoms of each of half of the wafers; cover with remaining wafers. Refrigerate 1 hour or until filling is firm.
2. Dip sandwiches in candy coating; allow excess to drip off. Place on waxed paper; top with sprinkles or colored sugar. Let stand until set. Store in an airtight container in the refrigerator.
1 SANDWICH COOKIE: 105 cal., 5g fat (3g sat. fat), 4mg chol., 39mg sod., 14g carb. (11g sugars, 0 fiber), 1g pro.

BUTTERSCOTCH BLONDIES

Toffee and chocolate dot the golden brown batter of these delightful brownies. I do a lot of cooking for the police officers I work with, and they always line up for these treats.
—*Jennifer Ann Sopko, Battle Creek, MI*

Prep: 15 min. • **Bake:** 20 min.
Makes: 2 dozen

- 2   cups all-purpose flour
- 2   cups packed brown sugar
- 2   tsp. baking powder
- ¼   tsp. salt
- ½   cup butter, melted and cooled
- 2   large eggs, room temperature
- 1   tsp. vanilla extract
- 1   cup semisweet chocolate chunks
- 4   Heath candy bars (1.4 oz. each), coarsely chopped

1. In a large bowl, combine the flour, brown sugar, baking powder and salt. In another bowl, beat the butter, eggs and vanilla until smooth. Stir into dry ingredients just until combined (batter will be thick).
2. Spread into a 13x9-in. baking pan coated with cooking spray. Sprinkle with chocolate chunks and chopped candy bars; press gently into batter.
3. Bake at 350° until a toothpick inserted in the center comes out clean, 20-25 minutes. Cool on a wire rack. Cut into bars.
1 PIECE: 218 cal., 9g fat (5g sat. fat), 29mg chol., 126mg sod., 35g carb. (26g sugars, 1g fiber), 2g pro.

BUTTERSCOTCH BLONDIES TIPS

- **How can you make butterscotch brownies your own?** You can make this brownie recipe your own by throwing in your favorite mix-ins. Try a handful of butterscotch chips or nuts (we highly recommend walnuts).

- **How else can you grease the pan to make butterscotch blondies?** If you don't have cooking spray on hand, use a few teaspoons of softened butter or shortening.

- **How do you store butterscotch blondies?** Butterscotch blondies will last 3 to 4 days at room temperature when stored in an airtight container. You can also store them, tightly wrapped, in the freezer for up to 2 months.

ENGLISH TEA CAKES

These unique cookies are baked in muffin cups, giving them a perfectly round shape. I sometimes omit the nuts on top and decorate them for holidays instead.
—*Beverly Christian, Fort Worth, TX*

- -

Prep: 15 min. • **Bake:** 10 min./batch
Makes: 5 dozen

    2   cups butter, softened
    1   cup sugar
    2   tsp. vanilla extract
    4   cups all-purpose flour
   60   walnut or pecan halves, toasted

1. In a large bowl, cream butter and sugar until light and fluffy, 5-7 minutes. Beat in the vanilla extract. Gradually add flour and mix well. Drop by heaping tablespoonfuls into greased miniature muffin cups; flatten slightly. Press a walnut half into the center of each.
2. Bake at 350° for 10-12 minutes or until edges are lightly browned. Cool for 2 minutes before removing from pans to wire racks.
1 TEA CAKE: 108 cal., 7g fat (4g sat. fat), 16mg chol., 49mg sod., 10g carb. (3g sugars, 0 fiber), 1g pro.

LEMON-LIME BARS

I baked these bars for a luncheon, and a gentleman made his way to the kitchen to compliment the cook who made them.
—*Holly Wilkins, Lake Elmore, VT*

- -

Prep: 20 min. • **Bake:** 20 min. + cooling
Makes: 4 dozen

    1   cup butter, softened
   ½   cup confectioners' sugar
    2   tsp. grated lime zest
   1¾   cups all-purpose flour
   ¼   tsp. salt
FILLING
    4   large eggs, room temperature
   1½   cups sugar
   ¼   cup all-purpose flour
   ½   tsp. baking powder
   ⅓   cup lemon juice
    2   tsp. grated lemon zest
          Confectioners' sugar

1. Preheat oven to 350°. In a large bowl, cream butter and confectioners' sugar until light and fluffy. Beat in lime zest. Combine flour and salt; gradually add to creamed mixture and mix well.
2. Press into a greased 13x9-in. baking dish. Bake just until edges are lightly browned, 13-15 minutes.
3. Meanwhile, in another large bowl, beat eggs and sugar. Combine flour and baking powder. Gradually add to egg mixture. Stir in lemon juice and zest; beat until frothy. Pour over the hot crust.
4. Bake 20-25 minutes or until light golden brown. Cool completely on a wire rack. Dust with confectioners' sugar. Cut into squares. Store in the refrigerator.
1 BAR: 88 cal., 4g fat (2g sat. fat), 28mg chol., 60mg sod., 12g carb. (7g sugars, 0 fiber), 1g pro.

SOFTENED BUTTER, STAT

To soften butter super quick, partially unwrap the stick (use the wrapped half as a handle to keep your hand clean) and shred it using the largest holes of your box grater. The butter will reduce to a fluffy heap and soften faster. Shredded butter is ready to use in your recipe right away.

WATCH
JOSH MAKE
CHRISTMAS
ONES
Just hover your
camera here.

FRENCH MACARONS

Even decorated simply—a sprinkle of sugar, a drizzle of icing—these stylish beauties are part of our creative Christmas cookies collection. They will be the showstoppers on any cookie tray.
—*Josh Rink, Milwaukee, WI*

- -

Prep: 1 hour + standing
Bake: 15 min./batch + cooling
Makes: 30 macarons

MACARON SHELLS
1⅓ cups almond flour
2¼ cups confectioners' sugar, divided
4 large egg whites,
    room temperature
⅛ tsp. salt
2 Tbsp. superfine sugar

BUTTERCREAM FILLING
¼ cup unsalted butter, softened
1 cup confectioners' sugar
2 Tbsp. heavy whipping cream
½ tsp. vanilla extract
⅛ tsp. salt

1. Place the almond flour and 1¾ cups confectioners' sugar in a food processor; pulse until thoroughly mixed to ensure almond flour is very fine. Pass almond flour mixture through a fine-mesh sieve; discard any large pieces that remain.
2. Place the egg whites and salt in a very clean bowl of a stand mixer fitted with a whisk attachment; whisk on medium-low speed until frothy. Slowly add superfine sugar; whisk until dissolved, 1-2 minutes. Slowly add remaining ½ cup confectioners' sugar; increase speed to high and whip until meringue is glossy and stiff peaks form, 1-2 minutes.
3. Gently fold the almond flour mixture into meringue, a third at a time. Using the side of a spatula, smooth batter up side of bowl several times to remove air bubbles and ensure there are no lumps; do not overmix. Run spatula down the center of the bowl; the line in the batter should remain visible for a moment before mixture runs back into itself.
4. Position rack in upper third of oven; preheat oven to 300°. Transfer batter into a pastry bag fitted with a #7 or #10 round tip. Pipe 1⅜-in. rounds onto a parchment-lined tray about 1 in. apart. Tap tray against counter 2-3 times to remove excess air bubbles. Let the macarons stand until no longer wet or sticky to the touch, 30-60 minutes. Bake, 1 tray at a time, until cookies rise about ⅛ in. to form feet, 14-16 minutes, rotating tray halfway through baking. Remove tray and let macarons cool completely; repeat with remaining trays. Once macarons have cooled completely, remove from parchment.
5. To make filling, cream butter in a stand mixer fitted with whisk attachment; slowly add confectioners' sugar until incorporated. Add heavy cream, vanilla and salt; mix until smooth. Pour frosting into a pastry bag fitted with a small round tip; pipe buttercream onto the bottoms of half the macarons. Top with remaining macaron shells. Refrigerate, covered, until ready to serve.

1 MACARON: 101 cal., 4g fat (1g sat. fat), 5mg chol., 26mg sod., 16g carb. (14g sugars, 0 fiber), 2g pro.

STRAWBERRY VARIATION: For macaron shells: Add pink gel food coloring (do not use liquid food coloring) to whipped meringue until desired color is reached. For filling: Add 1 Tbsp. strawberry powder to confectioners' sugar. If desired, add 2-3 drops strawberry flavoring to frosting. Pipe a circle of frosting onto bottoms of half the macaron shells. Place ¼ tsp. strawberry jam in center of each frosting circle. Top with remaining macaron shells.

CHOCOLATE VARIATION: For macaron shells: Add 2 Tbsp. dark cocoa powder to almond flour and confectioners' sugar before sifting.

FLOURLESS PEANUT BUTTER COOKIES

When my mother (who's now a great-grandmother) gave me this recipe for no-flour peanut butter cookies about 15 years ago, I was skeptical, because it calls for only three ingredients (and no flour?!). But since then I've never had a failure, and I make them all the time!
—Maggie Schimmel, Wauwatosa, WI

Prep: 15 min. • **Bake:** 15 min.
Makes: 2 dozen

1 large egg, room temperature, beaten
1 cup sugar
1 cup creamy peanut butter

1. Preheat oven to 350°. In a large bowl, mix all ingredients. Roll level tablespoons of dough into balls. Place on an ungreased baking sheet; flatten with a fork.
2. Bake until crisp, 12-15 minutes. Remove to a wire rack to cool.

1 COOKIE: 99 cal., 6g fat (1g sat. fat), 8mg chol., 48mg sod., 11g carb. (10g sugars, 1g fiber), 3g pro.

READER REVIEW

"I made it a four-ingredient recipe by throwing in a handful of chocolate chips. Yum!"
—RAY218, TASTEOFHOME.COM

CRANBERRY RUGELACH

These traditional Polish treats will keep for a long time in an airtight container. One year, I sent a batch to my sister, but the box got lost. She received it 12 days later and reported that the cookies were worth the wait!
—Jean Doxon, Omaha, NE

Prep: 25 min. + chilling
Bake: 20 min./batch
Makes: about 5 dozen

1 cup butter, softened
1 pkg. (8 oz.) cream cheese, softened
½ cup sugar
2¾ cups all-purpose flour
1 tsp. salt

FILLING

¾ cup sugar
⅔ cup dried cranberries, finely chopped
½ cup finely chopped walnuts, toasted
⅓ cup butter, melted
2 tsp. ground cinnamon
1 tsp. ground allspice
1 large egg, lightly beaten
Additional sugar

1. In a large bowl, cream the softened butter, cream cheese and sugar until light and fluffy, 5-7 minutes. Combine flour and salt; gradually add to the creamed mixture and mix well.
2. Turn onto a lightly floured surface; knead for 3 minutes or until smooth. Divide into 8 portions. Roll each portion into a ball; flatten into a 4-in. circle. Wrap and refrigerate at least 1 hour.
3. In a small bowl, combine the sugar, cranberries, walnuts, melted butter, cinnamon and allspice. On a lightly floured surface, roll 1 portion of dough into an 8-in. circle. Sprinkle with 3 Tbsp. of filling to within ½ in. of edges. Cut into 8 wedges.
4. Roll up wedges from the wide end and place point side down 2 in. apart on foil-lined baking sheets. Curve ends to form a crescent shape. Brush with egg; sprinkle with additional sugar.
5. Repeat with remaining dough and filling. Bake at 350° for 18-20 minutes or until golden brown. Remove to wire racks to cool.

1 COOKIE: 103 cal., 6g fat (3g sat. fat), 17mg chol., 80mg sod., 12g carb. (8g sugars, 0 fiber), 1g pro.

PECAN LOGS

Folks always expect to find these tender nutty logs on the cookie gift trays I give at Christmas. Not too sweet, they're just right with a steaming cup of coffee or tea.
—*Joyce Beck, Gadsden, AL*

Prep: 15 min. + chilling
Bake: 15 min./batch
Makes: 2½ dozen

1   cup butter, softened
5   Tbsp. confectioners' sugar
2   tsp. vanilla extract
2   cups all-purpose flour
1   cup finely chopped pecans
    Confectioners' sugar

1. In a small bowl, cream butter and sugar until light and fluffy, 5-7 minutes. Beat in vanilla. Add the flour, beating on low speed just until combined. Stir in pecans. Cover and refrigerate for 30 minutes or until easy to handle.
2. Shape ½ cups into ½-in.-thick logs. Cut logs into 2-in. pieces. Place 2 in. apart on greased baking sheets. Bake at 350° for 15-18 minutes or until lightly browned. Roll warm cookies in confectioners' sugar; cool on wire racks.

1 COOKIE: 117 cal., 9g fat (4g sat. fat), 16mg chol., 62mg sod., 8g carb. (1g sugars, 1g fiber), 1g pro.

Short & Sweet

MEMORABLE BISCOTTI

The enticing aroma of anise filled the kitchen and wafted through the house as Mom baked these crisp cookies when I was a girl. She always kept a big glass jar filled so we had a supply of these traditional cookies on hand.
—*Cookie Curci, San Jose, CA*

Prep: 20 min. • **Bake:** 55 min. + cooling
Makes: 2½ dozen

1   cup butter, softened
1   cup sugar
3   large eggs, room temperature
1   tsp. vanilla extract
1   tsp. anise extract
3   cups all-purpose flour
1   Tbsp. baking powder
½   tsp. salt
1   cup chopped almonds

1. Preheat oven to 300°. In a large bowl, cream butter and sugar until light and fluffy, 5-7 minutes. Add eggs, 1 at a time, beating well after each addition. Beat in extracts. Combine the flour, baking powder and salt; gradually add to creamed mixture and mix well. Stir in almonds.
2. Line a baking sheet with foil and grease the foil. Divide dough in half. On the foil, form each portion into an 11x3-in. rectangle.
3. Bake for 35 minutes or until lightly browned. Carefully remove to wire racks; cool for 15 minutes. Increase heat to 325°.
4. Transfer rectangles to a cutting board; cut diagonally with a serrated knife into ¾-in. slices. Place cut side down on ungreased baking sheets.
5. Bake for 10 minutes. Turn and bake 10 minutes longer or until firm. Remove to wire racks to cool completely. Store in an airtight container.

1 COOKIE: 159 cal., 9g fat (4g sat. fat), 35mg chol., 144mg sod., 17g carb. (7g sugars, 1g fiber), 3g pro.

READER REVIEW
"Great biscotti. I added 1 Tbsp. of aniseed and toasted the almonds. They are so good with coffee."
—DOZER77, TASTEOFHOME.COM

TENDER ITALIAN SUGAR COOKIES

These traditional cookies are moist and tender. To tie into the colors of the Italian flag, you could tint the icing red, green and white.
—Weda Mosellie, Phillipsburg, NJ

Prep: 20 min.
Bake: 10 min./batch + cooling
Makes: 3 dozen

- ¾ cup shortening
- ¾ cup sugar
- 3 large eggs
- 1 tsp. vanilla extract
- 3 cups all-purpose flour
- 3 tsp. baking powder
- ⅛ tsp. salt

ICING
- ¼ cup milk
- 2 Tbsp. butter, melted
- ½ tsp. vanilla extract
- 2½ cups confectioners' sugar
  Food coloring and coarse sugar, optional

1. Preheat oven to 400°. In a large bowl, cream shortening and sugar until light and fluffy, 5-7 minutes. Beat in eggs and vanilla. Combine flour, baking powder and salt; gradually add to creamed mixture and mix well.
2. Shape dough into 1½-in. balls. Place 1 in. apart on ungreased baking sheets. Bake 8-10 minutes or until lightly browned. Remove to wire racks to cool completely.
3. For icing, in a small bowl, combine milk, butter, vanilla and confectioners' sugar until smooth. Tint with food coloring if desired. Dip tops of cookies in icing; allow excess to drip off. Sprinkle with coarse sugar if desired. Place cookies on waxed paper; let stand until set.
1 COOKIE: 136 cal., 5g fat (2g sat. fat), 20mg chol., 54mg sod., 21g carb. (12g sugars, 0 fiber), 2g pro.

KEY LIME BLONDIE BARS

Here's my tropical take on a beloved treat. These key lime bars combine the taste of the classic pie with a blondie batter and cream cheese frosting. You can make a thicker crust if desired.
—Kristin LaBoon, Austin, TX

Prep: 35 min. + chilling
Bake: 25 min. + cooling
Makes: 16 servings

- 1⅓ cups graham cracker crumbs, divided
- ⅓ cup plus 2 Tbsp. melted butter, divided
- 3 Tbsp. plus ¼ cup packed brown sugar, divided
- ⅔ cup butter, softened
- 1 cup plus 1 Tbsp. sugar, divided
- 2 large eggs, room temperature
- 1 large egg white, room temperature
- 3 Tbsp. Key lime juice
- 4½ tsp. grated Key lime zest
- 1 cup all-purpose flour
- ½ tsp. plus ⅛ tsp. salt, divided
- 1 tsp. vanilla extract
- ⅛ tsp. ground cinnamon

FROSTING
- ¼ cup butter, softened
- ¼ cup cream cheese, softened
- 4 cups confectioners' sugar
- 2 Tbsp. 2% milk
- 1 tsp. vanilla extract
  Key lime slices, optional

1. Preheat oven to 350°. Line a 9-in. square baking pan with parchment, letting ends extend up sides. Combine 1 cup cracker crumbs, ⅓ cup melted butter and 3 Tbsp. brown sugar; press onto bottom of prepared pan. Bake 10 minutes. Cool on a wire rack.
2. For blondie layer, in a large bowl, cream softened butter and 1 cup sugar until light and fluffy, 5-7 minutes. Beat in eggs, egg white, and lime juice and zest. In a small bowl, mix flour and ½ tsp. salt; gradually add to creamed mixture, mixing well.
3. Spread over crust. Bake until a toothpick inserted in center comes out clean, 25-30 minutes (do not overbake). Cool completely in pan on a wire rack.
4. For streusel, combine the remaining ⅓ cup cracker crumbs, 2 Tbsp. melted butter, ¼ cup brown sugar, 1 Tbsp. sugar and ⅛ tsp. salt, along with the vanilla and cinnamon, until crumbly. Reserve ½ cup for topping.
5. In a large bowl, combine the 5 frosting ingredients; beat until smooth. Stir in ½ cup streusel. Spread over bars. Sprinkle with the reserved topping. Refrigerate at least 4 hours before cutting. Lifting with the parchment, remove from pan. Cut into bars. Store in an airtight container in the refrigerator. If desired, garnish with sliced Key limes.
1 BLONDIE: 422 cal., 19g fat (11g sat. fat), 69mg chol., 283mg sod., 62g carb. (51g sugars, 1g fiber), 3g pro.

KEY LIME
BLONDIE BARS

WHITE CHOCOLATE CRANBERRY COOKIES

These sweet cookies feature white chocolate and cranberries for a delightful taste. And the red and white coloring add a festive holiday feel to any cookie tray.
—Donna Beck, Scottdale, PA

Prep: 20 min. • **Bake:** 10 min./batch
Makes: 3 dozen

- ⅓ cup butter, softened
- ½ cup packed brown sugar
- ⅓ cup sugar
- 1 large egg, room temperature
- 1 tsp. vanilla extract
- 1½ cups all-purpose flour
- ½ tsp. salt
- ½ tsp. baking soda
- ¾ cup dried cranberries
- ½ cup white baking chips

1. In a large bowl, beat butter and sugars until crumbly, about 2 minutes. Beat in egg and vanilla. Combine the flour, salt and baking soda; gradually add to butter mixture and mix well. Stir in cranberries and chips.
2. Drop by tablespoonfuls 2 in. apart onto baking sheets coated with cooking spray. Bake at 375° until lightly browned, 8-10 minutes. Cool for 1 minute before removing to wire racks.

1 COOKIE: 78 cal., 3g fat (2g sat. fat), 10mg chol., 69mg sod., 13g carb. (9g sugars, 0 fiber), 1g pro.

SPUMONI SLICES

My sweet rectangles get their name from the old-fashioned tricolored ice cream. Our whole family loves them.
—Mary Chupp, Chattanooga, TN

Prep: 40 min. + chilling
Bake: 5 min./batch + cooling
Makes: about 7 dozen

- 1 cup butter, softened
- 1½ cups confectioners' sugar
- 1 large egg, room temperature
- 1 tsp. vanilla extract
- 2½ cups all-purpose flour
- 2 oz. semisweet chocolate, melted
- ½ cup chopped pecans
- 3 to 5 drops green food coloring
- ¼ cup finely chopped candied red cherries
- ½ tsp. almond extract
- 3 to 5 drops red food coloring

1. In a large bowl, cream butter and sugar until light and fluffy, 5-7 minutes. Beat in egg and vanilla. Gradually add flour and mix well. Divide dough into 3 portions. Stir chocolate into 1 portion. Add pecans and green food coloring to the second portion. Add the cherries, almond extract and red food coloring to the third.
2. Roll each portion between 2 pieces of waxed paper into an 8x6-in. rectangle. Remove waxed paper. Place chocolate rectangle on a piece of plastic wrap. Top with the green and pink rectangles; press together lightly. Wrap with plastic and chill overnight.
3. Preheat oven to 375°. Cut chilled dough in half lengthwise. Return 1 rectangle to the refrigerator. Cut remaining rectangle into ⅛-in. slices. Place 1 in. apart on ungreased baking sheets.
4. Bake until set, 5-7 minutes. Cool 2 minutes before removing to wire racks to cool completely. Repeat with remaining dough.

1 COOKIE: 52 cal., 3g fat (2g sat. fat), 8mg chol., 19mg sod., 6g carb. (3g sugars, 0 fiber), 1g pro.

PICK THE BEST BUTTER

Unsalted, or sweet, butter is ideal in recipes that highlight a rich, buttery flavor, such as shortbread cookies and buttercream frosting. In these preparations, unwanted salt could detract from the buttery taste desired.

PEANUT CARAMEL BROWNIE BITES

With their three irresistible layers, these brownies are my family's absolute favorite.
—*Ella Agans, Birch Tree, MO*

- -

Prep: 1 hour + chilling
Bake: 20 min. + cooling
Makes: 4 dozen

- ¾ cup butter, cubed and softened
- ⅔ cup sugar
- 2 Tbsp. water
- 1 cup semisweet chocolate chips
- 2 large eggs, room temperature
- 1 tsp. vanilla extract
- 1 cup all-purpose flour
- ½ tsp. baking powder

CANDY BAR TOPPING

- 1 cup sugar
- ¼ cup butter, cubed
- ¼ cup 2% milk
- 1 cup marshmallow creme
- ½ cup creamy peanut butter, divided
- ½ tsp. vanilla extract
- 2½ cups dry roasted peanuts, divided
- 40 caramels
- 2 Tbsp. water
- 1¼ cups semisweet chocolate chips

1. Preheat oven to 350°. Line a 13x9-in. baking pan with foil, letting ends extend up sides; coat foil with cooking spray.

2. Microwave butter, sugar and water on high just until mixture comes to a boil, 3-4 minutes; stir until blended. Stir in chocolate chips until melted. Whisk in eggs, 1 at a time, stirring well after each addition. Whisk in vanilla. Stir in flour and baking powder.

3. Spread into prepared pan. Bake until a toothpick inserted in center comes out clean, 18-20 minutes. Cool 30 minutes.

4. For topping, combine sugar, butter and milk in a large saucepan; bring to a boil, stirring constantly, over medium heat. Boil 5 minutes, stirring frequently. Stir in the marshmallow creme, ¼ cup peanut butter and vanilla; pour over brownies. Sprinkle with 2 cups peanuts.

5. In a small saucepan, combine caramels and water; cook, stirring, over medium-high heat until blended. Pour over peanuts.

6. Microwave chocolate chips on high until softened, about 1 minute. Stir in remaining peanut butter until smooth; pour over caramel layer. Chop remaining peanuts; sprinkle on top. Refrigerate at least 1 hour.

7. Lifting with foil, remove brownies from pan. Cut into bites. Store in an airtight container in the refrigerator.

1 BAR: 212 cal., 12g fat (5g sat. fat), 19mg chol., 135mg sod., 24g carb. (19g sugars, 1g fiber), 4g pro.

EASY LIFT
Lining a pan with parchment or foil makes the treats easy to remove and cut after baking. After cooling as directed, simply lift brownies or bars out of the pan and cut. This helps preserve your pan's finish too.

MACAROON BARS

Guests will never recognize the refrigerated crescent roll dough that goes into these almond-flavored bars. You can assemble these chewy coconut treats in no time.
—*Carolyn Kyzer, Alexander, AR*

Prep: 10 min. • **Bake:** 30 min. + cooling
Makes: 3 dozen

- 3¼ cups sweetened shredded coconut, divided
- 1 can (14 oz.) sweetened condensed milk
- 1 tsp. almond extract
- 1 tube (8 oz.) refrigerated crescent rolls

1. Preheat oven to 350°. Grease a 13x9-in. baking pan; line pan with nonstick foil, allowing foil to hang over edges of pan. Grease foil; sprinkle 1½ cups coconut into pan. Combine milk and extract; drizzle half over the coconut. Unroll crescent dough into 1 long rectangle; seal seams and perforations. Place in pan. Drizzle with remaining milk mixture; sprinkle with remaining coconut.
2. Bake bars until golden brown, 30-35 minutes. Cool completely on a wire rack before cutting. Store in the refrigerator.
1 BAR: 103 cal., 5g fat (4g sat. fat), 4mg chol., 85mg sod., 12g carb. (9g sugars, 0 fiber), 2g pro.

Short & Sweet

ANISE SUGAR COOKIES

As much as I love sharing my baked goods, sometimes I want to keep these cookies just for me. The light anise flavor and melt-in-your-mouth texture make them a perfect Christmas treat.
—*P. Marchesi, Rocky Point, NY*

Prep: 40 min. • **Bake:** 10 min./batch
Makes: 5 dozen

- 1 cup butter, softened
- 1½ cups sugar
- 2 large eggs, room temperature
- ¼ to ½ tsp. anise extract
- 3 cups all-purpose flour
- 1 to 1½ tsp. aniseed
- 1 tsp. salt
- 1 tsp. baking powder
- 1 tsp. baking soda
- Optional: Frosting of choice and sprinkles

1. Preheat oven to 375°. In a large bowl, cream butter and sugar until light and fluffy, 5-7 minutes. Beat in eggs and extract. Combine the flour, aniseed, salt, baking powder and baking soda; gradually add to creamed mixture and mix well.
2. Shape into 1-in. balls; place on greased baking sheets. Dip the bottom of glass in sugar; use to flatten cookies. Bake for 8-10 minutes or until set. Cool on wire racks. If desired, decorate cookies with frosting and sprinkles.
1 COOKIE: 72 cal., 3g fat (2g sat. fat), 14mg chol., 95mg sod., 10g carb. (5g sugars, 0 fiber), 1g pro.

ANISE SUGAR COOKIES TIPS

- **How do you store anise sugar cookies?** You can store these and other sugar cookies for up to a week in an airtight container at room temperature.

- **Can you make this dough ahead of time?** Yes. Cookie dough usually lasts for about 3 months in the freezer. Tightly wrap, label and freeze the dough. Thaw overnight in the refrigerator before slicing.

CARAMEL CHIP BISCOTTI

The combination of caramel and chocolate in these delicate Italian biscuits is to die for. It's divine dunked in coffee or a sweet wine, or even enjoyed on its own. Feel free to use any flavor chocolate chips.
—*Tami Kuehl, Loup City, NE*

Prep: 30 min. • **Bake:** 30 min. + cooling
Makes: 2 dozen

- ½ cup butter, softened
- 1 cup sugar
- 2 large eggs, room temperature
- 1 tsp. vanilla extract
- 2½ cups all-purpose flour
- 1½ tsp. baking powder
- ¼ tsp. salt
- 1 cup Kraft caramel bits
- 1 cup semisweet chocolate chips
- 3 oz. white candy coating, melted

1. Preheat oven to 325°. Cream the butter and sugar until light and fluffy, 5-7 minutes; beat in eggs and vanilla. In another bowl, whisk together flour, baking powder and salt; gradually beat into creamed mixture (dough will be stiff). Stir in caramel bits and chocolate chips.
2. Divide dough into 3 portions. On parchment-lined baking sheets, shape each portion into a 7x3-in. rectangle. Bake until a toothpick inserted in the center comes out clean, 20-25 minutes. Cool on pans on wire racks 5 minutes.
3. On a cutting board, use a serrated knife to cut each rectangle crosswise into 8 slices. Place slices on baking sheets, cut side down. Bake until crisp, 10-12 minutes per side. Remove from pans to wire racks; cool completely.
4. Drizzle melted candy coating over tops; let stand until set. Store between pieces of waxed paper in airtight containers.
1 COOKIE: 206 cal., 8g fat (5g sat. fat), 26mg chol., 115mg sod., 32g carb. (21g sugars, 1g fiber), 2g pro.

DIPPED CHERRY COOKIES

Our children and grandchildren declared this festive, flavorful cookie a keeper. We gave a batch to our mail carrier to thank her for trudging through so much snow, and she requested the recipe.
—*Ruth Anne Dale, Titusville, PA*

Prep: 30 min.
Bake: 10 min./batch + cooling
Makes: about 4 dozen

- 2½ cups all-purpose flour
- ¾ cup sugar, divided
- 1 cup cold butter, cubed
- ½ cup finely chopped maraschino cherries, patted dry
- 12 oz. white baking chocolate, finely chopped, divided
- ½ tsp. almond extract
- 2 tsp. shortening
     Coarse clear and red sugars

1. In a large bowl, combine flour and ½ cup sugar; cut in the butter until crumbly. Knead in cherries, ⅔ cup white chocolate and the extract until dough forms a ball.
2. Shape into ¾-in. balls. Place 2 in. apart on ungreased baking sheets. Flatten slightly with a glass dipped in remaining ¼ cup sugar. Bake at 325° for 10-12 minutes or until edges are lightly browned. Remove to wire racks to cool completely.
3. In a microwave, melt shortening and remaining white chocolate; stir until smooth.
4. Dip half of each cookie into chocolate; allow excess to drip off. Place on waxed paper; sprinkle with coarse sugar. Let stand until set. Store in an airtight container.
1 COOKIE: 108 cal., 6g fat (4g sat. fat), 11mg chol., 34mg sod., 12g carb. (7g sugars, 0g fiber), 1g pro.

READER REVIEW
"Delicious recipe! It takes a little bit of work to incorporate all of the flour, but they are worth it. Instead of dipping, I drizzled the white chocolate on top. They looked great and were a bit less sweet."
—BLTRITTIN, TASTEOFHOME.COM

Short & Sweet

CLASSIC LEMON BARS

These bars are simple enough for no-fuss dinners yet elegant enough for special celebrations. Regardless of when you serve them, I'm sure they'll be a hit at your home.
—Melissa Mosness, Loveland, CO

- -

Prep: 15 min. • **Bake:** 25 min. + cooling
Makes: 9 servings

- ½ cup butter, softened
- ¼ cup sugar
- 1 cup all-purpose flour

FILLING

- ¾ cup sugar
- 2 large eggs
- 3 Tbsp. lemon juice
- 2 Tbsp. all-purpose flour
- 1 tsp. grated lemon zest
- ¼ tsp. baking powder
  Confectioners' sugar

1. Preheat oven to 350°. In a small bowl, cream butter and sugar until light and fluffy, 5-7 minutes; gradually beat in flour until blended.
2. Press into an ungreased 8-in. square baking dish. Bake for 15-20 minutes or until edges are lightly browned.
3. For filling, in a small bowl, beat the sugar, eggs, lemon juice, flour, lemon zest and baking powder until frothy. Pour over crust.
4. Bake 10-15 minutes longer or until set and lightly browned. Cool completely on a wire rack. Sprinkle with confectioners' sugar. Cut into squares.
1 PIECE: 250 cal., 11g fat (7g sat. fat), 74mg chol., 99mg sod., 35g carb. (23g sugars, 0 fiber), 3g pro.

FUDGY BROWNIES WITH PEANUT BUTTER PUDDING FROSTING

Rich brownies are topped with a peanut butter pudding frosting to make this a recipe the whole family will love. These are perfect for a potluck, bake sale or yummy after-dinner treat.
—Amy Crook, Syracuse, UT

- -

Prep: 20 min. • **Bake:** 25 min. + chilling
Makes: 2½ dozen

- 1 pkg. fudge brownie mix (13x9-in. pan size)
- 1½ cups confectioners' sugar
- ½ cup butter, softened
- 2 to 3 Tbsp. peanut butter
- 2 Tbsp. cold 2% milk
- 4½ tsp. instant vanilla pudding mix
- 1 can (16 oz.) chocolate fudge frosting

1. Prepare and bake brownies according to package directions. Cool on a wire rack.
2. Meanwhile, in a small bowl, beat the confectioners' sugar, butter, peanut butter, milk and pudding mix until smooth. Spread over brownies. Refrigerate for 30 minutes or until firm. Frost with chocolate frosting just before cutting.
1 BROWNIE: 236 cal., 12g fat (4g sat. fat), 23mg chol., 145mg sod., 31g carb. (23g sugars, 1g fiber), 2g pro.

READER REVIEW
"Very easy to make. For boxed brownies and canned frosting, this was pretty tasty. The peanut butter filling was really good and creamy. I used chunky peanut butter. I would make this quick and easy 'take to a church function' dessert again."
—JOYFULME2, TASTEOFHOME.COM

PEANUT BUTTER BROWNIE CUPS

I used to make these brownie bites with a cherry in the center. Then I discovered that my granddaughter Lily is big on peanut butter, so I switched it up. Now she loves to help me make them.
—Donna McGinnis, Taylor Ridge, IL

Prep: 20 min. • **Bake:** 20 min. + cooling
Makes: 3½ dozen

- 1 pkg. fudge brownie mix (13x9-in. pan size)

FROSTING
- ½ cup creamy peanut butter
- 3 oz. cream cheese, softened
- 2 cups confectioners' sugar
- 4 tsp. 2% milk
- 1 tsp. vanilla extract
  Chopped salted peanuts, optional

1. Preheat oven to 350°. Line 42 mini-muffin cups with paper or foil liners.
2. Prepare brownie mix batter according to package directions. Fill prepared cups two-thirds full. Bake 18-22 minutes or until a toothpick inserted in center comes out clean (do not overbake).
3. Place pans on wire racks. Using the end of a wooden spoon handle, make a ½-in.-deep indentation in the center of each brownie. Cool 10 minutes before removing from pans.
4. For frosting, in a large bowl, beat peanut butter and cream cheese until blended. Gradually beat in the confectioners' sugar, milk and vanilla until smooth. Spoon or pipe frosting into indentations. If desired, sprinkle with chopped peanuts. Refrigerate the leftovers.

1 BROWNIE BITE: 134 cal., 7g fat (1g sat. fat), 11mg chol., 71mg sod., 16g carb. (12g sugars, 0 fiber), 2g pro.

BLACK FOREST ICEBOX COOKIES

These rich chocolate wafers are the perfect complement to the creamy filling's sweet-tart tones. Chill for up to four hours; any longer and the wafers get too soft to pick up with your hands.
—Taste of Home Test Kitchen

Prep: 15 min. + chilling
Cook: 5 min. + cooling
Makes: 20 cookies

- 3 Tbsp. sugar
- 4 tsp. cornstarch
  Dash salt
- ¾ cup fresh or frozen pitted tart cherries (thawed), coarsely chopped
- ¾ cup cherry juice blend
- 1½ tsp. lemon juice
- 1 to 2 drops red food coloring, optional
- ½ cup mascarpone cheese
- 1 Tbsp. confectioners' sugar
- 1 tsp. cherry brandy
- 1 pkg. (9 oz.) chocolate wafers
- ½ cup semisweet chocolate chips
- ¼ cup heavy whipping cream

1. In a small saucepan, combine the sugar, cornstarch and salt. Add the cherries, juice blend and lemon juice. Bring to a boil; cook and stir until thickened, about 2 minutes. Remove from the heat; if desired, stir in food coloring. Cool to room temperature.
2. In a small bowl, combine the mascarpone cheese, confectioners' sugar and brandy. Spread about 1 tsp. cheese mixture onto each of 20 wafers; layer each with 2 tsp. cherry mixture. Top with remaining wafers. Place on a waxed paper-lined baking pan.
3. Place chocolate chips in a small bowl. In a small saucepan, bring cream just to a boil. Pour over chips; whisk until smooth. Drizzle over cookies. Refrigerate, covered, for up to 4 hours before serving.

1 SANDWICH COOKIE: 139 cal., 9g fat (4g sat. fat), 17mg chol., 81mg sod., 15g carb. (9g sugars, 1g fiber), 2g pro.

ITALIAN RAINBOW COOKIES

My family has made these classic Italian cookies for generations, and this homemade version is so much better than the bakery version. They remain a much-anticipated treat during the holidays.
—*Cindy Casazza, Hopewell, NJ*

Prep: 35 min. + chilling
Bake: 10 min./batch + cooling
Makes: about 11 dozen

    1   cup sugar
    3½ oz. almond paste, cut into small
        pieces
    4   large eggs, room temperature
    1   cup all-purpose flour
    1   cup butter, melted and cooled
    ½   tsp. salt
    ½   tsp. almond extract
    6   to 8 drops red food coloring
    6   to 8 drops green food coloring
    ¼   cup seedless raspberry jam
GLAZE
    1   cup semisweet chocolate chips
    1   tsp. shortening

1. Preheat oven to 375°. Place sugar and almond paste in a food processor; process until combined. Transfer to a large bowl, beat eggs and sugar mixture 2-3 minutes or until thick and lemon-colored. Gradually add flour, butter, salt and extract.

2. Divide batter into thirds. Tint one portion red and one portion green; leave remaining portion plain. Spread one portion into each of 3 well-greased 11x7-in. baking dishes.

3. Bake 7-11 minutes or until a toothpick inserted in center comes out clean and edges begin to brown. Cool 10 minutes before removing from pans to wire racks to cool completely.

4. Place red layer on waxed paper; spread with 2 Tbsp. jam. Top with plain layer and remaining jam. Add green layer; press down gently.

5. For glaze, in a microwave, melt chocolate chips and shortening; stir until smooth. Spread half over green layer. Refrigerate 20 minutes or until set. Turn over; spread remaining glaze over red layer. Refrigerate 20 minutes or until set.

6. With a sharp knife, trim edges. Cut rectangle lengthwise into fourths. Cut each portion into ¼-in. slices.

1 COOKIE: 35 cal., 2g fat (1g sat. fat), 10mg chol., 21mg sod., 4g carb. (3g sugars, 0 fiber), 0 pro.

ITALIAN RAINBOW COOKIES TIPS

• **Can you make Italian rainbow cookies without almond paste?** The flavor that almond paste and almond extract work together to create is what Italian rainbow cookies are known for. We don't recommend skipping the almond paste—not only would you be missing out on flavor, but the texture of each layer would be different as well.

• **How can you make Italian rainbow cookies your own?** Raspberry jam is typically spread between the layers in Italian rainbow cookies, but another popular option is apricot. However, you could experiment with your favorite jams to see what you like best!

• **How should you store Italian rainbow cookies?** Store Italian rainbow cookies in an airtight container in the fridge for up to a week. You can also make them ahead of time and freeze them for up to 3 months.

FROSTED MOLASSES COOKIES

If my family knows I've baked these cookies, they're sure to gobble them up in a hurry.
—Sarah Byler, Harrisville, PA

Prep: 40 min. + chilling
Bake: 10 min./batch + standing
Makes: 8 dozen

- 1 cup butter, softened
- 1 cup sugar
- 3 large egg yolks, room temperature
- 1 cup molasses
- ½ cup water
- 5 cups all-purpose flour
- 3 tsp. baking soda
- 1½ tsp. ground cinnamon
- 1 tsp. baking powder

FROSTING
- 1½ cups sugar
- 3 large egg whites
- ¼ cup water
- 1 cup confectioners' sugar

1. In a large bowl, cream butter and sugar until light and fluffy, 5-7 minutes. Beat in the egg yolks, molasses and water. Combine the flour, baking soda, cinnamon and baking powder; gradually add to creamed mixture and mix well. Cover and refrigerate for 2 hours or until easy to handle.
2. On a lightly floured surface, roll out dough to ⅛-in. thickness. Cut with a floured 2½-in. round cookie cutter. Place 1 in. apart on ungreased baking sheets. Bake at 375° for 8-10 minutes or until edges are firm. Remove to wire racks to cool.

3. For frosting, combine the sugar, egg whites and water in a small heavy saucepan over low heat. With a hand mixer, beat on low speed for 1 minute. Continue beating on low over low heat 8-10 minutes or until frosting reaches 160°. Pour into the bowl of a heavy-duty stand mixer; add the confectioners' sugar. Beat on high until frosting forms stiff peaks, about 7 minutes. Frost cookies. Let stand until dry.
1 COOKIE: 78 cal., 2g fat (1g sat. fat), 11mg chol., 63mg sod., 14g carb. (9g sugars, 0 fiber), 1g pro.

PISTACHIO MERINGUE SANDWICH COOKIES

Traditional macarons are confections made with egg whites, sugar and almonds. Our easy version calls for pistachios and features a rich chocolate filling.
—Taste of Home *Test Kitchen*

Prep: 35 min. + cooling
Bake: 10 min./batch + cooling
Makes: about 1½ dozen

- 3 large egg whites
- 1¼ cups confectioners' sugar
- ¾ cup pistachios
- Dash salt
- ¼ cup sugar
- Green paste food coloring, optional

CHOCOLATE FILLING
- 4 oz. bittersweet chocolate, chopped
- ½ cup heavy whipping cream
- 2 tsp. corn syrup
- 1 Tbsp. butter

1. Let egg whites stand at room temperature for 30 minutes. Pulse confectioners' sugar and pistachios in a food processor until powdery.
2. Preheat oven to 350°. Add salt to egg whites; beat on medium speed until soft peaks form. Gradually add sugar, 1 Tbsp. at a time, beating on high until stiff peaks form. Fold in pistachio mixture and, if desired, green food coloring.
3. Transfer pistachio mixture to a pastry bag fitted with a round tip. Pipe 1-in.-diameter cookies 1 in. apart onto parchment-lined baking sheets. Bake until lightly browned and firm to the touch, 10-12 minutes. Cool completely on pans on wire racks.

4. Place chocolate in a small bowl. In a small saucepan, bring cream and corn syrup just to a boil. Pour over chocolate; whisk until smooth. Whisk in butter. Cool, stirring occasionally, to room temperature or until filling reaches a spreading consistency, about 45 minutes. Spread on the bottoms of half the cookies; cover with remaining cookies. If desired, roll edges in additional chopped pistachios.
1 SANDWICH COOKIE: 160 cal., 9g fat (4g sat. fat), 10mg chol., 135mg sod., 16g carb. (14g sugars, 1g fiber), 3g pro.

PISTACHIO MERINGUE
SANDWICH COOKIES

CHERRY & ALMOND CRISPY BARS

A grown-up version of the crisp rice square will please the whole party. Everyone will agree it's delicious!
—Taste of Home *Test Kitchen*

- -

Takes: 20 min. • **Makes:** 2 dozen

1	pkg. (10 oz.) large marshmallows
3	Tbsp. butter
1	tsp. almond extract
6	cups crisp rice cereal
3	cups salted roasted almonds, divided
1½	cups dried cherries, divided

1. In a Dutch oven, combine marshmallows and butter. Cook and stir over medium-low heat until melted. Remove from the heat; stir in extract. Stir in the cereal, 1 cup almonds and 1 cup cherries.

2. Press into a greased 13x9-in. pan. Sprinkle with remaining 2 cups almonds and ½ cup cherries; gently press onto cereal mixture. Cool. Cut into bars.

1 BAR: 205 cal., 11g fat (2g sat. fat), 4mg chol., 137mg sod., 25g carb. (13g sugars, 2g fiber), 5g pro.

Short & Sweet

LEMONY GINGERBREAD WHOOPIE PIES

These whoopie pies are spiced just right. They combine two popular flavors in one fun treat. Roll the chewy cookies in sugar before baking for a bit of crunch.
—*Jamie Jones, Madison, GA*

- -

Prep: 25 min. + chilling
Bake: 10 min./batch + cooling
Makes: about 2 dozen

¾	cup butter, softened
¾	cup packed brown sugar
½	cup molasses
1	large egg, room temperature
3	cups all-purpose flour
2	tsp. ground ginger
1	tsp. ground cinnamon
1	tsp. baking soda
¼	tsp. salt
½	cup sugar

FILLING
¾	cup butter, softened
¾	cup marshmallow creme
1½	cups confectioners' sugar
¾	tsp. lemon extract

1. In a large bowl, cream butter and brown sugar until light and fluffy, 5-7 minutes. Beat in molasses and egg. Combine flour, ginger, cinnamon, baking soda and salt; gradually add to creamed mixture and mix well. Cover and refrigerate at least 3 hours.

2. Preheat oven to 350°. Shape dough into 1-in. balls; roll in sugar. Place 3 in. apart on ungreased baking sheets. Flatten to ½-in. thickness with a glass dipped in sugar. Bake 8-10 minutes or until set. Cool for 2 minutes before removing from pans to wire racks to cool completely.

3. For filling, in a small bowl, beat butter and marshmallow creme until light and fluffy. Gradually beat in confectioners' sugar and extract.

4. Spread filling on the bottoms of half of the cookies, about 1 Tbsp. on each; top with remaining cookies.

1 WHOOPIE PIE: 286 cal., 13g fat (8g sat. fat) 42mg chol., 184mg sod., 41g carb. (26g sugars, 1g fiber), 2g pro.

HAWAIIAN SUNSET
CAKE, PAGE 64

Cakes & Cupcakes

Each frosted, layered or sprinkled creation here is sure to be the belle of any ball. Breathtaking delights abound for every baker's skill level and the season.

MAJESTIC PECAN CAKE

This recipe truly lives up to its name. The pecan-dotted cake is stacked in three layers, and made-from-scratch frosting is the crowning touch.

—*Karen Jones, Claypool, IN*

Prep: 1½ hours
Bake: 20 min. + cooling
Makes: 16 servings

- ½   cup butter, softened
- ¼   cup shortening
- 2   cups sugar, divided
- 2   tsp. vanilla extract
- 3   cups cake flour
- 5   tsp. baking powder
- ½   tsp. salt
- 1⅓ cups 2% milk
- 6   large egg whites, room temperature
- 1   cup chopped pecans

FILLING
- ⅓   cup sugar
- 3   Tbsp. cornstarch
- 2   cups whole milk
- 3   large egg yolks, beaten
- 1   Tbsp. butter
- 1½ tsp. vanilla extract

FROSTING
- 1¾ cups sugar
- 4   large egg whites
- ½   cup water
- ½   tsp. cream of tartar
- 1   tsp. vanilla extract

1. Grease and flour three 9-in. round baking pans; set aside. In a large bowl, cream the butter, shortening and 1¾ cups sugar until light and fluffy, 5-7 minutes. Beat in vanilla. Combine the flour, baking powder and salt; add to the creamed mixture alternately with milk, beating well after each addition.

2. In a large bowl with clean beaters, beat egg whites until soft peaks form. Gradually beat in remaining sugar, 1 Tbsp. at a time, on high until stiff peaks form. Fold into batter. Fold in nuts.

3. Transfer to prepared pans. Bake at 350° until a toothpick inserted in the center comes out clean, 18-22 minutes. Cool for 10 minutes before removing from pans to wire racks to cool completely.

4. For filling, in a small heavy saucepan, combine sugar and cornstarch; gradually stir in milk until smooth. Cook and stir over medium-high heat until thickened and bubbly. Reduce heat to low; cook and stir 2 minutes longer.

5. Remove from the heat. Stir a small amount of hot mixture into egg yolks; return all to the pan, stirring constantly. Bring to a gentle boil; cook and stir for 2 minutes. Remove from the heat; stir in butter and vanilla. Cool.

6. For frosting, in a large heavy saucepan, combine the sugar, egg whites, water and cream of tartar over low heat. With a hand mixer, beat on low speed for 1 minute. Continue beating on low over low heat until frosting reaches 160°, 8-10 minutes. Pour into a large bowl; add vanilla. Beat on high until stiff peaks form, about 7 minutes.

7. Spread filling between cake layers. Frost cake. Store in the refrigerator.

1 PIECE: 486 cal., 17g fat (7g sat. fat), 60mg chol., 301mg sod., 76g carb. (54g sugars, 1g fiber), 7g pro.

SLOW-COOKER SPUMONI CAKE

I created this cake for a holiday potluck one year. It has become one of my most requested desserts. If you prefer, you can use all semisweet chips instead of a mix.
—Lisa Renshaw, Kansas City, MO

- -

Prep: 10 min. • **Cook:** 4 hours + standing
Makes: 10 servings

- 3 cups cold 2% milk
- 1 pkg. (3.4 oz.) instant pistachio pudding mix
- 1 pkg. white cake mix (regular size)
- ¾ cup chopped maraschino cherries
- 1 cup white baking chips
- 1 cup semisweet chocolate chips
- 1 cup pistachios, chopped

1. In a large bowl, whisk milk and pudding mix for 2 minutes. Transfer to a greased 5-qt. slow cooker. Prepare cake mix batter according to package directions, folding cherries into batter. Pour into slow cooker.
2. Cook, covered, on low for 4 hours or until edges of cake are golden brown.
3. Remove slow-cooker insert; sprinkle cake with baking chips and chocolate chips. Let cake stand, uncovered, 10 minutes. Sprinkle with pistachios before serving.
1 SERVING: 588 cal., 27g fat (9g sat. fat), 9mg chol., 594mg sod., 79g carb. (54g sugars, 3g fiber), 10g pro.

Short & Sweet

MINI BLUEBERRY BUNDT CAKES

These pretty little blueberry cakes are topped with a yummy lemon-flavored glaze. The recipe makes 12 tiny cakes, so one batch gives you plenty of sweet treats to share with friends.
—Cathy Isaak, Rivers, MB

- -

Prep: 20 min. • **Bake:** 30 min. + cooling
Makes: 1 dozen

- 1 cup butter, softened
- 2 cups sugar
- 4 large eggs, room temperature
- 2 tsp. vanilla extract
- 4 cups all-purpose flour
- 1 tsp. baking powder
- 1 tsp. salt
- 1 cup 2% milk
- 4 cups fresh blueberries

LEMON ICING
- 2 cups confectioners' sugar
- 2 Tbsp. 2% milk
- 4 tsp. lemon juice

1. Preheat oven to 350°. In a large bowl, cream butter and sugar until light and fluffy, 5-7 minutes. Beat in the eggs and vanilla. In another bowl, combine flour, baking powder and salt; add to creamed mixture alternately with milk, beating well after each addition. Fold in blueberries.
2. Scoop into 12 greased 4-in. fluted tube pans. Place pans on a large baking sheet. Bake until a toothpick inserted in the center comes out clean, 30-35 minutes. Cool for 10 minutes before removing from tube pans to wire racks to cool completely.
3. For icing, in a small bowl, combine the confectioners' sugar, milk and lemon juice; drizzle over cakes. If desired, garnish the cakes with additional blueberries.
1 MINI CAKE: 560 cal., 18g fat (11g sat. fat), 105mg chol., 395mg sod., 94g carb. (59g sugars, 2g fiber), 8g pro.

NOT JUST A PRETTY SHAPE

The hole in a Bundt pan puts more of the cake's surface area in contact with the oven's heat. This lets a rich, high-in-sugar batter fully cook in the center before browning too much on the outside.

SACHER TORTE

Guests will be surprised to hear that this dessert starts with a convenient cake mix. Each bite features the heavenly combo of chocolate, almonds and apricots.
—Taste of Home *Test Kitchen*

- -

Prep: 30 min.+ chilling
Bake: 25 min. + cooling
Makes: 16 servings

- ½ cup chopped dried apricots
- ½ cup amaretto
- 1 pkg. devil's food cake mix (regular size)
- 3 large eggs, room temperature
- ¾ cup water
- ⅓ cup canola oil

FILLING
- ⅔ cup apricot preserves
- 1 Tbsp. amaretto

GLAZE
- 1 cup heavy whipping cream
- ¼ cup light corn syrup
- 12 oz. semisweet chocolate, chopped
- 4 tsp. vanilla extract
- 1 cup toasted sliced almonds, optional

1. Preheat oven to 350°. Combine apricots and amaretto; let stand 15 minutes. In another bowl, combine cake mix, eggs, water, oil and apricot mixture. Beat on low speed for 30 seconds; beat on medium 2 minutes.
2. Pour into 2 greased and floured 9-in. round baking pans. Bake until a toothpick inserted in center comes out clean, 22-27 minutes. Cool in pans 10 minutes before removing to a wire rack to cool completely.
3. For filling, heat apricot preserves and amaretto on low in a small saucepan, stirring occasionally, until preserves are melted; set aside.
4. For glaze, combine cream and corn syrup in a small saucepan. Bring just to a boil. Pour over chocolate; whisk until smooth. Stir in vanilla.
5. Using a long serrated knife, cut each cake horizontally in half. Place 1 layer on a serving plate; spread with half of the filling. Top with another layer; spread with a third of the glaze. Cover with third layer and remaining filling. Top with remaining layer; spread top and side of torte with remaining glaze. If desired, spread toasted almonds on edge or side of torte. Refrigerate torte for several hours
before slicing.
1 PIECE: 415 cal., 21g fat (9g sat. fat), 52mg chol., 281mg sod., 44g carb. (30g sugars, 2g fiber), 5g pro.

SACHER TORTE TIPS

- **Why is Sacher torte famous?** Sacher torte is one of the few recipes we actually know the true origin of, unlike many other desserts from around the world. In 1832, the Austrian chancellor's head chef became ill, forcing him to ask his young apprentice chef to create a special dessert for his dinner party. The 16-year-old chef created a simple yet deceptively delicious cake that impressed the chancellor and his guests. To this day, Sacher torte has an almost cult-like following.

- **Does Sacher torte have nuts?** Traditional Sacher torte doesn't have nuts. But over the years, chefs around the world have added their personal touches to this elegant dessert. If you want to gild the lily by adding nuts, place toasted sliced almonds on the top or side of the Sacher torte after frosting it. To toast the almonds, bake them in a shallow pan at 350° for 5-10 minutes, or cook them in a skillet over low heat until lightly browned, stirring frequently.

- **What's the traditional decoration for Sacher torte?** Walk into any bakery in Austria and you'll have no doubt about which desserts are the Sacher tortes—they literally have the name Sacher written on top of them in ganache. If you feel up to the challenge, give this a try. Otherwise, a simple coating of ganache on the outside tastes just as good.

- **Does Sacher torte have to be refrigerated?** If the temperature in your house is 60-70°, then it's fine to let a Sacher torte sit out at room temperature—just press parchment or waxed paper against the cut edges of the exposed cake to keep it moist.

FUN & FESTIVE CAKE POPS

When looking for a little nibble at a coffee shop, lots of people go for a cake pop. With this recipe, you can make your own, even changing flavors to match the occasion or season of the year.

—Taste of Home *Test Kitchen*

- -

Prep: 1 hour • **Bake:** 35 min. + freezing
Makes: 4 dozen

1   pkg. cake mix of your choice (regular size)
1   cup prepared frosting of your choice
48 lollipop sticks
2½ lbs. dark chocolate, milk chocolate white or pink candy coating, coarsely chopped
    Optional toppings: Nonpareils, crushed peppermint candies, finely chopped cashews, unsweetened coconut, assorted sprinkles, finely chopped crystallized ginger, crushed gingersnap cookies, melted caramels and coarse sea salt

1. Prepare and bake cake mix according to package directions, using a greased 13x9-in. baking pan. Cool completely on a wire rack.
2. Crumble cake into a large bowl. Add frosting and mix well. Shape into 1½-in. balls. Place on baking sheets; insert sticks. Freeze for at least 2 hours or refrigerate for at least 3 hours or until cake balls are firm.
3. In a microwave, melt candy coating. Dip each cake ball in coating; allow excess to drip off. Roll, sprinkle or drizzle with toppings of your choice. Insert cake pops into a foam block to stand. Let stand until set.

1 CAKE POP: 213 cal., 11g fat (7g sat. fat), 13mg chol., 97mg sod., 28g carb. (23g sugars, 1g fiber), 1g pro.

CAKE POP TIPS

- **How do you decorate cake pops if you're a beginner?** If you are new to making cake pops, keep the decorating simple and organized from the get-go. Keep various sprinkles and toppings in their own dishes and have them ready to go before you begin. Rather than dealing with chocolates, which require complex processes such as tempering to retain proper snap and shine, use confectioners' candy coatings or melting disks. Be sure to let the formed cake balls chill for a bit in the refrigerator before you dip and decorate them.

- **How do you make cake pops smooth?** When forming cake pops, tightly compact the scoop of cake crumbs and frosting in the palm of your hand and roll it into a very compact, round ball. Once it has chilled, if you still find the cake ball a little bumpy, try gently rolling and compacting it again while cold. When dipping the cake ball, stir the coating well first to make sure there are no lumps. If the coating seems a little thick, stir in a bit of vegetable shortening and reheat it gently, stirring until smooth.

- **Can you leave cake pops in the fridge overnight before dipping?** Absolutely! Keep them covered so they don't dry out.

TOFFEE POKE CAKE

This toffee poke cake is a favorite among my family and friends. I love making it because it is so simple.
—*Jeanette Hoffman, Oshkosh, WI*

Prep: 25 min. • **Bake:** 25 min. + chilling
Makes: 15 servings

- 1   pkg. chocolate cake mix (regular size)
- 1   jar (17 oz.) butterscotch-caramel ice cream topping
- 1   carton (12 oz.) frozen whipped topping, thawed
- 3   Heath candy bars (1.4 oz. each), chopped

1. Prepare and bake cake according to package directions, using a greased 13x9-in. baking pan. Cool on a wire rack.
2. Using the handle of a wooden spoon, poke holes in the cake. Pour ¾ cup caramel topping into holes. Spoon remaining caramel over cake. Top with whipped topping. Sprinkle with candy. Refrigerate for at least 2 hours before serving.

1 PIECE: 404 cal., 16g fat (8g sat. fat), 48mg chol., 322mg sod., 60g carb. (39g sugars, 1g fiber), 4g pro.

Short & Sweet

APRICOT ALMOND TORTE

This pretty cake takes a bit of time, so I like to make the layers in advance and assemble it the day of serving, which makes it easier when entertaining.
—*Trisha Kruse, Eagle, ID*

Prep: 45 min. • **Bake:** 25 min. + cooling
Makes: 12 servings

- 3   large eggs, room temperature
- 1½ cups sugar
- 1   tsp. vanilla extract
- 1¾ cups all-purpose flour
- 1   cup ground almonds, toasted
- 2   tsp. baking powder
- ½   tsp. salt
- 1½ cups heavy whipping cream, whipped

FROSTING
- 1   pkg. (8 oz.) cream cheese, softened
- 1   cup sugar
- ⅛   tsp. salt
- 1   tsp. almond extract
- 1½ cups heavy whipping cream, whipped
- 1   jar (10 to 12 oz.) apricot preserves
- ½   cup slivered almonds, toasted

1. Preheat oven to 350°. In a large bowl, beat eggs, sugar and vanilla on high speed until thick and lemon-colored. Combine flour, almonds, baking powder and salt; gradually fold into egg mixture alternately with the whipped cream.
2. Transfer to 2 greased and floured 9-in. round baking pans. Bake until a toothpick inserted in the center comes out clean, 22-28 minutes. Cool 10 minutes before removing from pans to wire racks to cool completely.
3. In a large bowl, beat cream cheese, sugar and salt until smooth. Beat in extract. Fold in whipped cream.
4. Cut each cake horizontally into 2 layers. Place bottom layer on a serving plate; spread with 1 cup frosting. Top with another cake layer; spread with half the preserves. Repeat layers. Frost side of cake; decorate the top edge with remaining frosting. Sprinkle with almonds.

1 PIECE: 546 cal., 25g fat (12g sat. fat), 115mg chol., 284mg sod., 75g carb. (51g sugars, 2g fiber), 8g pro.

READER REVIEW

"The apricot preserves pair so nicely with the almond flavoring! Can use this recipe for very special occasions."
—KARENKEEFE, TASTEOFHOME.COM

OLD-FASHIONED CARROT CAKE WITH CREAM CHEESE FROSTING

A pleasingly moist cake, this treat is the one I requested that my mom make each year for my birthday. It's dotted with sweet carrots and a hint of cinnamon. The fluffy buttery frosting is scrumptious with chopped walnuts stirred in. One piece of this cake is never enough!
—*Kim Orr, West Grove, PA*

Prep: 30 min. • **Bake:** 35 min. + cooling
Makes: 16 servings

- 4 large eggs, room temperature
- 2 cups sugar
- 1 cup canola oil
- 2 cups all-purpose flour
- 2 to 3 tsp. ground cinnamon
- ¾ tsp. baking soda
- ½ tsp. baking powder
- ¼ tsp. salt
- ¼ tsp. ground nutmeg
- 2 cups grated carrots

FROSTING
- ½ cup butter, softened
- 3 oz. cream cheese, softened
- 1 tsp. vanilla extract
- 3¾ cups confectioners' sugar
- 2 to 3 Tbsp. 2% milk
- 1 cup chopped walnuts, optional
  Optional: Orange and green food coloring

1. In a large bowl, combine the eggs, sugar and oil. Combine the flour, cinnamon, baking soda, baking powder, salt and nutmeg; beat into egg mixture. Stir in carrots.

2. Pour into 2 greased and floured 9-in. round baking pans. Bake at 350° for 35-40 minutes or until a toothpick inserted in center comes out clean. Cool for 10 minutes before removing from pans to wire racks to cool completely.

3. For frosting, in another large bowl, cream butter and cream cheese until light and fluffy, 3-4 minutes. Beat in vanilla. Gradually beat in confectioners' sugar. Add enough milk to achieve desired spreading consistency. If desired, reserve ½ cup frosting for decorating. Stir walnuts into remaining frosting, if desired.

4. Spread the frosting between layers and over top and side of cake. If decorating the cake, tint ¼ cup reserved frosting orange and ¼ cup green. Cut a small hole in the corner of pastry bag; insert #7 round pastry tip. Fill the bag with orange frosting. Pipe 16 carrots on top of cake, so each piece will have a carrot. Using #67 leaf pastry tip and the green frosting, pipe a leaf at the top of each carrot.

5. Store cake in the refrigerator.

1 PIECE: 531 cal., 28g fat (7g sat. fat), 67mg chol., 203mg sod., 68g carb. (54g sugars, 1g fiber), 5g pro.

CARROT CAKE WITH CREAM CHEESE FROSTING TIPS

- **What's the trick to a moist carrot cake?** Cakes made with oil tend to retain more moisture than those made with butter or shortening. Ingredients such as sour cream or buttermilk are also key ingredients to a moist carrot cake because they contain acids that tenderize the developing gluten in the flour.

- **How do I make the frosting less sweet?** To keep the frosting from becoming too sweet, cut back on the confectioners' sugar slightly (a few tablespoons may be enough to make a difference). As you prepare the frosting, add a little sugar at a time and taste as you go. Also, you could add a teaspoon of lemon juice to the frosting because the acidity in the juice counters the sweetness of the sugar. If the frosting still seems too sweet, simply decrease the amount you use on your cake.

- **How do I prevent my frosting from getting runny?** Because it is made in a mixer, cream cheese frosting can become runny if overbeaten. Mix just until all of the confectioners' sugar has been incorporated and you have whipped in some air for fluffiness and stability. To thicken your frosting, pop the bowl in the refrigerator for 5-10 minutes. This will allow the butter and cream cheese in it to firm up a bit more.

SPARKLING CIDER POUND CAKE

This pound cake is incredible and completely reminds me of fall with every bite. Using sparkling apple cider in the batter and the glaze gives it a delicious and unique flavor. I love everything about it!
—*Nikki Barton, Providence, UT*

Prep: 20 min. • **Bake:** 40 min. + cooling
Makes: 12 servings

- ¾ cup butter, softened
- 1½ cups sugar
- 3 large eggs, room temperature
- 1½ cups all-purpose flour
- ¼ tsp. baking powder
- ¼ tsp. salt
- ½ cup sparkling apple cider

GLAZE
- ¾ cup confectioners' sugar
- 3 to 4 tsp. sparkling apple cider

1. Preheat oven to 350°. Line bottom of a greased 9x5-in. loaf pan with parchment; grease parchment.
2. In a large bowl, cream butter and sugar until light and fluffy, 5-7 minutes. Add eggs, 1 at a time, beating well after each addition. In another bowl, whisk flour, baking powder and salt; add to creamed mixture alternately with cider, beating well after each addition.
3. Transfer to prepared pan. Bake until a toothpick inserted in center comes out clean, 40-50 minutes. Cool in pan 10 minutes before removing to a wire rack to cool completely.
4. In a small bowl, mix glaze ingredients until smooth; spoon over top of cake, allowing it to flow over the sides.

1 PIECE: 308 cal., 13g fat (8g sat. fat), 77mg chol., 169mg sod., 46g carb. (34g sugars, 0 fiber), 3g pro.

CHOCOLATE HAZELNUT TORTE

Most cakes feed a crowd. So we came up with this elegant little cake that serves six. That's enough for a small household—with a little bit left over!
—*Taste of Home Test Kitchen*

Prep: 30 min. + chilling
Bake: 25 min. + cooling
Makes: 6 servings

- ⅓ cup butter, softened
- 1 cup packed brown sugar
- 1 large egg, room temperature
- 1 tsp. vanilla extract
- 1 cup all-purpose flour
- ¼ cup baking cocoa
- 1 tsp. baking soda
- ⅛ tsp. salt
- ½ cup sour cream
- ½ cup brewed coffee, room temperature

FROSTING
- 7 oz. semisweet chocolate, chopped
- 1 cup heavy whipping cream
- 2 Tbsp. sugar
- ⅓ cup Nutella
  Optional: Chocolate curls and hazelnuts

1. In a small bowl, cream butter and brown sugar until light and fluffy, 5-7 minutes. Beat in egg and vanilla. Combine the flour, cocoa, baking soda and salt; gradually add to creamed mixture alternately with sour cream and coffee. Beat just until combined.
2. Pour into 2 greased and floured 6-in. round baking pans. Bake at 350° for 25-30 minutes or until a knife inserted in the center comes out clean. Cool for 10 minutes before removing from pans to wire racks to cool completely.
3. For frosting, in a small saucepan, melt chocolate with cream and sugar over low heat; stir until smooth. Remove from the heat; whisk in Nutella. Transfer to a small bowl; cover and refrigerate until frosting reaches spreading consistency, stirring occasionally.
4. Spread frosting between the layers and over top and side of cake. Garnish with chocolate curls and hazelnuts if desired.

1 PIECE: 768 cal., 45g fat (25g sat. fat), 130mg chol., 386mg sod., 89g carb. (66g sugars, 4g fiber), 9g pro.

PEANUT BUTTER CUP CHOCOLATE CUPCAKES

Chocolate and peanut butter—it's a match made in heaven. And these dreamy cupcakes are to die for! Let the kids help you frost and decorate them.
—Taste of Home *Test Kitchen*

Prep: 30 min. • **Bake:** 20 min. + cooling
Makes: 2 dozen

- 1 pkg. chocolate cake mix (regular size)
- 1¼ cups water
- ⅓ cup canola oil
- 3 large eggs, room temperature
- 24 miniature peanut butter cups

FROSTING
- 6 oz. semisweet chocolate, chopped
- ⅔ cup heavy whipping cream
- ⅓ cup peanut butter
  Additional miniature peanut butter cups, chopped

1. In a large bowl, combine the cake mix, water, peanut butter, oil and eggs; beat on low speed for 30 seconds. Beat on medium for 2 minutes or until smooth.
2. Fill paper-lined muffin cups half full. Place a peanut butter cup in the center of each cupcake. Cover each with 1 Tbsp. batter.
3. Bake at 350° for 18-22 minutes or until a toothpick inserted in the center of the cupcake comes out clean. Cool for 10 minutes before removing from pans to wire racks to cool completely.
4. Place chocolate in a small bowl. In a small saucepan, bring cream just to a boil. Pour over chocolate; whisk until smooth. Stir in the peanut butter. Cool, stirring occasionally, to room temperature or until mixture reaches a spreading consistency, about 10 minutes.
5. Spread frosting over cupcakes; immediately sprinkle with additional peanut butter cups. Let stand until set.
1 CUPCAKE: 269 cal.,17g fat (6g sat. fat), 36mg chol., 220mg sod., 27g carb. (18g sugars, 2g fiber), 5g pro.

STRAWBERRY POKE CAKE

Strawberry shortcake takes on a wonderful new twist with this super simple recipe. Strawberries liven up each pretty slice.
—Mary Jo Griggs, West Bend, WI

Prep: 25 min. • **Bake:** 25 min. + chilling
Makes: 12 servings

- 1 pkg. white cake mix (regular size)
- 1¼ cups water
- 2 large eggs, room temperature
- ¼ cup canola oil
- 2 pkg. (10 oz. each) frozen sweetened sliced strawberries, thawed
- 2 pkg. (3 oz. each) strawberry gelatin
- 1 carton (12 oz.) frozen whipped topping, thawed, divided
  Fresh strawberries, optional

1. Preheat oven to 350°. In a large bowl, combine the cake mix, water, eggs and oil; beat on low speed for 30 seconds. Beat on medium speed for 2 minutes.
2. Pour into 2 greased and floured 9-in. round baking pans. Bake until a toothpick inserted in the center comes out clean, 25-35 minutes. Cool for 10 minutes; remove from pans to wire racks to cool completely.
3. Using a serrated knife, level tops of cakes if necessary. Return layers, top side up, to 2 clean 9-in. round baking pans. Pierce cakes with a meat fork or wooden skewer at ½-in. intervals.
4. Drain juice from strawberries into a 2-cup measuring cup; refrigerate berries. Add water to juice to measure 2 cups; pour into a small saucepan. Bring to a boil; stir in gelatin until dissolved. Chill for 30 minutes. Gently spoon over each cake layer. Chill for 2-3 hours.
5. Dip bottom of 1 pan into warm water for 10 seconds. Invert the cake onto a serving platter. Top with chilled strawberries and 1 cup whipped topping. Place second cake layer over topping.
6. Frost cake with remaining whipped topping. Chill for at least 1 hour. Serve with fresh strawberries if desired. Refrigerate leftovers.
1 PIECE: 376 cal., 14g fat (7g sat. fat), 35mg chol., 301mg sod., 56g carb. (37g sugars, 1g fiber), 4g pro.

Short &
Sweet

PRETTY
PETITS FOURS

CHAI CUPCAKES

You'll get a double dose of the spicy blend that's frequently used to flavor tea in these tender single-sized cakes. Both the cupcake and frosting use the sweet blend of spices.
—Taste of Home *Test Kitchen*

- -

Prep: 25 min. • **Bake:** 25 min. + cooling
Makes: 1 dozen

- ½ tsp. each ground ginger, cinnamon, cardamom and cloves
- ⅛ tsp. pepper
- ½ cup butter, softened
- 1 cup sugar
- 1 large egg, room temperature
- ½ tsp. vanilla extract
- 1½ cups cake flour
- 1½ tsp. baking powder
- ¼ tsp. salt
- ⅔ cup 2% milk

FROSTING
- 6 Tbsp. butter, softened
- 3 cups confectioners' sugar
- ¾ tsp. vanilla extract
- 3 to 4 Tbsp. 2% milk

1. In a small bowl, combine the ginger, cinnamon, cardamom, cloves and pepper.
2. In a large bowl, cream butter and sugar until light and fluffy, 5-7 minutes. Beat in egg and vanilla. Combine the flour, baking powder, salt and 1½ tsp. spice mixture. Gradually add to the creamed mixture alternately with milk, beating well after each addition.
3. Fill 12 paper-lined muffin cups two-thirds full. Bake at 350° until a toothpick inserted in the center comes out clean, 24-28 minutes. Cool for 10 minutes before removing from pans to wire racks to cool completely.
4. In a large bowl, beat butter until fluffy; beat in the confectioners' sugar, vanilla and remaining spice mixture until smooth. Add enough milk to reach desired consistency. Pipe frosting over cupcakes.
1 CUPCAKE: 377 cal., 14g fat (9g sat. fat), 54mg chol., 209mg sod., 61g carb. (46g sugars, 0 fiber), 3g pro.

PRETTY PETITS FOURS

Add a delicate touch to your dessert table with these bite-sized cakes. We decorated the tops with simple buttercream rosettes and gold sugar pearls, but feel free to try your hand at other designs.
—Taste of Home *Test Kitchen*

- -

Prep: 1½ hours • **Bake:** 20 min. + cooling
Makes: about 4 dozen (3 cups frosting)

- ¼ cup butter, softened
- ¼ cup shortening
- 1 cup sugar
- 1 tsp. vanilla extract
- 1⅓ cups all-purpose flour
- 2 tsp. baking powder
- ½ tsp. salt
- ⅔ cup whole milk
- 3 large egg whites, room temperature

GLAZE
- 2 lbs. confectioners' sugar
- ⅔ cup plus 2 Tbsp. water
- 2 tsp. orange extract

FROSTING
- 6 Tbsp. butter, softened
- 2 Tbsp. shortening
- ½ tsp. vanilla extract
- 3 cups confectioners' sugar
- 3 to 4 Tbsp. whole milk
  Gel, liquid or paste food coloring
  Gold sugar pearls, optional

1. In a large bowl, cream butter, shortening and sugar until light and fluffy, 5-7 minutes. Beat in vanilla. Combine flour, baking powder and salt; add to creamed mixture alternately with milk, beating well after each addition. In a small bowl, beat egg whites until soft peaks form; gently fold into batter.
2. Pour into a greased 9-in. square baking pan. Bake at 350° until a toothpick inserted in the center comes out clean, 20-25 minutes. Cool for 10 minutes before removing from pan to a wire rack to cool completely.
3. Cut a thin slice off each side of cake. Cut cake into 1¼-in. squares. Place ½ in. apart on a rack in a 15x10x1-in. baking pan.
4. In a large bowl, combine glaze ingredients. Beat on low speed just until blended; beat on high until smooth. Apply glaze evenly over tops and sides of cake squares, allowing excess to drip off. Let dry. Repeat if necessary to thoroughly coat squares. Let dry completely.
5. For frosting, in a small bowl, cream the butter, shortening and vanilla. Beat in confectioners' sugar and enough milk to achieve desired consistency. Place ⅓ cup in each of 2 bowls; tint 1 pink and 1 green. Leave the remaining frosting plain.
6. Using a small star tip, decorate petits fours with frosting. If desired, garnish with sugar pearls.
1 PETIT FOUR: 171 cal., 4g fat (2g sat. fat), 7mg chol., 70mg sod., 33g carb. (30g sugars, 0 fiber), 1g pro.

HAWAIIAN SUNSET CAKE

This three-layer orange cake is pretty enough for company, but it's so simple to fix that you'll find yourself making it all the time. A boxed mix keeps it convenient while the pineapple-coconut filling makes it feel special.
—*Kara de la Vega, Santa Rosa, CA*

- -

Prep: 20 min. + chilling
Bake: 25 min. + cooling
Makes: 16 servings

1 pkg. white or orange cake mix (regular size)
1½ cups milk
1 pkg. (3.4 oz.) instant vanilla pudding mix
1 pkg. (3 oz.) orange gelatin
4 large eggs, room temperature
½ cup canola oil
FILLING
1 can (20 oz.) crushed pineapple, well drained
2 cups sugar
3½ cups sweetened shredded coconut (about 10 oz.)
1 cup sour cream
1 carton (8 oz.) frozen whipped topping, thawed
Optional: Additional toasted coconut, fresh pineapple, orange slices and fresh mint leaves

1. Preheat oven to 350°. In a large bowl, combine the first 6 ingredients; beat on low speed for 30 seconds. Beat on medium speed for 2 minutes.
2. Pour into 3 greased and floured 9-in. round baking pans. Bake until a toothpick inserted in the center comes out clean, 25-30 minutes. Cool for 10 minutes before removing from pans to wire racks to cool completely.
3. In a large bowl, combine the pineapple, sugar, 3½ cups coconut and sour cream. Set aside 1 cup for frosting. Place 1 cake on a serving plate; top with half of the remaining pineapple mixture. Repeat layers once; top with remaining cake.
4. Fold whipped topping into the reserved pineapple mixture. Spread over top and side of cake. If desired, top with additional coconut, sliced pineapple, orange slices and mint. Refrigerate until serving.

1 PIECE: 548 cal., 23g fat (12g sat. fat), 66mg chol., 384mg sod., 80g carb. (61g sugars, 2g fiber), 5g pro.

HAWAIIAN SUNSET CAKE TIPS

- **What is the best way to thoroughly drain the pineapple?** Place pineapple in a fine mesh sieve over a bowl. Press pineapple against the sieve with a spoon to extract liquid. If you don't have a sieve, you can scoop the pineapple onto several layers of paper towel or cheesecloth, then squeeze out the juice into a bowl.

- **How do you store Hawaiian sunset cake?** This cake can be stored in a cake carrier or airtight container in the refrigerator for up to 3 days.

- **How can you make Hawaiian sunset cake your own?** Try turning this sunset cake into pretty cupcakes! Fill cupcake liners in a muffin tin to ⅔ full with cake batter. Bake for about 20 minutes (test with a toothpick to make sure they're done). Cool completely, then hollow out centers with a small paring knife or melon scoop and fill with a spoonful of pineapple filling. Frost the tops of cupcakes with the whipped topping-pineapple mixture and decorate!

BOSTON CREAM CUPCAKES

Boston cream Bismarcks have been my favorite bakery treat since I was a child, so I put together this easy-to-make cupcake version.
—*Jeanne Holt, St. Paul, MN*

Prep: 25 min. • **Bake:** 15 min. + cooling
Makes: ½ dozen

- 3 Tbsp. shortening
- ⅓ cup sugar
- 1 large egg, room temperature
- ½ tsp. vanilla extract
- ½ cup all-purpose flour
- ½ tsp. baking powder
- ¼ tsp. salt
- 3 Tbsp. 2% milk
- ⅔ cup prepared vanilla pudding
- ½ cup semisweet chocolate chips
- ¼ cup heavy whipping cream

1. Preheat oven to 350°. In a small bowl, cream shortening and sugar until light and fluffy, 5-7 minutes. Beat in egg and vanilla. Combine the flour, baking powder and salt; add to the creamed mixture alternately with milk, beating well after each addition.
2. Fill paper-lined muffin cups half full. Bake until a toothpick inserted in the center comes out clean, 15-20 minutes. Cool for 10 minutes before removing from pan to a wire rack to cool completely.
3. Cut a small hole in the corner of a pastry bag; insert a small tip. Fill with pudding. Push the tip through the top to fill each cupcake.
4. Place chocolate chips in a small bowl. In a small saucepan, bring cream just to a boil. Pour over chocolate; whisk until smooth. Cool, stirring occasionally, to room temperature or until ganache thickens slightly, about 10 minutes. Spoon over cupcakes. Let stand until set. Store in an airtight container in the refrigerator.
1 CUPCAKE: 283 cal., 15g fat (7g sat. fat), 45mg chol., 204mg sod., 34g carb. (20g sugars, 1g fiber), 4g pro.

CREAM CHEESE SHEET CAKE

This tender, buttery sheet cake with a thin layer of fudge frosting is perfect for a crowd. It's always popular at potlucks and parties. It's common to see folks going back for second and even third pieces.
—*Gaye Mann, Rocky Mount, NC*

Prep: 20 min. + cooling
Bake: 30 min. + cooling
Makes: 30 servings

- 1 cup plus 2 Tbsp. butter, softened
- 6 oz. cream cheese, softened
- 2¼ cups sugar
- 6 large eggs, room temperature
- ¾ tsp. vanilla extract
- 2¼ cups cake flour

FROSTING
- 1 cup sugar
- ⅓ cup evaporated milk
- ½ cup butter, cubed
- ½ cup semisweet chocolate chips
  Sprinkles, optional

1. In a large bowl, cream the butter, cream cheese and sugar until light and fluffy, 5-7 minutes. Add eggs 1 at a time, beating well after each addition. Beat in vanilla. Add flour until well blended.
2. Pour into a greased 15x10x1-in. baking pan. Bake at 325° for 30-35 minutes or until a toothpick inserted in the center comes out clean. Cool completely on a wire rack.
3. For frosting, in a small saucepan, combine sugar and milk; bring to a boil over medium heat. Cover and cook for 3 minutes (do not stir). Stir in butter and chocolate chips until melted. Cool slightly. Stir frosting; spread over top of cake. If desired, top with sprinkles.
1 PIECE: 250 cal., 13g fat (8g sat. fat), 73mg chol., 125mg sod., 32g carb. (23g sugars, 0 fiber), 3g pro.

DIY CAKE FLOUR SUBSTITUTE

For each cup of cake flour needed, use 1 cup minus 2 Tbsp. of all-purpose flour and 2 Tbsp. cornstarch. Sift mixture together.

CHOCOLATE TRUFFLE CAKE

This tender, luxurious layer cake is perfect for chocolate lovers. With a ganache glaze and a wonderful bittersweet filling, the indulgence is so worth it!
—*JoAnn Koerkenmeier, Damiansville, IL*

- -

Prep: 35 min. + standing
Bake: 25 min. + cooling
Makes: 16 servings

2½ cups 2% milk
1 cup butter, cubed
8 oz. semisweet chocolate, chopped
3 large eggs, room temperature
2 tsp. vanilla extract
2⅔ cups all-purpose flour
2 cups sugar
1 tsp. baking soda
½ tsp. salt

FILLING
6 Tbsp. butter, cubed
4 oz. bittersweet chocolate, chopped
2½ cups confectioners' sugar
½ cup heavy whipping cream

GANACHE
10 oz. semisweet chocolate, chopped
⅔ cup heavy whipping cream

1. In a large saucepan, cook milk, butter and chocolate over low heat until melted. Remove from the heat; let stand for 10 minutes.
2. Preheat oven to 325°. In a large bowl, beat eggs and vanilla; stir in chocolate mixture until smooth. Combine flour, sugar, baking soda and salt; gradually add to chocolate mixture and mix well (batter will be thin).
3. Transfer to 3 greased and floured 9-in. round baking pans. Bake until a toothpick inserted in center comes out clean, 25-30 minutes. Cool 10 minutes before removing from pans to wire racks to cool completely.
4. For filling, in a small saucepan, melt the butter and chocolate. Stir in confectioners' sugar and heavy whipping cream until smooth.
5. For ganache, place the chocolate in a small bowl. In a small saucepan, bring cream just to a boil. Pour over chocolate; whisk until smooth. Cool, stirring occasionally, until ganache reaches a spreading consistency.
6. Place 1 cake layer on a serving plate; spread with half of the filling. Repeat layers. Top with remaining cake layer. Spread ganache over top and side of cake. Store in the refrigerator.
1 PIECE: 676 cal., 38g fat (22g sat. fat), 109mg chol., 299mg sod., 84g carb. (63g sugars, 3g fiber), 8g pro.

LEAF GARNISH

To garnish the cake with chocolate leaves, brush lemon leaves with 2 coats of melted milk chocolate, refrigerating until set between layers. Once the second coat is set, remove lemon leaves from chocolate and press chocolate leaves onto frosted cake. Lemon leaves can be found at most supermarket florists.

PUMPKIN CAKE ROLL

This lovely cake is a slice of heaven—especially if you like cream cheese and pumpkin together. With such excellent attributes, it's worth considering as a fancy alternative to pumpkin pie for Thanksgiving dessert.

—*Elizabeth Montgomery, Allston, MA*

- -

Prep: 25 min. • **Bake:** 15 min. + chilling
Makes: 10 servings

- 3   large eggs
- 1   cup sugar
- ⅔   cup canned pumpkin
- 1   tsp. lemon juice
- ¾   cup all-purpose flour
- 2   tsp. ground cinnamon
- 1   tsp. baking powder
- ½   tsp. salt
- ¼   tsp. ground nutmeg
- 1   cup finely chopped walnuts

CREAM CHEESE FILLING

- 6   oz. cream cheese, softened
- 1   cup confectioners' sugar
- ¼   cup butter, softened
- ½   tsp. vanilla extract
    Additional confectioners' sugar

1. In a large bowl, beat eggs on high for 5 minutes. Gradually beat in sugar until thick and lemon-colored. Add pumpkin and lemon juice. Combine the flour, cinnamon, baking powder, salt and nutmeg; fold into the pumpkin mixture.
2. Grease a 15x10x1-in. baking pan and line with parchment. Grease and flour the paper. Spread batter into pan; sprinkle with walnuts. Bake at 375° for 15 minutes or until cake springs back when lightly touched.

3. Immediately turn out onto a clean dish towel dusted with confectioners' sugar. Peel off paper and roll cake up in towel, starting with a short end. Cool.
4. Meanwhile, in a large bowl, beat the cream cheese, sugar, butter and vanilla until fluffy. Carefully unroll the cake. Spread filling over cake to within 1 in. of edges. Roll up again. Cover and chill until serving. Dust with confectioners' sugar.
1 PIECE: 365 cal., 20g fat (8g sat. fat), 85mg chol., 279mg sod., 44g carb. (33g sugars, 2g fiber), 6g pro.

CAKE ROLL POINTERS

Cool the rolled cake seam-side down to prevent it from unrolling. This cake is tender and can tear easily, so work slowly when spreading the filling.

HUMMINGBIRD CUPCAKES

Turn the traditional hummingbird cake—flavored with pineapple, bananas and walnuts—into a bite-sized treat with these lovely cupcakes.
—*Jessie Oleson, Santa Fe, NM*

Prep: 40 min. • **Bake:** 20 min. + cooling
Makes: 2 dozen

- 1 cup butter, softened
- 2 cups sugar
- 3 large eggs, room temperature
- 2 tsp. vanilla extract
- 2 cups mashed ripe bananas
- ½ cup drained canned crushed pineapple
- 3 cups all-purpose flour
- 1 tsp. baking soda
- 1 tsp. ground cinnamon
- ½ tsp. salt
- 1 cup sweetened shredded coconut
- 1 cup chopped walnuts

CREAM CHEESE FROSTING
- 1 pkg. (8 oz.) cream cheese, softened
- ½ cup butter, softened
- 3¾ cups confectioners' sugar
- 1 tsp. vanilla extract

1. In a large bowl, cream butter and sugar until light and fluffy, 5-7 minutes. Add eggs, 1 at a time, beating well after each addition. Beat in vanilla. In a small bowl, combine bananas and pineapple.
2. Combine the flour, baking soda, cinnamon and salt; add to the creamed mixture alternately with banana mixture, beating well after each addition. Fold in coconut and walnuts.
3. Fill 24 paper-lined muffin cups about two-thirds full. Bake at 350° until a toothpick inserted in the center comes out clean, 20-25 minutes. Cool the cupcakes for 10 minutes before removing from pans to wire racks to cool completely.
4. In a small bowl, beat the cream cheese and butter until fluffy. Add confectioners' sugar and vanilla; beat until smooth. Frost cupcakes.
1 CUPCAKE: 410 cal., 20g fat (11g sat. fat), 67mg chol., 230mg sod., 56g carb. (39g sugars, 2g fiber), 4g pro.

UPSIDE-DOWN STRAWBERRY SHORTCAKE

For a tasty twist, this special shortcake has a berry layer on the bottom. Our family has savored this tempting cake for many years.
—*Debra Falkiner, St. Charles, MO*

Prep: 20 min. • **Bake:** 45 min. + cooling
Makes: 15 servings

- 1 cup miniature marshmallows
- 1 pkg. (16 oz.) frozen sweetened sliced strawberries, thawed
- 1 pkg. (3 oz.) strawberry gelatin
- ½ cup shortening
- 1½ cups sugar
- 3 large eggs, room temperature
- 1 tsp. vanilla extract
- 2¼ cups all-purpose flour
- 3 tsp. baking powder
- ½ tsp. salt
- 1 cup 2% milk
   Fresh strawberries and whipped cream

1. Preheat oven 350°. Sprinkle marshmallows evenly into a greased 13x9-in. baking dish; set aside. In a small bowl, combine strawberries and gelatin powder; set aside.
2. In a large bowl, cream the shortening and sugar until light and fluffy, 5-7 minutes. Add eggs, 1 at a time, beating well after each addition. Beat in vanilla. Combine the flour, baking powder and salt; add to the creamed mixture alternately with milk, beating well after each addition.
3. Pour batter over the marshmallows. Spoon strawberry mixture evenly over batter. Bake 45-50 minutes or until a toothpick inserted in the center comes out clean. Cool 10 minutes before removing from pan to a wire rack to cool completely. Invert onto a serving platter (strawberry layer will be on bottom). Garnish with strawberries and whipped cream.

1 PIECE: 288 cal., 8g fat (2g sat. fat), 39mg chol., 214mg sod., 51g carb. (35g sugars, 1g fiber), 4g pro.

READER REVIEW
"Delicious! This was the perfect summer dessert. It would be good with whipped topping or ice cream, but it is wonderful on its own! I will make this again and again. It is easy and pretty enough for company. I am going to try it with blueberries next time."
—GITRUMM, TASTEOFHOME.COM

BLOOD ORANGE UPSIDE-DOWN CUPCAKES

When blood oranges are in season, this is one of my favorite ways to use them. I start with a cake mix and bump up the flavor with essential oil. No one knows these cupcakes are not from scratch.
—*Monica Chadha, Fremont, CA*

- -

Prep: 20 min. • **Bake:** 15 min. + cooling
Makes: 2 dozen

- 4   medium blood oranges
- ¼   cup whole-berry cranberry sauce
- 1   pkg. orange cake mix (regular size)
- 1   cup water
- ⅓   cup olive oil
- 3   large eggs, room temperature
- 3   to 4 drops orange oil, optional
    Optional: Creme fraiche or sour cream

1. Preheat oven to 350°. Grease or line 24 muffin cups with paper or foil liners.

Cut a thin slice from the top and bottom of each orange; stand orange upright on a cutting board. With a knife, cut off peel and outer membrane from orange. Thinly slice oranges; trim to fit muffin cups. Place 1 slice in each cup; top each with ½ tsp. cranberry sauce. Bake 8 minutes.
2. Meanwhile, in a large bowl, combine cake mix, water, olive oil, eggs and, if desired, orange oil; beat on low speed 30 seconds. Beat on medium speed 2 minutes. Remove pans from oven; fill with prepared batter.
3. Bake until a toothpick inserted in center comes out clean, 15-20 minutes. Cool cupcakes in pans for 10 minutes before removing to wire racks to cool completely. Remove liners; serve with creme fraiche if desired.
1 CUPCAKE: 130 cal., 5g fat (1g sat. fat), 23mg chol., 137mg sod., 19g carb. (11g sugars, 0 fiber), 2g pro. **DIABETIC EXCHANGES:** 1½ starch, 1 fat.

MILLION DOLLAR CAKE

Pineapple and mandarin oranges give this easy cake a refreshing, tropical twist. With cake mix and pudding mix as ingredients, it is a breeze to put together when you're short on prep time. Plus, it needs to chill before serving, so it's a perfect make-ahead dessert for potlucks and parties!
—*Rashanda Cobbins, Aurora, CO*

- -

Prep: 15 min. + chilling
Bake: 30 min. + cooling
Makes: 16 servings

- 1   can (11 oz.) mandarin oranges, undrained
- 1   pkg. yellow cake mix (regular size)
- 1¼ cups cold 2% milk
- 1   pkg. (3.4 oz.) instant vanilla pudding mix
- 1   can (20 oz.) crushed pineapple, well drained
- 2   cups whipped topping
- 8   oz. cream cheese, softened
- ½   cup confectioners' sugar
- 1   tsp. vanilla extract

1. Drain mandarin oranges and reserve liquid. Add reserved liquid to a liquid measuring cup (there should be about ½ cup) and fill with water to measure 1 cup. Prepare cake mix according to package directions, using the juice and water mixture in place of the water called for on the package. Bake in two greased 9-in. round baking pans according to package directions. Cool for 10 minutes before removing from pans to wire racks to cool completely.
2. In a large bowl, whisk milk and pudding mix for 2 minutes. Stir in pineapple. Spread 1 cup between cake layers.
3. In a small bowl, beat cream cheese, sugar and vanilla until smooth. Beat in 1 cup whipped topping. Fold in remaining topping. Spread on top and side of cake. Cover and refrigerate for 3 hours or overnight. Decorate with mandarin oranges prior to serving.
1 PIECE: 319 cal., 13g fat (6g sat. fat), 51mg chol., 317mg sod., 46g carb. (33g sugars, 0 fiber), 4g pro.

SANDY'S CHOCOLATE CAKE

Years ago, I drove four hours to a cake contest, holding my entry on my lap the whole way. But it paid off. One bite and you'll see why this velvety beauty was named the best chocolate cake recipe and won first prize.
—*Sandy Johnson, Tioga, PA*

- -

Prep: 30 min. • **Bake:** 30 min. + cooling
Makes: 16 servings

  1 cup butter, softened
  3 cups packed brown sugar
  4 large eggs, room temperature
  2 tsp. vanilla extract
2⅔ cups all-purpose flour
 ¾ cup baking cocoa
  3 tsp. baking soda
 ½ tsp. salt
1⅓ cups sour cream
1⅓ cups boiling water

FROSTING
 ½ cup butter, cubed
  3 oz. unsweetened chocolate, chopped
  3 oz. semisweet chocolate, chopped
  5 cups confectioners' sugar
  1 cup sour cream
  2 tsp. vanilla extract

1. Preheat oven to 350°. Grease and flour three 9-in. round baking pans.
2. In a large bowl, cream butter and brown sugar until light and fluffy, 5-7 minutes. Add eggs, 1 at a time, beating well after each addition. Beat in vanilla. In another bowl, whisk flour, cocoa, baking soda and salt; add to creamed mixture alternately with the sour cream, beating well after each addition. Stir in water until blended.
3. Transfer batter to prepared pans. Bake until a toothpick comes out clean, 30-35 minutes. Cool in pans for 10 minutes; remove to wire racks to cool completely.
4. For frosting, in a metal bowl over simmering water, melt the butter and chopped chocolates; stir until smooth. Cool slightly.
5. In a large bowl, combine the confectioners' sugar, sour cream and vanilla. Add chocolate mixture; beat until smooth. Spread frosting between layers and over top and side of cake. Refrigerate leftovers.
1 PIECE: 685 cal., 29g fat (18g sat. fat), 115mg chol., 505mg sod., 102g carb. (81g sugars, 3g fiber), 7g pro.

CREAM-FILLED PUMPKIN CUPCAKES

Here's a deliciously different use for pumpkin. Bursting with flavor and plenty of eye-catching appeal, these sweet and spicy filled cupcakes are bound to dazzle your family.
—*Ali Johnson, Petersburg, PA*

- -

Prep: 35 min. • **Bake:** 20 min. + cooling
Makes: 1½ dozen

  2 cups sugar
 ¾ cup canola oil
  1 can (15 oz.) pumpkin
  4 large eggs, room temperature
  2 cups all-purpose flour
  2 tsp. baking soda
  1 tsp. salt
  1 tsp. baking powder
  1 tsp. ground cinnamon

FILLING
  1 Tbsp. cornstarch
  1 cup whole milk
 ½ cup shortening
 ¼ cup butter, softened
2¾ cups confectioners' sugar
 ½ tsp. vanilla extract, optional
    Whole cloves, optional

1. Preheat oven to 350°. In a large bowl, beat sugar, oil, pumpkin and eggs until well blended. Combine flour, baking soda, salt, baking powder and cinnamon; gradually beat into pumpkin mixture until well blended.
2. Fill paper-lined muffin cups two-thirds full. Bake until a toothpick inserted in center comes out clean, 18-22 minutes. Cool 10 minutes before removing from pans to wire racks to cool completely.
3. For filling, combine cornstarch and milk in a small saucepan until smooth. Bring to a boil, stirring constantly. Remove from heat; cool to room temperature.
4. In a large bowl, cream shortening, butter and confectioners' sugar until light and fluffy, 3-4 minutes. Beat in vanilla if desired. Gradually add cornstarch mixture, beating until smooth, 3-5 minutes.
5. Using a sharp knife, cut a 1-in. circle 1 in. deep in the top of each cupcake. Carefully remove tops and set aside. Spoon or pipe filling into cupcakes. Replace tops. If desired, add a clove pumpkin stem to the tops.
1 CUPCAKE: 397 cal., 19g fat (4g sat. fat), 49mg chol., 342mg sod., 54g carb. (42g sugars, 1g fiber), 4g pro.

CREAM-FILLED
PUMPKIN CUPCAKES

WATERMELON
CUPCAKES

SWEET POTATO POUND CAKE

Since we are originally from Texas, we naturally love sweet potatoes, but this pound cake deserves to be a tradition in any home, whether you're from the South, East, North or West.
—Diane Mannix, Helmville, MT

- -

Prep: 25 min. • **Bake:** 50 min. + cooling
Makes: 16 servings

- 1 cup butter, softened
- 2 cups sugar
- 4 large eggs, room temperature
- 1 tsp. vanilla extract
- 3 cups all-purpose flour
- 2 tsp. baking powder
- 1 tsp. ground cinnamon
- ½ tsp. baking soda
- ¼ tsp. salt
- ¼ tsp. ground nutmeg
- 2 cups cold mashed sweet potatoes

GLAZE
- 1 cup confectioners' sugar
- 1 tsp. grated orange zest
- 3 to 5 tsp. orange juice

1. Preheat oven to 350°. Grease and flour a 10-in. fluted tube pan. In a large bowl, beat butter and sugar until light and fluffy, 5-7 minutes. Add eggs, 1 at a time, beating well after each addition. Beat in vanilla. Combine flour, baking powder, cinnamon, baking soda, salt and nutmeg; add to creamed mixture alternately with sweet potatoes. Beat just until combined (batter will be thick). Transfer to prepared pan.
2. Bake for 50-60 minutes or until a toothpick inserted in the center comes out clean. Cool 10 minutes before removing from pan to a wire rack to cool completely.
3. For glaze, in a small bowl, combine confectioners' sugar, orange zest and enough juice to achieve desired consistency. Drizzle over cake.
1 PIECE: 365 cal., 13g fat (8g sat. fat), 77mg chol., 257mg sod., 58g carb. (35g sugars, 2g fiber), 5g pro.

WATERMELON CUPCAKES

My granddaughter and I bake together each week. She was inspired by all of her mommy's flavored syrups, so we came up with this fun watermelon cupcake. If you have watermelon syrup, it can replace some of the lemon-lime soda in the cake batter and frosting, but the gelatin adds a lot of watermelon flavor on its own. If you are not going to pipe the frosting, you can reduce the amount of frosting by half.
—Elizabeth Bramkamp, Gig Harbor, WA

- -

Prep: 30 min. • **Bake:** 20 min. + cooling
Makes: 2 dozen

- 1 pkg. white cake mix (regular size)
- 1 cup lemon-lime soda
- 3 large egg whites, room temperature
- ¼ cup canola oil
- 1 pkg. (3 oz.) watermelon gelatin
- 2 drops watermelon oil, optional

FROSTING
- 2 cups butter, softened
- 6 cups confectioners' sugar
- 1 pkg. (3 oz.) watermelon gelatin
- 5 to 6 Tbsp. lemon-lime soda
- 15 drops red food coloring
- 3 Tbsp. miniature semisweet chocolate chips

1. Preheat oven to 350°. Line 24 muffin cups with paper liners. In a large bowl, combine cake mix, soda, egg whites, canola oil, gelatin and, if desired, watermelon oil; beat on low speed 30 seconds. Beat on medium speed 2 minutes. Transfer to prepared pans. Bake 18-21 minutes or until a toothpick inserted in center comes out clean. Cool in pans 10 minutes before removing to wire racks to cool completely.
2. For frosting, in a large bowl, combine the butter, confectioners' sugar, gelatin, soda and food coloring; beat until smooth. Frost cupcakes. Sprinkle with chocolate chips. Store in the refrigerator.
1 CUPCAKE: 385 cal., 19g fat (11g sat. fat), 41mg chol., 282mg sod., 54g carb. (46g sugars, 1g fiber), 2g pro.

CARROT SHEET CAKE

We sold pieces of this to-die-for carrot cake at an art show. Before long, we sold all 10 cakes we had made!
—*Dottie Cosgrove, South El Monte, CA*

Prep: 20 min. • **Bake:** 35 min. + cooling
Makes: 30 servings

- 4 large eggs, room temperature
- 1 cup canola oil
- 2 cups sugar
- 2 cups all-purpose flour
- 2 tsp. baking soda
- ¼ tsp. baking powder
- 2 tsp. ground cinnamon
- ½ tsp. salt
- 3 cups shredded carrots
- ⅔ cup chopped walnuts

FROSTING
- 1 pkg. (8 oz.) cream cheese, softened
- ½ cup butter, softened
- 1 tsp. vanilla extract
- 4 cups confectioners' sugar
- ⅔ cup chopped walnuts

1. Preheat oven to 350°. In a bowl, beat eggs, oil and sugar until smooth. Combine flour, baking soda, baking powder, cinnamon and salt; add to egg mixture and beat well. Stir in carrots and walnuts. Pour into a greased 15x10x1-in. baking pan. Bake until a toothpick inserted in the center comes out clean, about 35 minutes. Cool on a wire rack.

2. For frosting, beat cream cheese, butter and vanilla in a bowl until smooth; beat in confectioners' sugar. Spread over cake. Sprinkle with nuts. Decorate as desired. Store in the refrigerator.

1 PIECE: 311 cal., 17g fat (5g sat. fat), 45mg chol., 193mg sod., 38g carb. (29g sugars, 1g fiber), 4g pro.

CITRUS CORNMEAL CAKE

Cornmeal adds a rustic quality to this delicate dessert flavored with citrus and almond. It's sure to be a staple in your recipe collection. It also makes a great holiday party hostess gift.
—*Roxanne Chan, Albany, CA*

Prep: 25 min. • **Bake:** 25 min. + cooling
Makes: 8 servings

- ½ cup lemon yogurt
- ⅓ cup honey
- ¼ cup olive oil
- 1 large egg, room temperature
- 2 large egg whites, room temperature
- ¼ tsp. almond extract
- ¾ cup all-purpose flour
- ½ cup cornmeal
- 1 tsp. baking powder
- ½ tsp. grated orange zest
- 1 can (15 oz.) mandarin oranges, drained
- 3 Tbsp. sliced almonds

1. Coat a 9-in. fluted tart pan with removable bottom with cooking spray. In a large bowl, beat the yogurt, honey, oil, egg, egg whites and extract until well blended. Combine the flour, cornmeal and baking powder; gradually beat into yogurt mixture until blended. Stir in orange zest.

2. Pour into prepared pan. Arrange oranges over batter; sprinkle with almonds. Bake at 350° until a toothpick inserted in the center comes out clean, 25-30 minutes. Cool on a wire rack for 10 minutes before cutting. Serve warm or at room temperature.

1 PIECE: 240 cal., 9g fat (1g sat. fat), 27mg chol., 85mg sod., 36g carb. (20g sugars, 2g fiber), 5g pro.

PUMPKIN PIE CAKE

No one will guess this stunning dessert with yummy cinnamon frosting started with a cake mix. It's a perfect treat year-round.
—*Linda Murray, Allenstown, NH*

Prep: 25 min. • **Bake:** 25 min. + cooling
Makes: 12 servings

- 1   pkg. yellow cake mix (regular size)
- 3   large eggs, room temperature
- 1   cup water
- 1   cup canned pumpkin
- 1¾ tsp. ground cinnamon, divided
- ¼   tsp. ground ginger
- ¼   tsp. ground nutmeg
- 2½ cups vanilla frosting
- 1¼ cups chopped walnuts
     Additional ground cinnamon, optional

1. In a large bowl, combine the cake mix, eggs, water, pumpkin, 1 tsp. cinnamon, ginger and nutmeg; beat on low speed for 30 seconds. Beat on medium for 2 minutes.

2. Pour into 2 well-greased and floured 9-in. round baking pans. Bake at 375° for 25-30 minutes or until a toothpick inserted in each center comes out clean. Cool for 10 minutes before removing from pans to wire racks to cool completely.

3. Combine frosting and remaining cinnamon; spread between layers and over top and side of cake. Press the walnuts lightly into frosting on side of cake. If desired, dust top of cake with additional ground cinnamon.

1 PIECE: 500 cal., 19g fat (6g sat. fat), 47mg chol., 447mg sod., 78g carb. (52g sugars, 3g fiber), 5g pro.

Short & Sweet

RED VELVET CUPCAKES WITH COCONUT FROSTING

There's no better way to celebrate being together than with these fun-loving cupcakes.
—*Marie Rizzio, Interlochen, MI*

Prep: 25 min. • **Bake:** 20 min. + cooling
Makes: 2 dozen

- ¾   cup butter, softened
- 1½ cups sugar
- 2   large eggs, room temperature
- 1   Tbsp. red food coloring
- 1   tsp. vanilla extract
- 1¾ cups all-purpose flour
- ¼   cup baking cocoa
- ¾   tsp. baking soda
- ¾   tsp. salt
- 1   cup buttermilk
- 1   tsp. white vinegar

FROSTING
- 2   pkg. (8 oz. each) cream cheese, softened
- ¼   cup butter, softened
- 1½ cups confectioners' sugar
- 1   tsp. vanilla extract
- 2   cups sweetened shredded coconut, divided

1. Preheat oven to 350°. In a large bowl, cream butter and sugar until light and fluffy, 5-7 minutes. Add eggs, 1 at a time, beating well after each addition. Stir in food coloring and vanilla. Combine flour, cocoa, baking soda and salt. Combine buttermilk and vinegar. Add dry ingredients to creamed mixture alternately with buttermilk mixture, beating well after each addition.

2. Fill foil or paper-lined muffin cups two-thirds full. Bake until a toothpick inserted in center comes out clean, 18-22 minutes. Cool 10 minutes before removing from pans to wire rack to cool completely.

3. For frosting, in a large bowl, beat cream cheese and butter until fluffy, 3-5 minutes. Add confectioners' sugar and vanilla; beat until smooth. Stir in 1 cup coconut. Frost cupcakes.

4. Toast remaining 1 cup coconut; sprinkle over cupcakes. Store in the refrigerator.

1 CUPCAKE: 296 cal., 18g fat (12g sat. fat), 59mg chol., 260mg sod., 32g carb. (23g sugars, 1g fiber), 4g pro.

CLASSIC LEMON MERINGUE
PIE, PAGE 110

Pies & Tarts

From classic cherry and lemon meringue to root beer float and caramel macchiato, you'll find plenty of gorgeous pies here.

CRANBERRY-APPLE LATTICE PIE

Two popular fall fruits bring out the best in each other, while rum works its own magic. Few people pass up a piece of this pie.

—*Sonja Blow, Sherman Oaks, CA*

Prep: 40 min. + chilling
Bake: 65 min. + cooling
Makes: 8 servings

2½ cups all-purpose flour
1 Tbsp. sugar
¾ tsp. salt
½ cup cold unsalted butter, cubed
⅓ cup cold shortening
5 to 7 Tbsp. ice water

FILLING
½ cup dried currants or raisins
2 Tbsp. dark rum or water
1 cup fresh or frozen cranberries, divided
¾ cup sugar, divided
6 medium baking apples, such as Fuji or Braeburn (about 2 lbs.), peeled and cut into ¼-in. slices
2 Tbsp. quick-cooking tapioca
1 Tbsp. lemon juice
2 tsp. grated lemon zest
½ tsp. ground cinnamon

EGG WASH
2 tsp. sugar
Dash ground cinnamon
1 large egg
1 Tbsp. 2% milk or heavy whipping cream

1. In a small bowl, mix the flour, sugar and salt; cut in butter and shortening until crumbly. Gradually add ice water, tossing with a fork until dough holds together when pressed. Divide dough in half. Shape each half into a disk; wrap. Refrigerate for 30 minutes or overnight.

2. In a small bowl, combine currants and rum; let stand for 20 minutes.

3. Place ¾ cup cranberries and ¼ cup sugar in a food processor; pulse until cranberries are coarsely chopped. Transfer to a large bowl. Add the apples, tapioca, lemon juice, lemon zest, cinnamon, remaining ½ cup sugar and currant mixture; toss to combine. Let stand for 15 minutes. Preheat oven to 400°.

4. On a lightly floured surface, roll half the dough to a ⅛-in.-thick circle; transfer to a 9-in. deep-dish pie plate. Trim crust to ½ in. beyond rim of plate. Add filling.

5. Roll remaining dough to a ⅛-in.-thick circle; cut into ½-in.-wide strips. Arrange over filling in a lattice pattern. Trim and seal strips to edge of bottom crust; if desired flute edge. Place the remaining cranberries in spaces between lattice strips.

6. For egg wash, in a small bowl, mix sugar and cinnamon; set aside. In another bowl, whisk egg and milk; brush over lattice top. Sprinkle with sugar mixture.

7. Bake on a lower oven rack for 25 minutes. Reduce oven temperature to 325°; until crust is golden brown and filling is bubbly, 40-45 minutes longer.

8. Cool on a wire rack for 30 minutes; serve warm.

1 PIECE: 508 cal., 21g fat (9g sat. fat), 54mg chol., 235mg sod., 75g carb. (38g sugars, 4g fiber), 6g pro.

HUCKLEBERRY CHEESE PIE

To us Idahoans, huckleberries are a treasure! We've enjoyed this recipe a lot and serve it as a special treat when we have out-of-state guests.
—Pat Kuper, McCall, ID

Prep: 30 min. • Bake: 20 min. + cooling
Makes: 10 servings

BUTTER CRUNCH CRUST
1   cup all-purpose flour
¼   cup packed brown sugar
½   cup finely chopped nuts
½   cup cold butter
CHEESE FILLING
1   pkg. (8 oz.) cream cheese, softened
¾   cup confectioners' sugar
1   tsp. vanilla extract
1   cup whipped cream or 1 cup whipped topping

FRUIT TOPPING
½   cup sugar
4½ tsp. cornstarch
    Dash salt
½   cup water
2   cups fresh huckleberries or blueberries, divided
1½ tsp. butter
    Additional whipped cream, optional

1. In a bowl, combine the flour, brown sugar and nuts. Cut in butter until mixture resembles coarse crumbs. Spread on baking sheet; bake at 400° for 20 minutes, stirring occasionally.
2. Remove from oven. While mixture is still hot, press into a 9-in. pie plate, forming a pie shell. Cool completely.
3. For cheese filling, beat cream cheese, confectioners' sugar and vanilla until smooth; gently fold in whipped cream. Pour or spoon filling into cooled crust; refrigerate.
4. For topping, combine the sugar, cornstarch and salt in saucepan. Stir in water until smooth; add 1 cup berries. Bring to a boil. Cook and stir for 1-2 minutes or until thickened. Add butter and remaining berries. Cool; pour over cheese filling. Top with additional whipped cream if desired.
1 PIECE: 379 cal., 23g fat (12g sat. fat), 56mg chol., 192mg sod., 41g carb. (28g sugars, 1g fiber), 5g pro.

CONTEST-WINNING GERMAN CHOCOLATE CREAM PIE

I've won quite a few awards in recipe contests over the years, and I was truly delighted when this luscious pie sent me to the Great American Pie Show finals in Branson, Missouri.
—Marie Rizzio, Interlochen, MI

Prep: 20 min. • Bake: 45 min. + cooling
Makes: 8 servings

    Dough for single-crust pie
4   oz. German sweet chocolate, chopped
¼   cup butter, cubed
1   can (12 oz.) evaporated milk
1½ cups sugar
3   Tbsp. cornstarch
    Dash salt
2   large eggs
1   tsp. vanilla extract

1⅓ cups sweetened shredded coconut
½   cup chopped pecans
TOPPING
2   cups heavy whipping cream
2   Tbsp. confectioners' sugar
1   tsp. vanilla extract

1. Preheat oven to 375°. On a lightly floured surface, roll the dough to a ⅛-in.-thick circle; transfer to a 9-in. pie plate. Trim crust to ½ in. beyond rim of plate; flute edge. Refrigerate while preparing filling.
2. Place chocolate and butter in a small saucepan. Cook and stir over low heat until smooth. Remove from the heat; stir in milk. In a large bowl, combine sugar, cornstarch and salt. Add eggs, vanilla and chocolate mixture; mix well. Pour into crust. Sprinkle with coconut and pecans.
3. Bake 45-50 minutes or until a knife inserted in the center comes out clean. Cool completely on a wire rack.
4. For topping, in a large bowl, beat cream until it begins to thicken. Add confectioners' sugar and vanilla; beat until stiff peaks form. Spread over pie; sprinkle with additional coconut and pecans. Refrigerate until serving.
DOUGH FOR SINGLE-CRUST PIE:
Combine 1¼ cups all-purpose flour and ¼ tsp. salt; cut in ½ cup cold butter until crumbly. Gradually add 3-5 Tbsp. ice water, tossing with a fork until dough holds together when pressed. Shape into a disk; wrap and refrigerate 1 hour.
1 PIECE: 808 cal., 53g fat (30g sat. fat), 168mg chol., 280mg sod., 78g carb. (58g sugars, 3g fiber), 9g pro.

BANANA CREAM PIE

Made from our farm-fresh dairy products, this pie was a sensational creamy treat any time Mom served it. Her recipe is a real treasure, and I've never found one that tastes better!
—*Bernice Morris, Marshfield, MO*

- -

Prep: 35 min. + chilling
Cook: 10 min. + cooling
Makes: 8 servings

    Dough for single-crust pie
¾ cup sugar
⅓ cup all-purpose flour
¼ tsp. salt
2 cups whole milk
3 large egg yolks, lightly beaten
2 Tbsp. butter
1 tsp. vanilla extract
3 firm medium bananas
    Whipped cream, optional

1. On a lightly floured surface, roll dough to a ⅛-in.-thick circle; transfer to a 9-in. pie plate. Trim to ½ in. beyond rim of plate; flute edge. Refrigerate 30 minutes. Preheat oven to 425°.

2. Line crust with a double thickness of foil. Fill with pie weights, dried beans or uncooked rice. Bake on a lower oven rack 20-25 minutes or the until edge is golden brown. Remove foil and weights; bake 3-6 minutes longer or until bottom is golden brown. Cool on a wire rack.

3. Meanwhile, in a saucepan, combine sugar, flour and salt; stir in milk and mix well. Cook over medium-high heat until mixture is thickened and bubbly. Cook and stir 2 minutes longer. Remove from the heat. Stir a small amount into egg yolks; return all to saucepan. Bring to a gentle boil. Cook and stir 2 minutes;

remove from the heat. Add butter and vanilla; cool slightly.

4. Slice bananas into crust; pour filling over top. Cool on wire rack for 1 hour. Store in the refrigerator. If desired, garnish with whipped cream and additional sliced bananas.

DOUGH FOR SINGLE-CRUST PIE: Combine 1¼ cups all-purpose flour and ¼ tsp. salt; cut in ½ cup cold butter until crumbly. Gradually add 3-5 Tbsp. ice water, tossing with a fork until dough holds together when pressed. Shape into a disk; wrap and refrigerate 1 hour.

1 PIECE: 338 cal., 14g fat (7g sat. fat), 101mg chol., 236mg sod., 49g carb. (30g sugars, 1g fiber), 5g pro.

FLAKY BUMBLEBERRY PIE

When you want to make an impression, make this pie! The recipe produces one of the flakiest crusts ever, and the combination of rhubarb and different berries in the filling is delicious.
—*Suzanne Alberts, Onalaska, WI*

- -

Prep: 20 min. + chilling
Bake: 1 hour + cooling
Makes: 8 servings

1½ cups all-purpose flour
1 tsp. salt
1 tsp. sugar
1 cup cold butter
¼ cup cold water

FILLING
1 medium tart apple, peeled and diced
1 cup diced fresh or frozen rhubarb, thawed
1 cup fresh or frozen raspberries, thawed and drained
1 cup fresh or frozen blueberries, thawed and drained
1 cup sliced fresh or frozen strawberries, thawed and drained
1 cup sugar
½ cup all-purpose flour
1 Tbsp. lemon juice

1. In a small bowl, combine flour, salt and sugar. Cut in butter until mixture resembles coarse crumbs. Gradually add water, tossing with a fork until a ball forms. Cover and refrigerate 1 hour or until easy to handle.

2. Preheat oven to 400°. On a lightly floured surface, roll out half the dough to fit a 9-in. pie plate. Transfer crust to pie plate. Trim to ½ in. beyond edge of plate.

3. In a large bowl, combine filling ingredients; pour into crust. Roll out the remaining dough; cut out decorative shapes with cookie cutters. Place over filling. Cover edge loosely with foil.

4. Bake 20 minutes. Reduce heat to 350°; remove foil. Bake 40-45 minutes or until crust is golden brown and filling is bubbly. Cool on a wire rack.

1 PIECE: 449 cal., 23g fat (14g sat. fat), 61mg chol., 528mg sod., 58g carb. (31g sugars, 3g fiber), 4g pro.

FLAKY
BUMBLEBERRY PIE

FRESH CHERRY PIE

If you're looking to learn how to make a cherry pie, this recipe is the place to start. This ruby-red cherry pie is just sweet enough, with a hint of almond flavor and a good level of cinnamon. The cherries peeking out of the lattice crust make it so pretty too. I like to make a few of these pies throughout the summer.
—*Josie Bochek, Sturgeon Bay, WI*

Prep: 25 min. • **Bake:** 55 min. + cooling
Makes: 8 servings

- 1¼ cups sugar
- ⅓ cup cornstarch
- 1 cup cherry juice blend
- 4 cups fresh or frozen pitted tart cherries, thawed
- ½ tsp. ground cinnamon
- ¼ tsp. ground nutmeg
- ¼ tsp. almond extract

DOUGH
- 2 cups all-purpose flour
- ½ tsp. salt
- ⅔ cup shortening
- 5 to 7 Tbsp. cold water
- 1 large egg, beaten, optional

1. Preheat oven to 425°. In a large saucepan, combine sugar and cornstarch; gradually stir in cherry juice until smooth. Bring to a boil; cook and stir until thickened, about 2 minutes. Remove from the heat. Add cherries, cinnamon, nutmeg and extract; set aside.
2. In a large bowl, combine flour and salt; cut in shortening until crumbly. Gradually add cold water, tossing with a fork until a ball forms. Divide dough in half so that 1 ball is slightly larger than the other.
3. On a lightly floured surface, roll out the larger ball to fit a 9-in. pie plate. Transfer dough to pie plate; trim even with edge of plate. Add filling. Roll out remaining dough; make a lattice crust. Trim, seal and flute edge. If desired, brush with egg wash.
4. Bake for 10 minutes. Reduce heat to 375°; bake until crust is golden brown, 45-50 minutes. Cool on a wire rack.

1 PIECE: 466 cal., 17g fat (4g sat. fat), 23mg chol., 161mg sod., 73g carb. (41g sugars, 2g fiber), 5g pro.

READER REVIEW
"Awesome! An old-fashioned cherry pie from scratch. I've always loved the combo of cherry and almond together. Simply the best."
—SUEFALK, TASTEOFHOME.COM

ROOT BEER FLOAT PIE

This is the kind of recipe your kids will look back on and always remember. And you don't even need to use an oven.
—*Cindy Reams, Philipsburg, PA*

Prep: 15 min. + freezing
Makes: 8 servings

- 1 carton (8 oz.) frozen reduced-fat whipped topping, thawed, divided
- ¾ cup cold diet root beer
- ½ cup fat-free milk
- 1 pkg. (1 oz.) sugar-free instant vanilla pudding mix
- 1 graham cracker crust (9 in.) Maraschino cherries, optional

1. Set aside and refrigerate ½ cup whipped topping for garnish. In a large bowl, whisk the root beer, milk and pudding mix for 2 minutes. Fold in half the remaining whipped topping. Spread into graham cracker crust.
2. Spread remaining whipped topping over pie. Freeze for at least 8 hours or overnight.
3. Dollop reserved whipped topping over each serving; top each serving with a maraschino cherry if desired.
1 PIECE: 184 cal., 8g fat (4g sat. fat), 0 chol., 268mg sod., 27g carb. (14g sugars, 0 fiber), 1g pro. **DIABETIC EXCHANGES:** 2 starch, 1½ fat.

BOURBON CHOCOLATE PECAN PIE

When my fiance first made this for me, I declared it to be the best pie ever! Creamy chocolate combines with crunchy nuts in a great, gooey filling.
—*Tanya Taylor, Cary, NC*

Prep: 25 min. + chilling
Bake: 50 min. + cooling
Makes: 8 servings

- 1¼ cups all-purpose flour
- 1 Tbsp. sugar
- ½ tsp. salt
- ½ cup cold butter, cubed
- 3 to 5 Tbsp. ice water

FILLING
- 3 large eggs
- 1 cup packed dark brown sugar
- ½ cup light corn syrup
- ½ cup dark corn syrup
- ¼ cup bourbon
- 2 Tbsp. butter, melted
- ½ tsp. salt
- 1½ cups pecan halves, divided
- ¾ cup 60% cacao bittersweet chocolate baking chips, divided

1. Combine flour, sugar and salt; cut in butter until crumbly. Gradually add water, tossing with a fork until dough holds together when pressed. Flatten into a disk. Wrap; refrigerate until easy to handle, about 1 hour.
2. Preheat oven to 325°. On a floured surface, roll dough to a ⅛-in.-thick circle; transfer to a 9-in. pie plate. Trim the crust to ½ in. beyond rim of plate; flute edge.
3. Beat first 7 filling ingredients until blended. Stir in 1 cup pecans and ½ cup chocolate chips. Pour filling into crust; sprinkle with remaining pecans and chocolate chips. Bake until crust is golden brown and filling is puffed, 50-60 minutes. Cool completely on a wire rack.
1 PIECE: 676 cal., 35g fat (14g sat. fat), 108mg chol., 490mg sod., 89g carb. (70g sugars, 3g fiber), 7g pro.

CUTTING IN BUTTER

Cutting butter into dry ingredients results in tiny bits of flour-coated butter throughout the dough, creating a pie crust that is both tender and crumbly at the same time. If you don't have a pastry blender, use two knives to cut in the cold butter.

APPLE PIE TARTLETS

Sweet and cinnamony, these apple-pie morsels are a delightful addition to a dessert buffet or snack tray. You can prebake the shells a day or two in advance.
—*Mary Kelley, Minneapolis, MN*

Prep: 35 min. + cooling
Makes: 20 servings

- 1   sheet refrigerated pie crust
- 1   Tbsp. sugar
      Dash ground cinnamon

FILLING
- 2   tsp. butter
- 2   cups diced peeled tart apples
- 3   Tbsp. sugar
- 3   Tbsp. fat-free caramel ice cream topping
- 2   Tbsp. all-purpose flour
- ½   tsp. ground cinnamon
- ½   tsp. lemon juice
- ⅛   tsp. salt

1. Preheat oven to 350°. On a lightly floured surface, roll out crust; cut into twenty 2½-in. circles. Press onto the bottom and up the sides of miniature muffin cups coated with cooking spray. Prick crusts with a fork. Spray lightly with cooking spray. Combine sugar and cinnamon; sprinkle over crusts.
2. Bake 6-8 minutes or until golden brown. Cool for 5 minutes before removing from pans to wire racks.
3. In a large saucepan, melt butter. Add apples; cook and stir over medium heat until crisp-tender, 4-5 minutes. Stir in sugar, caramel topping, flour, cinnamon, lemon juice and salt. Bring to a boil; cook and stir until sauce is thickened and apples are tender, about 2 minutes. Cool for 5 minutes. Spoon into tart shells.
1 PIECE: 74 cal., 3g fat (1g sat. fat), 3mg chol., 62mg sod., 11g carb. (5g sugars, 0 fiber), 1g pro.

PEACH & BLUEBERRY GALETTE

My husband's favorite pie is blueberry, made with fresh-picked northern Ontario blueberries. Adding peaches and a rustic crust creates a bit of summer fun, perfect for a picnic.
—*Christine Kropp, London, ON*

Prep: 30 min. + chilling
Bake: 50 min. + cooling
Makes: 8 servings

- 1½   cups all-purpose flour
- 1   Tbsp. sugar
- ½   tsp. salt
- 10   Tbsp. cold unsalted butter
- 4   Tbsp. 2% milk
- 1   large egg yolk

FILLING
- 1   lb. medium peaches, peeled and cut into ½-in. slices (about 3 cups)
- 2   cups fresh or frozen blueberries
- ¼   cup packed light brown sugar
- 2   Tbsp. all-purpose flour
- ¼   tsp. ground cinnamon
- ⅛   tsp. salt
- 1   large egg, beaten
- 2   Tbsp. demerara sugar
        Blueberry ice cream, optional

1. In a large bowl, mix flour, sugar and salt; cut in butter until crumbly. Combine milk and egg yolk; gradually add to flour mixture, tossing with a fork until dough holds together when pressed. Shape into a disk; cover and refrigerate for 1 hour or overnight.
2. Preheat oven to 350°. On a lightly floured surface, roll dough to a 13-in. circle. Transfer to a parchment-lined 14-in. pizza pan. Refrigerate, covered, while preparing filling.
3. For filling, combine peaches, blueberries, brown sugar, flour, cinnamon and salt. Arrange over crust to within 1½ in. of edge. Fold crust edge over filling, pleating as you go and leaving an opening in the center. Brush beaten egg over folded crust; sprinkle with demerara sugar.
4. Bake until crust is golden and filling is bubbly, 50-55 minutes. Transfer tart to a wire rack to cool for 10 minutes before cutting. Serve warm, with ice cream, if desired.
1 PIECE: 319 cal., 16g fat (9g sat. fat), 68mg chol., 196mg sod., 42g carb. (20g sugars, 2g fiber), 4g pro.

KEY LIME CREAM PIE

I am very proud of this luscious no-bake beauty. It's so cool and refreshing—perfect for any summer potluck or get-together. Wherever I take this pie, it quickly disappears, and everyone asks for the recipe.
—*Shirley Rickis, The Villages, FL*

Prep: 40 min. + chilling
Makes: 12 servings

- 1   pkg. (11.3 oz.) pecan shortbread cookies, crushed (about 2 cups)
- ⅓   cup butter, melted
- 4   cups heavy whipping cream
- ¼   cup confectioners' sugar
- 1   tsp. coconut extract
- 1   pkg. (8 oz.) cream cheese, softened
- 1   can (14 oz.) sweetened condensed milk
- ½   cup Key lime juice
- ¼   cup sweetened shredded coconut, toasted
      Sliced Key limes, optional

1. In a small bowl, mix crushed cookies and butter. Press onto bottom and up side of a greased 9-in. deep-dish pie plate. In a large bowl, beat cream until it begins to thicken. Add confectioners' sugar and extract; beat until stiff peaks form. In another large bowl, beat cream cheese, condensed milk and lime juice until blended. Fold in 2 cups whipped cream. Spoon into prepared crust.
2. Top with remaining whipped cream; sprinkle with toasted coconut. Refrigerate for at least 4 hours before serving. If desired, garnish with sliced Key limes.

1 PIECE: 646 cal., 52g fat (30g sat. fat), 143mg chol., 252mg sod., 41g carb. (29g sugars, 0 fiber), 8g pro.

STRAWBERRY TART

This creamy strawberry tart boasts a crunchy chocolate layer tucked next to the crust. Try making individual tartlets instead of one big dessert.
—*Dawn Tringali, Hamilton Square, NJ*

Prep: 30 min. + chilling
Makes: 8 servings

- 1 sheet refrigerated pie crust
- 3 oz. German sweet chocolate, melted
- 2 pkg. (8 oz. each) cream cheese, softened
- 3 Tbsp. heavy whipping cream
- 2 tsp. vanilla extract
- 1¾ cups confectioners' sugar
- 2½ cups sliced fresh strawberries
- ¼ cup red currant jelly

1. Preheat oven to 450°. Unroll crust and press onto the bottom and up the side of an ungreased 9-in. fluted tart pan with a removable bottom. Place on a baking sheet. Bake crust until golden brown, 10-12 minutes. Cool on a wire rack.
2. Spread melted chocolate over bottom of crust. Refrigerate until almost set, 5-10 minutes. Meanwhile, in a large bowl, beat cream cheese, cream and vanilla until smooth. Gradually beat in confectioners' sugar. Spread over chocolate layer.
3. Arrange strawberries over filling; brush strawberries with jelly. Refrigerate for at least 2 hours. Remove side of pan before serving.
1 PIECE: 545 cal., 32g fat (18g sat. fat), 69mg chol., 283mg sod., 55g carb. (40g sugars, 1g fiber), 6g pro.

LEMON TART WITH ALMOND CRUST

Our state produces an abundance of lemons, and everyone is always looking for new ways to use them. This beautiful tart is my delicious solution to the excess-lemon problem!
—*Lois Kinneberg, Phoenix, AZ*

Prep: 40 min. • **Bake:** 10 min. + cooling
Makes: 8 servings

- 1 cup all-purpose flour
- ½ cup sliced almonds, toasted
- ¼ cup sugar
- 6 Tbsp. cold butter
- ½ tsp. almond extract
- ¼ tsp. salt
- 2 to 3 Tbsp. cold water

FILLING
- 3 large eggs
- 3 large egg yolks
- 1 cup sugar
- ¾ cup lemon juice
- 2 Tbsp. grated lemon zest
  Dash salt
- 6 Tbsp. butter, cubed

1. Place the flour, almonds, sugar, butter, extract and salt in a food processor. Cover and pulse until blended. Gradually add water, 1 Tbsp. at a time, pulsing until mixture forms a soft dough.
2. Press onto the bottom and up the side of a greased 9-in. fluted tart pan with a removable bottom. Bake at 400° for 15-20 minutes or until golden brown. Cool on a wire rack. Reduce heat to 325°.
3. In a small heavy saucepan over medium heat, whisk the eggs, egg yolks, sugar, lemon juice, zest and salt until blended. Add butter; cook, whisking constantly, until mixture is thickened. Pour into crust.
4. Bake for 8-10 minutes or until set. Cool on a wire rack. Refrigerate the leftovers.
1 PIECE: 419 cal., 24g fat (12g sat. fat), 185mg chol., 424mg sod., 47g carb. (32g sugars, 1g fiber), 6g pro.

PEACH TARTLETS

Tarts are special treats that show off any fruit perfectly. The pastry is rich, tender and crunchy, almost like a cookie. I use it for every type of tart I can think of.
—Leanne Wheless, Borger, TX

- -

Prep: 30 min. • **Bake:** 15 min. + cooling
Makes: 8 servings

3⅓ cups all-purpose flour
¼ cup sugar
½ tsp. salt
1 cup cold butter, cubed
½ cup plus 2 Tbsp. cold water
2 large egg yolks

FILLING
⅔ cup sugar
2 Tbsp. cornstarch
  Dash salt
1 cup water
1 can (29 oz.) sliced peaches, drained
1 tsp. lemon juice
  Whipped cream, optional

1. In a large bowl, combine the flour, sugar and salt; cut in butter until mixture resembles coarse crumbs. Add water and egg yolks; stir until dough forms a ball.
2. Divide into 8 portions; press onto the bottom and up the sides of eight 4-in. tart pans. Bake at 400° until golden brown, 15-20 minutes. Cool on wire racks.

3. For filling, in a large saucepan, combine the sugar, cornstarch and salt. Stir in water until smooth. Bring to a boil; cook and stir for 2 minutes or until thickened. Remove from the heat. Stir in peaches and lemon juice.
4. Spoon into tart shells. Chill until serving. Garnish with whipped cream if desired.
1 TARTLET: 557 cal., 24g fat (15g sat. fat), 111mg chol., 336mg sod., 78g carb. (37g sugars, 2g fiber), 6g pro.
APRICOT TARTLETS: Substitute canned apricot halves for the peaches.
PEAR TARTLETS: Substitute canned sliced pears for the peaches.

MAPLE PUMPKIN PIE

Tired of traditional pumpkin pie? The maple syrup in this special pie provides a subtle but terrific enhancer.
—Lisa Varner, El Paso, TX

- -

Prep: 25 min. • **Bake:** 1 hour + chilling
Makes: 8 servings

  Dough for single-crust pie
2 large eggs
1 can (15 oz.) pumpkin
1 cup evaporated milk
¾ cup sugar
½ cup maple syrup
1 tsp. pumpkin pie spice
¼ tsp. salt
MAPLE WHIPPED CREAM
1 cup heavy whipping cream
2 Tbsp. confectioners' sugar
1 Tbsp. maple syrup
¼ tsp. pumpkin pie spice
  Chopped pecans, optional

1. Preheat oven to 425°. On a lightly floured surface, roll dough to a ⅛-in.-thick circle; transfer to a 9-in. pie plate. Trim crust to ½ in. beyond rim of plate; flute edge. Refrigerate while preparing filling.
2. In a large bowl, combine the next 7 ingredients; beat until smooth. Pour into crust. Bake for 15 minutes. Reduce heat to 350°. Bake 45-50 minutes longer or until crust is golden brown and top of pie is set (cover edge with foil during the last 15 minutes to prevent overbrowning if necessary). Cool on a wire rack for 1 hour. Refrigerate overnight or until set.
3. In a small bowl, beat the cream, confectioners' sugar, syrup and pumpkin pie spice until stiff peaks form. Pipe or dollop onto pie. Sprinkle with pecans if desired.
DOUGH FOR SINGLE-CRUST PIE: Combine 1¼ cups all-purpose flour and ¼ tsp. salt; cut in ½ cup cold butter until crumbly. Gradually add 3-5 Tbsp. ice water, tossing with a fork until dough holds together when pressed. Shape into a disk; wrap and refrigerate 1 hour.
1 PIECE: 489 cal., 26g fat (16g sat. fat), 121mg chol., 290mg sod., 59g carb. (40g sugars, 2g fiber), 7g pro.

READER REVIEW
"I made two pies for Thanksgiving and both came from Taste of Home. Of the seven pies at this year's gathering, mine were the only ones that were completely gone. This was one of them. The pumpkin with the maple was delicious, and I got many compliments. It was very easy to make. I think I only had to buy the pumpkin. Perfect pie."
—JUDONTMESSWITHME, TASTEOFHOME.COM

MAPLE PUMPKIN PIE.

MACAROON
CHERRY PIE

S'MORE TARTS

Short & Sweet

Kids of all ages will go crazy for these little graham cracker tarts filled with fudge brownies and golden marshmallows.
—*Trish Quinn, Cheyenne, WY*

Prep: 10 min. • **Bake:** 25 min.
Makes: 1 dozen

1 pkg. fudge brownie mix (13x9-in. pan size)
12 individual graham cracker shells
1½ cups miniature marshmallows
1 cup milk chocolate chips

1. Prepare brownie batter according to package directions. Place graham cracker shells on a baking sheet and fill with brownie batter.
2. Bake at 350° for 20-25 minutes or until a toothpick inserted in the center comes out with moist crumbs. Immediately sprinkle with marshmallows and chocolate chips. Bake 3-5 minutes longer or until marshmallows are puffed and golden brown.
1 TART: 503 cal., 24g fat (6g sat. fat), 35mg chol., 334mg sod., 66g carb. (40g sugars, 3g fiber), 6g pro.

FLAME-FINISHED FINALE

S'more tarts make a delicious cookout treat. You can gently reheat the tarts on a covered grill over low heat while guests are eating the main course. The tarts will be warm and gooey come dessert time, ready to top with chocolate sauce, whipped cream in a can, ice cream, bits of Hershey bar, Teddy Grahams or whatever else your crew dreams up.

MACAROON CHERRY PIE

In summer, I use homegrown cherries in this amazing pie with a crunchy coconut topping. But canned tart cherries yield a dessert that's almost as delicious. I always bake this pie around Presidents Day or Valentine's Day, but it's popular with my family the whole year through.
—*Lori Daniels, Beverly, WV*

Prep: 25 min. • **Bake:** 35 min. + chilling
Makes: 8 servings

Dough for single-crust pie
3 cans (14½ oz. each) pitted tart cherries
1 cup sugar
⅓ cup cornstarch
½ tsp. ground cinnamon
¼ tsp. red food coloring, optional
TOPPING
1 large egg, lightly beaten
2 Tbsp. 2% milk
1 Tbsp. butter, melted
¼ tsp. almond extract
¼ cup sugar
⅛ tsp. salt
1 cup sweetened shredded coconut
½ cup sliced almonds

1. Preheat oven to 400°. On a lightly floured surface, roll dough to a ⅛-in.-thick circle; transfer to a 9-in. cast-iron skillet or deep-dish pie plate. Trim to ½ in. beyond edge of plate; flute edge. Bake 6 minutes; set aside.
2. Drain cherries, reserving 1 cup juice. Set cherries aside. In a large saucepan, combine sugar and cornstarch; gradually stir in cherry juice until blended. Bring to a boil over medium heat; cook and stir until thickened, about 2 minutes.
3. Remove from heat; stir in cinnamon and, if desired, food coloring. Gently fold in cherries. Pour into crust. Cover edge loosely with foil. Bake at 400° for 20 minutes.
4. Meanwhile, in a large bowl, combine first 6 topping ingredients. Stir in coconut and almonds.
5. Remove foil from pie; spoon topping over pie. Reduce oven to 350°; bake until topping is lightly browned, 15-20 minutes. Cool on a wire rack 1 hour. Chill 4 hours or overnight before cutting.
DOUGH FOR SINGLE-CRUST PIE: Combine 1¼ cups all-purpose flour and ¼ tsp. salt; cut in ½ cup cold butter until crumbly. Gradually add 3-5 Tbsp. ice water, tossing with a fork until dough holds together when pressed. Shape into a disk; wrap and refrigerate 1 hour.
1 PIECE: 434 cal., 16g fat (8g sat. fat), 36mg chol., 199mg sod., 70g carb. (48g sugars, 3g fiber), 5g pro.
CLASSIC CRUMB-TOPPED CHERRY PIE: Preheat oven to 425°. Omit topping ingredients. Mix ½ cup all-purpose flour and ½ cup sugar; cut in ¼ cup cold butter until crumbly. Sprinkle over filling. Bake 35-45 minutes or until crust is golden brown and filling is bubbly. Cover edge loosely with foil if pie is browning too quickly.

VANILLA CREAM FRUIT TART

It's well worth the effort to whip up this creamy tart bursting with juicy summer berries. A friend gave me the recipe, and it always receives rave reviews at gatherings.
—*Susan Terzakis, Andover, MA*

Prep: 25 min. + chilling • **Bake:** 25 min.
Makes: 12 servings

- ¾ cup butter, softened
- ½ cup confectioners' sugar
- 1½ cups all-purpose flour
- 1 pkg. (10 to 12 oz.) white baking chips, melted and cooled
- ¼ cup heavy whipping cream
- 1 pkg. (8 oz.) cream cheese, softened
- ½ cup pineapple juice
- ¼ cup sugar
- 1 Tbsp. cornstarch
- ½ tsp. lemon juice
- 4 cups assorted fresh fruit

1. Preheat oven to 300°. Cream butter and confectioners' sugar until light and fluffy. Beat in flour (mixture will be crumbly). Pat onto a greased 12-in. pizza pan. Bake until lightly browned, 25-28 minutes. Cool.

2. Beat melted chips and cream until smooth. Beat in cream cheese until smooth. Spread over crust. Refrigerate 30 minutes. Meanwhile, in a small saucepan, combine pineapple juice, sugar, cornstarch and lemon juice. Bring to a boil over medium heat; cook and stir until thickened, about 2 minutes. Cool.

3. Arrange fruit over cream cheese layer; brush with pineapple mixture. Refrigerate 1 hour before serving.

1 PIECE: 433 cal., 28g fat (17g sat. fat), 60mg chol., 174mg sod., 43g carb. (28g sugars, 2g fiber), 5g pro.

FRUIT TART TIPS

How do you make a tart without a tart pan? This particular tart recipe calls for a flat pizza pan! If you don't have that, you can shape the tart into a rectangle and bake it on a cookie sheet. For other tart recipes, try using a springform pan if you don't have a tart pan. Lacking that, a pie pan will do the trick. Keep in mind that if you use a pie plate that is glass or ceramic, you may need to adjust your baking time, as traditional tart pans are metal.

How do you keep fruit tarts from getting soggy? Most fruit tarts are best eaten the day they are made, to avoid sogginess. However, if you plan on keeping your fruit tart longer than a day, consider coating the crust with a thin layer of melted chocolate—it can be white, semisweet, milk or dark chocolate—prior to filling. Not only does it coat the crust and keep it from absorbing moisture, but it also adds an additional surprise element of flavor!

How long does a fruit tart last in the fridge? Fresh fruit tarts really last only 1-2 days in the fridge, loosely covered with food wrap. It's best eaten sooner rather than later! If you want to prep this fruit tart ahead of time, make the filling and crust in advance and assemble on the day that you're serving it.

What fruits can you use on a fruit tart? The beauty of this fruit tart recipe is that you can use nearly any fruit. Berries, stone fruit and tropical fruits like mango all work very well to top a tart. The only fruits you should really steer clear of are ones that brown when they are sliced, like apples, bananas and pears. These will still taste fine, but they won't look as appealing.

GET OTHER
IDEAS FOR
DECORATING
THE TOP
Just hover your
camera here.

RUSTIC APPLE TART

Like an apple pie without the pan, this scrumptious tart has a crispy crust that cuts nicely. Add caramel topping for a yummy final touch.
—Betty Fulks, Onia, AR

Prep: 20 min. + chilling • **Bake:** 25 min.
Makes: 4 servings

⅔ cup all-purpose flour
1 Tbsp. sugar
⅛ tsp. salt
¼ cup cold butter, cubed
6½ tsp. cold water
⅛ tsp. vanilla extract
FILLING
1½ cups sliced or chopped peeled
    tart apples
3 Tbsp. sugar
1 Tbsp. all-purpose flour
TOPPING
1 tsp. sugar
¼ tsp. ground cinnamon
1 large egg
1 Tbsp. water

2 Tbsp. caramel ice cream topping, warmed

1. In a large bowl, combine flour, sugar and salt; cut in butter until crumbly. Gradually add water and vanilla, tossing with a fork until dough forms a ball. Cover and refrigerate until easy to handle, about 30 minutes.
2. Preheat oven to 400°. On a lightly floured surface, roll dough into a 10-in. circle. Transfer to a parchment-lined baking sheet. Combine the filling ingredients; spoon over crust to within 2 in. of edge. Fold up edge of crust over filling, leaving center uncovered. Combine sugar and cinnamon; sprinkle over filling. Whisk egg and water; brush over crust.
3. Bake until crust is golden and filling is bubbly, 25-30 minutes. Using parchment, slide tart onto a wire rack. Drizzle with caramel topping. Serve warm.
1 PIECE: 298 cal., 13g fat (8g sat. fat), 77mg chol., 218mg sod., 42g carb. (24g sugars, 1g fiber), 4g pro.

DARK CHOCOLATE-CARAMEL MACCHIATO PIE

One of my first entries in the National Pie Championship was this impressive pie with coffee flavor and cool chocolate curls on top.
—Amy Freeze, Avon Park, FL

Prep: 30 min. + freezing
Makes: 10 servings

8 undipped biscotti (about 6 oz.)
¼ cup butter, melted
FILLING AND TOPPING
1 pkg. (8 oz.) softened cream
    cheese, divided
4 oz. dark chocolate candy bar,
    melted

¼ cup strong brewed coffee, cooled
1 carton (12 oz.) frozen whipped
    topping, thawed, divided
4 oz. milk chocolate, melted
¼ cup caramel sundae syrup
    Shaved chocolate
    Additional caramel syrup, optional

1. Preheat oven to 350°. Pulse biscotti in a food processor until fine crumbs form (about 1¼ cups). Add butter; pulse until blended. Press onto bottom and up side of a greased 9-in. pie plate. Bake 8-10 minutes or until lightly browned. Cool on a wire rack.
2. Beat 4 oz. cream cheese until creamy. Gradually beat in melted dark chocolate and coffee until blended.

Fold in ¾ cup whipped topping. Spread in crust. Freeze 30 minutes or until set.
3. Beat remaining cream cheese until creamy. Gradually beat in melted milk chocolate until blended. Fold in ¾ cup whipped topping. Spread over first layer. Freeze until set, about 30 minutes.
4. Place remaining whipped topping in a large bowl; fold in caramel syrup. Spread over pie; top with shaved chocolate. Refrigerate until serving. If desired, drizzle with additional caramel syrup before serving.
1 PIECE: 413 cal., 27g fat (18g sat. fat), 55mg chol., 186mg sod., 39g carb. (30g sugars, 1g fiber), 5g pro.

CLASSIC LEMON MERINGUE PIE

Love lemon meringue pie? This is the only recipe you'll ever need. The flaky, tender, made-from-scratch crust is worth the effort.
—*Lee Bremson, Kansas City, MO*

- -

Prep: 30 min. + standing
Bake: 25 min. + chilling
Makes: 8 servings

1⅓ cups all-purpose flour
½ tsp. salt
½ cup shortening
1 to 3 Tbsp. cold water

FILLING

1¼ cups sugar
¼ cup cornstarch
3 Tbsp. all-purpose flour
¼ tsp. salt
1½ cups water
3 large egg yolks, lightly beaten
2 Tbsp. butter
1½ tsp. grated lemon zest
⅓ cup lemon juice

MERINGUE

4 large egg whites
½ cup sugar, divided
1 Tbsp. cornstarch
½ cup cold water
¾ tsp. vanilla extract

1. In a small bowl, combine flour and salt; cut in shortening until crumbly. Gradually add 3 Tbsp. cold water, tossing with a fork until dough forms a ball.

2. Roll out dough to fit a 9-in. pie plate. Transfer crust to pie plate. Trim to ½ in. beyond rim of plate; flute edge. Bake at 425° for 12-15 minutes or until lightly browned.

3. Meanwhile, in a large saucepan, combine the sugar, cornstarch, flour and salt. Gradually stir in water until smooth. Cook and stir over medium-high heat until thickened and bubbly. Reduce heat; cook and stir 2 minutes longer.

4. Remove from the heat. Stir a small amount of hot filling into egg yolks; return all to the pan, stirring constantly. Bring to a gentle boil; cook and stir 2 minutes longer. Remove from the heat. Gently stir in butter and lemon zest. Gradually stir in lemon juice just until combined. Pour into the crust.

5. Place egg whites in a large bowl; let stand at room temperature for 30 minutes. For meringue, in a saucepan, combine 2 Tbsp. sugar and cornstarch. Gradually stir in cold water. Cook and stir over medium heat until mixture is clear. Transfer to a bowl; cool.

6. Beat egg whites and vanilla until soft peaks form. Gradually beat in the remaining sugar, 1 Tbsp. at a time. Beat in cornstarch mixture on high until stiff peaks form and sugar is dissolved (meringue will not be smooth). Spread evenly over hot filling, sealing edge to crust.

7. Bake at 350° for 25 minutes or until the meringue is golden brown. Cool on a wire rack for 1 hour. Refrigerate for at least 3 hours before serving.

1 PIECE: 444 cal., 17g fat (5g sat. fat), 87mg chol., 282mg sod., 68g carb. (43g sugars, 1g fiber), 5g pro.

PREVENT WEEPING MERINGUE PIES

To prevent that dreaded watery texture, make sure that you cook the filling long enough. Keep an eye on the clock and be sure to heat the filling for the full time the recipe indicates. Another way to prevent weepy filling is to seal the pie properly. That means spreading the meringue to the very edge of the pie crust, making sure no filling is exposed. Do it while the filling is hot. Finally, meringue pies and humidity are not friends. If you're serving this pie on a humid day, keep it covered and refrigerated until it's time to serve.

CHOCOLATE-GLAZED
RASPBERRY ECLAIRS, PAGE 129

Pastries

From elegant eclairs and tiny cream puffs to flaky strudels and specialty cannoli, you'll find the perfect pastry in this chapter.

BLUEBERRY TURNOVERS

Growing up, one of my favorite treats was to heat up a Pepperidge Farm Blueberry Tart after school. I decided I'd try my hand at making them for my kids. I think they are really close and my kids love them.
—*Christine Hair, Tampa, FL*

Prep: 45 min. • **Bake:** 15 min.
Makes: 8 servings

- 2 cups fresh or frozen blueberries, divided
- 2 Tbsp. sugar
- 1 Tbsp. cornstarch
- 2 tsp. grated lemon zest
- 2 Tbsp. butter
- 1 pkg. (17.3 oz.) frozen puff pastry, thawed
- 1 large egg
- 1 Tbsp. water
- ½ cup confectioners' sugar
- 1 Tbsp. 2% milk

1. Preheat oven to 450°. In a large saucepan, combine ½ cup blueberries, sugar, cornstarch and lemon zest. Mash well with a fork. Bring the mixture to a boil over low heat; cook and stir until thickened, 1-2 minutes. Remove from the heat. Stir in butter and remaining 1½ cups blueberries.
2. Unfold puff pastry. On a lightly floured surface, roll out each pastry sheet into a 12-in. square. Cut each into 4 squares; spoon 3 Tbsp. filling into the center of each. Fold diagonally in half and press edges to seal. Place on an ungreased baking sheet. Beat egg and water; brush over pastry.
3. Bake for 12-15 minutes or until golden brown. Combine confectioners' sugar and milk; drizzle over turnovers. Serve warm or at room temperature.
1 TURNOVER: 400 cal., 20g fat (6g sat. fat), 31mg chol., 235mg sod., 51g carb. (14g sugars, 5g fiber), 6g pro.

EASY APPLE STRUDEL

My family always loves it when I make this wonderful dessert. Old-fashioned strudel was too fattening and time-consuming, but this revised classic is just as good.
—*Joanie Fuson, Indianapolis, IN*

Prep: 30 min. • **Bake:** 35 min.
Makes: 6 servings

- ⅓ cup raisins
- 2 Tbsp. water
- ¼ tsp. almond extract
- 3 cups coarsely chopped peeled apples
- ⅓ cup plus 2 tsp. sugar, divided
- 3 Tbsp. all-purpose flour
- ¼ tsp. ground cinnamon
- 2 Tbsp. butter, melted
- 2 Tbsp. canola oil
- 8 sheets phyllo dough (14x9-in. size) Confectioners' sugar, optional

1. Preheat oven to 350°. Place raisins, water and almond extract in a large microwave-save bowl; microwave, uncovered, on high for 1½ minutes. Let stand 5 minutes. Drain. Add the apples, ⅓ cup sugar, flour and cinnamon; toss to combine.
2. In a small bowl, mix melted butter and oil; remove 2 tsp. mixture for brushing top. Place 1 sheet of phyllo dough on a work surface; brush lightly with some of the butter mixture. (Keep remaining phyllo covered with a damp towel to prevent it from drying out.) Layer with 7 additional phyllo sheets, brushing each layer with some of the butter mixture. Spread apple mixture over phyllo to within 2 in. of 1 long side.
3. Fold the short edges over filling. Roll up jelly-roll style, starting from the side with a 2-in. border. Transfer to a baking sheet coated with cooking spray. Brush with reserved butter mixture; sprinkle with remaining 2 tsp. sugar. With a sharp knife, cut diagonal slits in top of strudel.
4. Bake strudel until golden brown, 35-40 minutes. Cool on a wire rack. If desired, dust with confectioners' sugar before serving.
1 PIECE: 229 cal., 9g fat (3g sat. fat), 10mg chol., 92mg sod., 37g carb. (24g sugars, 2g fiber), 2g pro.

CHOCOLATE ECLAIRS

With creamy filling and decadent frosting, these eclairs are extra special. Now you can indulge in classic bakery treats without leaving the house!
—*Jessica Campbell, Viola, WI*

- -

Prep: 45 min. • **Bake:** 35 min. + cooling
Makes: 9 servings

- 1 cup water
- ½ cup butter, cubed
- ¼ tsp. salt
- 1 cup all-purpose flour
- 4 large eggs

FILLING
- 2½ cups cold 2% milk
- 1 pkg. (5.1 oz.) instant vanilla pudding mix
- 1 cup heavy whipping cream
- ¼ cup confectioners' sugar
- 1 tsp. vanilla extract

FROSTING
- 2 oz. semisweet chocolate
- 2 Tbsp. butter
- 1¼ cups confectioners' sugar
- 2 to 3 Tbsp. hot water

1. Preheat oven to 400°. In a large saucepan, bring water, butter and salt to a boil. Add flour all at once and stir until a smooth ball forms. Remove from heat; let stand 5 minutes. Add eggs, 1 at a time, beating well after each addition. Continue beating until mixture is smooth and shiny.

2. Using a tablespoon or a pastry tube with a #10 or large round tip, form dough into nine 4x1½-in. strips on a greased baking sheet. Bake 35-40 minutes
or until puffed and golden. Place on a wire rack. Immediately split eclairs open; remove tops and set aside. Discard soft dough from inside. Cool eclairs.

3. In a large bowl, beat milk and pudding mix according to package directions. In another bowl, whip cream until soft peaks form. Beat in the confectioners' sugar and vanilla; fold into pudding. Fill eclairs (chill any remaining filling for another use). Replace tops.

4. For frosting, in a microwave, melt chocolate and butter; stir until smooth. Stir in the confectioners' sugar and enough hot water to achieve a smooth consistency. Cool slightly. Frost eclairs. Store in refrigerator.

1 ECLAIR: 483 cal., 28g fat (17g sat. fat), 174mg chol., 492mg sod., 52g carb. (37g sugars, 1g fiber), 7g pro.

CHOCOLATE ECLAIRS TIPS

- **How can you tell when the choux pastry is ready?** Learning how to make choux pastry (pronounced like shoe) seems tricky, but it's pretty simple. The best way to tell when the batter is ready is to pull a spatula through it. When it drops off the spatula in a nice V-shape, the batter is ready to pipe onto the baking sheet.

- **Why did my eclairs collapse?** The common cause for eclair collapse is too much moisture in the batter. Make sure to stir the batter vigorously in the pot for several minutes until the mixture forms a firm, dry ball and an even, thin coating of batter remains on the side of the pot. Don't rush this; it's almost better for the dough to overcook than to undercook. Also, resist the temptation to open the oven door while the eclairs bake. That could allow steam that helps form the puffed shells to escape.

- **Why do my chocolate eclairs have cracks in them?** Cracks can happen when too much air is whipped into the choux pastry, or if there are variances in oven temperature. But don't worry. Cracks are a natural part of the baking process and give the eclairs a unique appearance.

- **What other fillings can you put in eclairs?** Try filling your eclairs with other flavored puddings, such as chocolate fudge, peppermint or butterscotch.

- **Can you make chocolate eclairs ahead of time?** Choux pastry and the filling for eclairs can both be made a day in advance, but don't fill the pastry until you're ready to serve. Store baked, unfilled eclairs in an airtight container overnight. The filling can be prepped, covered and refrigerated a day in advance.

NUTELLA HAND PIES

These pint-sized Nutella hand pies are too good to keep to yourself!
—Taste of Home *Test Kitchen*

Takes: 30 min. • **Makes:** 9 servings

- 1 large egg
- 1 Tbsp. water
- 1 sheet frozen puff pastry, thawed
- 3 Tbsp. Nutella
- 1 to 2 tsp. grated orange zest

ICING

- ⅓ cup confectioners' sugar
- ½ tsp. orange juice
- ⅛ tsp. grated orange zest
  Additional Nutella, optional

Short & Sweet

1. Preheat oven to 400°. In a small bowl, whisk egg with water.
2. Unfold the puff pastry; cut into 9 squares. Place 1 tsp. Nutella in center of each; sprinkle with orange zest. Brush edges of pastry with egg mixture. Fold 1 corner over filling to form a triangle; press edges to seal. Transfer to an ungreased baking sheet.
3. Bake until pastry is golden brown and cooked through, 17-20 minutes. Cool slightly.
4. In a small bowl, mix confectioners' sugar, orange juice and orange zest; drizzle over pies. If desired, warm additional Nutella in a microwave and drizzle over tops.

1 HAND PIE: 190 cal., 10g fat (2g sat. fat), 21mg chol., 100mg sod., 24g carb. (8g sugars, 2g fiber), 3g pro.

APPLE DUMPLINGS WITH SAUCE

These warm and comforting apple dumplings are incredible by themselves or served with ice cream. You can decorate each dumpling by cutting 1-inch leaves and a 1/2-inch stem from the leftover dough.
—*Robin Lendon, Cincinnati, OH*

Prep: 1 hour + chilling • **Bake:** 50 min.
Makes: 8 servings

- 3 cups all-purpose flour
- 1 tsp. salt
- 1 cup shortening
- ⅓ cup cold water
- 8 medium tart apples, peeled and cored
- 8 tsp. butter
- 9 tsp. cinnamon sugar, divided

SAUCE

- 1½ cups packed brown sugar
- 1 cup water
- ½ cup butter, cubed

1. In a large bowl, combine flour and salt; cut in shortening until crumbly. Gradually add water, tossing with a fork until dough forms a ball. Divide into 8 portions. Cover and refrigerate at least 30 minutes or until easy to handle.
2. Preheat oven to 350°. Roll each portion of dough between 2 lightly floured sheets of waxed paper into a 7-in. square. Place an apple on each square. Place 1 tsp. butter and 1 tsp. cinnamon sugar in the center of each apple.
3. Gently bring up corners of dough to each center, trimming any excess; pinch edges to seal. If desired, cut out apple leaves and stems from dough scraps; attach to dumplings with water. Place dumplings in a greased 13x9-in. baking dish. Sprinkle with half the remaining cinnamon sugar.
4. In a large saucepan, combine the sauce ingredients. Bring just to a boil, stirring until blended. Pour over apples; sprinkle with remaining cinnamon sugar.
5. Bake until apples are tender and pastry is golden brown, 50-55 minutes, basting occasionally with the sauce. Serve warm.

1 DUMPLING: 764 cal., 40g fat (16g sat. fat), 41mg chol., 429mg sod., 97g carb. (59g sugars, 3g fiber), 5g pro.

PECAN KRINGLE STICKS

My family loves that the kringle is flaky and not too sweet—it just melts in your mouth. This makes a beautiful presentation on a cookie platter along with other holiday sweets.
—*Connie Vjestica, Brookfield, IL*

Prep: 40 min. + chilling
Bake: 20 min.
Makes: 4 kringles (6 servings each)

- 2 cups all-purpose flour
- 1 cup cold butter, cubed
- 1 cup sour cream

FILLING
- 1 large egg white
- 1 tsp. vanilla extract
- ½ cup sugar
- 1 cup chopped pecans

ICING
- 1¼ cups confectioners' sugar
- 2 Tbsp. 2% milk

1. Place the flour in a large bowl; cut in butter until crumbly. Stir in the sour cream. Shape into a disk (mixture will be crumbly). Wrap and refrigerate overnight.
2. In a small bowl, beat egg white and vanilla on medium speed until soft peaks form. Gradually beat in sugar on high until stiff peaks form. Fold in pecans.
3. Divide dough into 4 portions. Roll 1 portion into a 12x6-in. rectangle; place on an ungreased rimmed baking sheet (keep remaining dough refrigerated). Spread a fourth of the filling lengthwise down the center. Fold in sides of pastry to meet in the center; pinch seam to seal. Repeat with remaining dough and filling.
4. Bake at 375° for 18-22 minutes or until lightly browned. Combine confectioners' sugar and milk; drizzle over pastries.

1 PIECE: 201 cal., 13g fat (6g sat. fat), 27mg chol., 60mg sod., 19g carb. (11g sugars, 1g fiber), 2g pro.

FINGER-LICKING GOOD MINI CREAM PUFFS

This recipe is quick and easy to whip up and the kids will love it! They are perfect to pack for a picnic or to have as a snack for family game night. I guarantee you can't eat just one—they are so addicting and will satisfy any sweet tooth!
—*Jennifer Erwin, Reynoldsburg, OH*

Prep: 45 min. • **Bake:** 25 min. + cooling
Makes: about 2½ dozen

- ½ cup water
- ¼ cup butter
- ½ cup all-purpose flour
- ¼ tsp. salt
- 2 large eggs

VANILLA FILLING
- 1 pkg. (3.4 oz.) instant vanilla pudding mix
- 1¾ cups 2% milk
- 1 cup frozen whipped topping, thawed
  Confectioners' sugar

1. Preheat oven to 400°. In a small saucepan, bring water and butter to a rolling boil over medium heat. Add flour and salt all at once; beat until blended. Cook, stirring vigorously, until a film forms at the bottom of the pan, about 4 minutes. Remove from heat; let stand 10 minutes.
2. Add eggs, 1 at a time, beating well after each addition until smooth. Continue beating until mixture is smooth and shiny. Drop dough by 1-in. balls 1½ in. apart onto parchment-lined baking sheets. Bake until puffed, very firm and golden brown, 25-30 minutes. Cool on wire racks.
3. Meanwhile, whisk together pudding mix and milk for 2 minutes or until thickened; let stand 5 minutes. Fold in whipped topping. Cut puffs in half. Fill cream puffs with vanilla filling; replace tops. Dust with confectioners' sugar; serve immediately.

1 FILLED CREAM PUFF: 52 cal., 3g fat (2g sat. fat), 18mg chol., 64mg sod., 6g carb. (4g sugars, 0 fiber), 1g pro.

EASY ELEPHANT EARS

The cinnamon-sugar combo in these crispy treats is classic. Even more, they call for just three ingredients and are so simple to assemble.
—*Bob Rose, Waukesha, WI*

- -

Prep: 20 min. + freezing
Bake: 15 min./batch
Makes: about 2½ dozen

- ½ cup sugar
- 2 tsp. ground cinnamon
- 1 pkg. (17.3 oz.) frozen puff pastry, thawed

1. Preheat oven to 375°. Mix sugar and cinnamon.
2. On a lightly floured surface, roll 1 sheet of pastry into an 11x8-in. rectangle. Sprinkle with ¼ cup cinnamon sugar. Working from short sides, roll up jelly-roll style toward the center. Securely wrap in waxed paper; freeze 10 minutes. Repeat.
3. Unwrap and cut dough into ½-in. slices; place on parchment-lined baking sheets. Bake 12-15 minutes or until crisp and golden brown. Remove to wire racks to cool.

1 ELEPHANT EAR: 87 cal., 4g fat (1g sat. fat), 0 chol., 51mg sod., 12g carb. (3g sugars, 1g fiber), 1g pro.

STRAWBERRY TUILE CANNOLI

My mom and I made up this recipe by combining two others. These cute cookies are crispy on the outside and light and fluffy inside. You could also bake the cookies flat and serve the filling as a cookie dip if you like.
—*Crystal Briddick, Colfax, IL*

- -

Prep: 40 min. + chilling
Bake: 5 min./batch + cooling
Makes: about 2 dozen

- 4 oz. cream cheese, softened
- ¼ cup sugar
- 2 Tbsp. seedless strawberry jam
- ¼ cup heavy whipping cream, whipped
- 1 to 3 drops red food coloring, optional

BATTER
- ½ cup sugar
- ⅓ cup all-purpose flour
- ⅛ tsp. salt
- 2 large egg whites, room temperature
- ¼ tsp. vanilla extract
- ¼ cup butter, melted and cooled
  Chopped fresh strawberries, optional

1. Preheat oven to 400°. Beat cream cheese, sugar and jam until blended. Fold in whipped cream and, if desired, food coloring. Refrigerate.
2. For batter, whisk sugar, flour and salt; stir in egg whites and vanilla until smooth. Whisk in butter until blended. Line baking sheets with parchment. Preparing 4 cookies at a time, drop batter by 1½ teaspoonfuls 4 in. apart onto prepared pans. Bake until edges are lightly browned, 5-8 minutes.

3. Loosen each cookie and curl around a wooden spoon handle. Press lightly to seal; hold 20 seconds or until set. Transfer to waxed paper to cool. Repeat with remaining cookies. If cookies become too cool to shape, return to oven for 1 minute to soften.
4. Just before serving, spoon filling into cookie shells. Or pipe it by cutting a small hole in the tip of a pastry bag and inserting a star tip, then transferring filling to bag. After filling shells, dip ends of the cookies into chopped strawberries if desired. Refrigerate the leftovers.

1 COOKIE: 72 cal., 4g fat (3g sat. fat), 12mg chol., 44mg sod., 8g carb. (7g sugars, 0 fiber), 1g pro.

ROASTED GRAPE & SWEET CHEESE PHYLLO GALETTE

Faced with an abundant crop of grapes, I had to come up with a creative way to use them. It's fun to work with phyllo dough, and it bakes up golden and flaky. In this recipe, a layer of orange-kissed cream cheese is topped with roasted grapes. Then a bit of honey is drizzled on, and a sprinkle of coarse sugar is added to finish it off. You can use berries for this too.
—Kallee Krong-McCreery, Escondido, CA

- -

Prep: 25 min. • **Bake:** 35 min. + cooling
Makes: 10 servings

- 1 pkg. (8 oz.) cream cheese, softened
- 2 Tbsp. orange marmalade
- 1 tsp. sugar
- 8 sheets phyllo dough (14x9-in. size)
- 4 Tbsp. butter, melted
- 1 cup seedless grapes
- 1 Tbsp. honey
- 2 tsp. coarse sugar

1. Preheat oven to 350°. In a large bowl, beat cream cheese, marmalade and sugar until smooth; set aside.
2. Place 1 sheet of phyllo on a parchment-lined baking sheet; brush with butter. Layer with remaining phyllo sheets, brushing each layer. (Keep remaining phyllo covered with a damp towel to prevent it from drying out.) Spread cream cheese mixture over phyllo to within 2 in. of edges. Arrange grapes over cream cheese.
3. Fold edges of phyllo over filling, leaving center uncovered. Brush folded phyllo with any remaining butter; drizzle with honey and sprinkle with coarse sugar. Bake until phyllo is golden brown, 35-40 minutes. Transfer to a wire rack to cool completely. Refrigerate leftovers.
1 PIECE: 177 cal., 13g fat (8g sat. fat), 35mg chol., 148mg sod., 15g carb. (9g sugars, 0 fiber), 2g pro.

BAKEWELL PIE TARTS

With my busy family of five, I'm always burning things in the oven because I get pulled into other things. But the air fryer, with its time-controlled powers, has been a godsend. Now when the inevitable family emergency pops up, I don't have to worry about setting off the smoke detector! My British heritage means I grew up on tea and Bakewell tarts. This easy rendition uses similar components of the iconic tart, but it's easier for busy families to make. You can use any type of jam you want!
—Kristin Bowers, Gilbert, AZ

- -

Prep: 25 min.
Bake: 10 min./batch + cooling
Makes: 4 servings

- 2 sheets refrigerated pie crust
- 2 Tbsp. lemon curd
- 2 Tbsp. red tart cherry fruit spread
- 4 oz. almond paste
  Cooking spray

ICING
- ¾ cup confectioners' sugar
- 1 Tbsp. 2% milk
- ⅛ tsp. vanilla extract
- 1 Tbsp. sliced almonds, toasted

1. Preheat air fryer to 350°. On a work surface, unroll crusts. Roll to ¼-in. thickness. Cut each crust into four 4-in. squares. Top 4 squares with 1½ tsp. lemon curd and 1½ tsp. fruit spread; swirl slightly. Roll almond paste into a 4-in. square. Cut into four 2-in. squares. Place each piece of almond paste on top of curd mixture. Brush edges of crust with water; top with remaining crust squares. Press edges with a fork to seal. Prick tops with a fork.
2. In batches, arrange tarts in a single layer on greased tray in air-fryer basket; spritz with cooking spray. Cook until golden brown, 8-10 minutes. Cool completely.
3. For icing, in a small bowl, combine confectioners' sugar, milk and vanilla; whisk until smooth. Spoon over cooled pastries; sprinkle with almonds. Let stand until set.
1 TART: 597 cal., 28g fat (9g sat. fat), 21mg chol., 273mg sod., 82g carb. (47g sugars, 2g fiber), 6g pro.

CHOCOLATE CANNOLI

We made two Italian treats into one with beautiful pizzelle cookies wrapped around a rich, chocolaty cannoli filling. The chopped pistachios are a pretty touch.
—Taste of Home *Test Kitchen*

Prep: 45 min. + cooling
Cook: 5 min./batch
Makes: 1 dozen

    1   large egg, room temperature
   ¼   cup sugar
   ¼   cup butter, melted
   ½   tsp. vanilla extract
   ¼   tsp. grated lemon zest
   ⅛   tsp. almond extract
   ½   cup all-purpose flour
   ¼   tsp. baking powder

FILLING
   ¾   cup sugar
    3   Tbsp. cornstarch
    1   cup whole milk
  1⅛   tsp. vanilla extract
    1   drop cinnamon oil, optional
  1¾   cups ricotta cheese
    1   milk chocolate candy bar with
        almonds (4¼ oz.), chopped
   ½   cup chopped pistachios

1. In a large bowl, beat the egg, sugar, butter, vanilla, lemon zest and almond extract until blended. Combine flour and baking powder; stir into egg mixture and mix well.
2. Bake in a preheated pizzelle iron according to manufacturer's directions until golden brown. Remove cookies and immediately shape into tubes. Place on wire racks to cool.
3. In a small saucepan, combine sugar and cornstarch. Stir in milk until smooth. Bring to a boil; cook and stir until thickened, about 2 minutes. Stir in vanilla and cinnamon oil if desired. Cool completely.
4. In a large bowl, beat ricotta cheese until smooth. Gradually beat in custard mixture. Fold in chocolate. Spoon or pipe into shells. Dip each side in pistachios. Serve immediately. Refrigerate leftovers.
1 FILLED PIZZELLE: 289 cal., 15g fat (8g sat. fat), 47mg chol., 124mg sod., 33g carb. (25g sugars, 1g fiber), 8g pro.

FUNNEL CAKES

These are much simpler to make than doughnuts but taste just as good. They have been a regular treat of ours since we came across them when we lived in the Ozarks.
—*Mary Faith Yoder, Unity, WI*

Prep: 15 min. • **Cook:** 5 min./batch
Makes: 8 cakes

    2   large eggs, room temperature
    1   cup 2% milk
    1   cup water
   ½   tsp. vanilla extract
    3   cups all-purpose flour
   ¼   cup sugar
    3   tsp. baking powder
   ¼   tsp. salt
        Oil for deep-fat frying
        Confectioners' sugar

1. In a large bowl, beat eggs. Add milk, water and vanilla extract until well blended. In another bowl, whisk flour, sugar, baking powder and salt; beat into egg mixture until smooth. In a deep cast-iron or electric skillet, heat the oil to 375°.
2. For each cake: Cover the bottom of a funnel spout with your finger; ladle ½ cup batter into the funnel. Holding the funnel several inches above the oil, release your finger and move the funnel in a spiral motion until all the batter is released, scraping with a rubber spatula if needed.
3. Fry until golden brown, 2 minutes on each side. Drain on paper towels. Dust with confectioners' sugar; serve warm.
1 FUNNEL CAKE: 316 cal., 12g fat (2g sat. fat), 50mg chol., 256mg sod., 44g carb. (8g sugars, 1g fiber), 7g pro.

HOW TO MAKE CHOUX PASTRY

Step 1: Once the water, butter, milk sugar and salt are boiling, add in flour and stir constantly until dough comes together in a mass. It will be lumpy at first.

Step 2: When adding the eggs, beat them in 1 at a time, working fast so they don't scramble.

Step 3: To pipe perfectly matched eclairs, first draw outlines on underside of the parchment in pencil.

Step 4: Pierce the side of each eclair as soon as they're finished baking. This releases the steam so that the pastry will stay crisp.

CHOCOLATE-GLAZED RASPBERRY ECLAIRS

I first made choux pastry in high school for a French class assignment, and I was fascinated. I loved watching it puff up in the oven and enjoyed eating my delicious eclairs! Since then, eclairs have been my favorite pastry to make. They're not as tricky as they might seem, and you can make so many amazing flavors. I garnish each eclair either with a single fresh raspberry or with a sprinkling of crushed freeze-dried raspberries.
—Elisabeth Larsen, Pleasant Grove, UT

Prep: 1 hour + chilling
Bake: 25 min. + cooling
Makes: 1 dozen

- ½ cup sugar
- ¼ cup cornstarch
- 2 cups whole milk
- 4 large egg yolks
- 2 Tbsp. unsalted butter

PASTRY
- ½ cup water
- 6 Tbsp. unsalted butter, cubed
- ¼ cup 2% milk
- 2 tsp. sugar
- ¼ tsp. salt
- ¾ cup all-purpose flour
- 3 large eggs

GLAZE
- ⅔ cup semisweet chocolate chips
- ½ cup heavy whipping cream
- 1 Tbsp. light corn syrup
- 1 cup fresh raspberries

1. In a small heavy saucepan, mix sugar and cornstarch. Whisk in milk. Cook and stir over medium heat until thickened and bubbly. Reduce heat to low; cook and stir 2 minutes longer. Remove from heat.
2. In a small bowl, whisk a small amount of hot mixture into egg yolks; return all to pan, whisking constantly. Bring to a gentle boil; cook and stir 2 minutes. Immediately transfer to a clean bowl; stir in butter. Press plastic wrap onto surface of the filling; refrigerate until cold.
3. Preheat oven to 425°. For pastry, in a large saucepan, bring water, butter, milk, sugar and salt to a rolling boil. Add flour all at once and beat until blended. Cook over medium heat, stirring vigorously until mixture pulls away from side of pan and forms a ball. Remove from heat; let stand 5 minutes.
4. Add eggs, 1 at a time, beating well after each addition until smooth. Continue beating until mixture is smooth and shiny. Transfer to a piping bag with a large round tip. Pipe twelve 4½-in. strips about 3 in. apart on parchment-lined baking sheets. Bake for 15 minutes. Reduce oven temperature to 350°; bake until golden brown, 8-10 minutes longer. Pierce side of each eclair with tip of knife. Cool completely on wire racks. Split eclairs open. Pull out and discard soft dough from inside tops and bottoms.
5. For the glaze, in a microwave, melt chocolate chips, cream and corn syrup; stir until smooth. Stir raspberries into chilled pastry filling, mashing berries lightly. Fill eclairs just before serving. Dip tops in chocolate glaze; replace tops. Top with additional fresh raspberries. Let stand until set. Refrigerate leftovers.

FREEZE OPTION: Freeze unfilled, unglazed eclairs. in a freezer bag or airtight container for up to 2 months. Thaw, fill and glaze just before serving.
1 ECLAIR: 295 cal., 18g fat (11g sat. fat), 144mg chol., 96mg sod., 29g carb. (19g sugars, 1g fiber), 6g pro.

OTHER GLAZE IDEAS

Chocolate ganache is a traditional topping for eclairs, but you don't need to stop there! Eclairs can also be topped with a simple glaze of confectioners' sugar and water flavored with the extract or citrus fruit zest of your choosing (and maybe even a little food coloring).

APPLE TURNOVERS

These traditional apple turnovers are tender and flaky, with apple pie-like filling and a thin white drizzle. I freeze the extras and warm them up in the microwave. They're great with coffee.
—Dorothy Bayes, Sardis, OH

- -

Prep: 50 min. + chilling • **Bake:** 20 min.
Makes: 4 servings

1 cup all-purpose flour
½ tsp. salt
½ cup cold butter, divided
¼ cup ice water

FILLING
⅓ cup sugar
2 tsp. cornstarch
⅛ tsp. ground cinnamon
2 medium tart apples, peeled and thinly sliced
1 tsp. lemon juice
1 large egg, beaten
1½ tsp. water

GLAZE
¼ cup confectioners' sugar
1 tsp. water

1. In a small bowl, combine flour and salt; cut in ¼ cup butter until crumbly. Gradually add water, tossing with a fork until a ball forms. On a lightly floured surface, roll dough into a 12x6-in. rectangle.
2. Cut remaining butter into thin slices. Starting at a short side of dough, arrange half of the butter slices over two-thirds of rectangle to within ½ in. of edges. Fold unbuttered third of dough over middle third. Fold remaining third over the middle, forming a 6x4-in. rectangle. Roll the dough into a 12x6-in. rectangle.

3. Repeat steps of butter layering and dough folding, ending with a 6x4-in. rectangle. Cover; refrigerate for 15 minutes. Roll dough into a 12x6-in. rectangle. Fold in half lengthwise and then widthwise. Cover; refrigerate for 1 hour.
4. Preheat oven to 450°. Meanwhile, in a small saucepan, combine the sugar, cornstarch and cinnamon. Add apples and lemon juice; toss to coat. Bring to a boil over medium heat, stirring constantly. Reduce heat; simmer, uncovered, until apples are tender, stirring often, 5-10 minutes. Remove from the heat.
5. In a small bowl, combine egg and water. Roll dough into a 12-in. square; cut into four squares. Brush with half of the egg mixture. Spoon about ¼ cup filling on half of each square; fold dough over filling. Press edges with a fork to seal. Place on an ungreased baking sheet. Brush with remaining egg mixture. With a sharp knife, cut three small slits in the top of each turnover.
6. Bake pastries 17-22 minutes or until golden brown. Remove to a wire rack. Combine glaze ingredients; drizzle over turnovers. Serve warm.

1 TURNOVER: 466 cal., 25g fat (15g sat. fat), 108mg chol., 496mg sod., 58g carb. (31g sugars, 2g fiber), 5g pro.

QUICK APPLE TURNOVERS: Substitute 1 sheet frozen puff pastry, thawed for the dough. Skip steps 1-3. Proceed as directed in steps 4-6. Check doneness after 15 minutes.

BLUEBERRY TURNOVERS: Omit filling. In a saucepan, combine ¼ cup blueberries, 1 Tbsp. sugar, 1½ tsp. cornstarch and 1 tsp. grated lemon peel. Mash well with a fork. Bring to a boil over low heat; cook and stir for 2 minutes or until thickened. Remove from the heat. Stir in 1 Tbsp. butter and ¾ cup blueberries. Fill and bake turnovers as directed.

APPLE TURNOVERS TIPS

- **How do you keep apple turnovers crispy?** Apple turnovers are best when enjoyed the day they're baked, and even better fresh out of the oven with some vanilla ice cream. The longer they're stored in the refrigerator, the less crisp they'll become.

- **How long do apple turnovers last?** Homemade apple turnovers will last up to 24 hours at room temperature, or you can store them in the fridge for 3-4 days. Wrapped tightly in foil and stored in a freezer-proof container, apple turnovers will last about 6 months in the freezer.

READER REVIEW
"First time that I made these, and it was a huge success. Flaky crust and my family loved them. I'm going to try this pastry with cherries as well. Can't wait."
—STACY, TASTEOFHOME.COM

LEMON MANGO
KANAFEH

CASHEW BAKLAVA

I always wanted to make baklava, but it seemed like so much work. The son of my neighbor's friend showed us both how to make it—it's really quite easy and so delicious. I like to mix up the nuts in the filling and use walnut, cashews or pecans.
—*Lorraine Caland, Shuniah, ON*

- -

Prep: 50 min.
Bake: 20 min. + standing
Makes: 2 dozen

1½ cups salted cashews
1½ cups chopped walnuts
½ cup sugar
1 tsp. ground cardamom
½ tsp. ground cinnamon
¼ tsp. ground allspice
⅔ cup butter, melted
16 sheets phyllo dough (14x9 in.)
SYRUP
1⅓ cups sugar
⅔ cup water
⅔ cup honey
3 lemon slices
2 whole cloves
½ tsp. ground cinnamon

1. Preheat oven to 350°. For filling, in a food processor, combine the cashews, walnuts, sugar, cardamom, cinnamon and allspice. Cover and pulse until nuts are finely chopped. Brush a 13x9-in. baking pan with some of the butter. Unroll phyllo dough; trim to fit into pan.
2. Layer 4 sheets of phyllo dough in prepared pan, brushing each with butter. (Keep remaining dough covered with a damp towel to prevent it from drying out.) Sprinkle with a third of the nut mixture. Repeat layers twice. Top with remaining phyllo dough, brushing each sheet with butter.
3. Using a sharp knife, cut baklava into 6 squares, then cut each square into 4 triangles. Bake until golden brown, 20-25 minutes.
4. Meanwhile, in a large saucepan, combine the syrup ingredients. Bring to a boil. Reduce heat; simmer, uncovered, for 10 minutes, stirring occasionally. Discard lemon slices and cloves. Pour over warm baklava. Cool completely on a wire rack. Cover and let stand overnight.

1 PIECE: 258 cal., 15g fat (4g sat. fat), 13mg chol., 128mg sod., 31g carb. (24g sugars, 1g fiber), 4g pro.

LEMON MANGO KANAFEH

Several years ago I came upon a little neighborhood restaurant making the most incredible Turkish food I'd ever seen or tasted. I was completely blown away by the dessert and had to learn how to make it.
—*Jodi Taffel, Altadena, CA*

- -

Prep: 35 min. + chilling
Bake: 40 min. + cooling
Makes: 12 servings

1 cup butter, melted
½ cup half-and-half cream
2 Tbsp. honey
1 tsp. ground cinnamon
1 tsp. vanilla extract
1 pkg. (16 oz.) frozen shredded phyllo dough (kataifi), thawed
FILLING
6 large egg yolks
½ cup sugar
½ cup mango nectar
⅓ cup lemon juice
1 Tbsp. cornstarch
2 tsp. grated lemon zest
½ cup butter, cubed
½ cup chopped peeled mango
½ cup mandarin oranges, drained
½ cup seedless red grapes, halved
Confectioners' sugar

1. Preheat oven to 350°. Place a greased 9-in. springform pan on a double thickness of heavy-duty foil (about 18 in. square). Wrap foil securely around pan. Place on a baking sheet.
2. In a large bowl, whisk the butter, cream, honey, cinnamon and vanilla. Gently pull phyllo apart and add to bowl; toss to coat. Press onto bottom and up the side of prepared pan. Bake 40-45 minutes or until golden brown. Cool on a wire rack. Remove foil.
3. Meanwhile, in a small heavy saucepan, whisk egg yolks, sugar, mango nectar, lemon juice, cornstarch and zest until blended. Add butter; cook over medium heat, whisking constantly, until mixture comes just to a boil and is thick enough to coat a metal spoon.
4. Remove from heat immediately. Strain through a fine-mesh strainer into a small bowl. Stir in mango; cool. Press plastic wrap onto surface of custard. Refrigerate until cold.
5. Spoon filling into crust. Garnish with mandarin oranges and grapes. Remove rim from pan. Dust with confectioners' sugar.

1 PIECE: 424 cal., 27g fat (16g sat. fat), 158mg chol., 360mg sod., 41g carb. (18g sugars, 1g fiber), 6g pro.

CONTEST-WINNING
WHITE CHOCOLATE
CHEESECAKE, PAGE 140

Cheesecakes & Custards

Surrender to the irresistible lure of sophisticated cheesecake, lavish creme brulee, frozen custard and gourmet gelato.

ORANGE CHOCOLATE MOUSSE MIRROR CAKE

A shiny, mirror-like orange glaze covers a chocolate mousse cake to create a delicious showstopping dessert your guests will be talking about for weeks to come.
—*Matthew Hass, Ellison Bay, WI*

Prep: 45 min. + freezing
Makes: 16 servings

- 2 cups crushed Oreo cookies (about 20 cookies)
- 1 tsp. grated orange zest
- ¼ cup butter, melted

FILLING
- 1 envelope unflavored gelatin
- 6 Tbsp. orange juice
- 8 oz. semisweet chocolate, chopped
- 2½ cups heavy whipping cream, divided
- 3 pkg. (8 oz. each) cream cheese, softened
- ¾ cup sugar
- ¼ cup dark baking cocoa
- 1 Tbsp. grated orange zest

GLAZE
- 1 envelope unflavored gelatin
- ½ cup plus 1 tsp. water, divided
- ¾ cup sugar
- ⅓ cup sweetened condensed milk
- 1 cup white baking chips
  Orange paste food coloring

1. Mix the crushed cookies, orange zest and butter; press onto bottom of a greased 9-in. springform pan. Set aside.

2. In a small saucepan, sprinkle gelatin over orange juice; let stand 1 minute. Stir over low heat until gelatin is dissolved. Set aside.

3. For filling, melt chocolate with ½ cup cream in microwave; stir until smooth. Cool slightly; stir in dissolved gelatin. In a large bowl, beat cream cheese, sugar and cocoa until smooth. Gradually add chocolate mixture and orange zest; mix well. In another bowl, beat remaining cream until stiff peaks form. Gently fold into cream cheese mixture. Spoon over crust. Refrigerate, covered, until set, about 4 hours. Freeze, covered, overnight.

4. For glaze, sprinkle gelatin over ¼ cup water in a small bowl; set aside (mixture will solidify). Meanwhile, in a small saucepan, combine sugar, milk and remaining water. Bring to a simmer over medium heat, stirring occasionally. Remove from heat. Stir in gelatin mixture until dissolved. Add baking chips; stir with a whisk until melted. Add food coloring; mix well. Cool glaze, stirring occasionally, until it reaches 90°, about 40 minutes.

5. Place cake on an inverted 9-in. pie plate in a foil-lined 15x10x1-in. pan. Remove the side of the springform. Pour cooled glaze over frozen cake, allowing excess to drip off. Let glaze set 15 minutes before removing drips from bottom edge of cake. Refrigerate 2 hours before serving.

1 PIECE: 610 cal., 43g fat (25g sat. fat), 97mg chol., 244mg sod., 47g carb. (40g sugars, 1g fiber), 7g pro.

SMOOTH AS GLASS

For a perfectly smooth mirror top, start pouring the glaze in the center of the cake and work your way out toward the edge. Let the glaze run over the edge, draping down the side of the cake.

LAVENDER PEACH GELATO

This sophisticated herbal gelato can be served as an appetizer, a palate-cleanser between courses or a dessert that tastes like heaven on a spoon.
—*Christine Wendland, Browns Mills, NJ*

Prep: 40 min. + chilling
Process: 20 min. + freezing
Makes: 3 cups

- 2 cups 2% milk
- 2 Tbsp. cardamom pods, crushed
- 1 Tbsp. dried lavender flowers
- 1 vanilla bean
- ¾ cup sugar
- 5 large egg yolks, beaten
- 2 medium peaches, peeled and finely chopped

1. In a large heavy saucepan, combine the milk, cardamom pods and dried lavender. Split vanilla bean and scrape seeds; add bean and seeds to milk mixture. Heat until bubbles form around side of pan. Remove from the heat; cover and let steep for 10 minutes. Strain, discarding the flowers and spices.

2. Return milk to the heat; stir in sugar. Cook until bubbles form around side of pan. Whisk a small amount of hot mixture into the egg yolks. Return all to the pan, whisking constantly.

3. Cook and stir over low heat until mixture is thickened and coats the back of a spoon. Quickly transfer to a bowl; place in ice water and stir for 2 minutes. Press waxed paper onto surface of custard. Refrigerate for several hours or overnight.

4. Fill cylinder of ice cream maker two-thirds full; freeze according to the manufacturer's directions. When the gelato is frozen, stir in peaches. Transfer to a freezer container; freeze for 2-4 hours before serving.

NOTE: Look for dried lavender flowers in spice shops. If using lavender from the garden, make sure it hasn't been treated with chemicals.

½ CUP: 206 cal., 5g fat (2g sat. fat), 177mg chol., 47mg sod., 35g carb. (32g sugars, 1g fiber), 5g pro.

NUTELLA CHEESECAKE

Creamy chocolate-hazelnut spread tops a crust made of crushed Oreo cookies to make this irresistible baked cheesecake.
—*Nick Iverson, Denver, CO*

Prep: 35 min. • **Bake:** 1¼ hours + chilling
Makes: 16 servings

- 2½ cups lightly crushed Oreo cookies (about 24 cookies)
- ¼ cup sugar
- ¼ cup butter, melted

FILLING
- 4 pkg. (8 oz. each) cream cheese, softened
- ½ cup sugar
- 2 jars (26½ oz. each) Nutella
- 1 cup heavy whipping cream
- 1 tsp. salt
- 4 large eggs, room temperature, lightly beaten
- ½ cup chopped hazelnuts, toasted

1. Preheat oven to 325°. Pulse cookies and sugar in a food processor until fine crumbs form. Continue processing while gradually adding butter in a steady stream. Press mixture onto bottom of a greased 10x3-in. springform pan. Securely wrap bottom and side of pan in a double thickness of heavy-duty foil (about 18 in. square).

2. For filling, beat cream cheese and sugar until smooth. Beat in Nutella, cream and salt. Add eggs; beat on low speed just until blended. Pour over crust.

3. Bake until a thermometer inserted in center reads 160°, about 1¼ hours. Cool 1¼ hours on a wire rack. Refrigerate overnight, covering when completely cooled.

4. Gently loosen rim from pan with a knife; remove rim. Top cheesecake with chopped hazelnuts.

1 PIECE: 900 cal., 62g fat (22g sat. fat), 129mg chol., 478mg sod., 84g carb. (71g sugars, 4g fiber), 12g pro.

LAYERED LEMON CHEESE PIE

This is a great ending for almost any meal that kids and adults all enjoy. The creamy lemon filling is always a hit with my husband.
—Elizabeth Yoder, Belcourt, ND

- -

Prep: 20 min. + chilling
Makes: 8 servings

- 1 pkg. (8 oz.) cream cheese, softened
- ½ cup sugar
- 1 can (15¾ oz.) lemon pie filling, divided
- 1 carton (8 oz.) frozen whipped topping, thawed
- 1 graham cracker crust (9 in.)

In a small bowl, beat cream cheese and sugar until smooth. Beat in half the pie filling. Fold in the whipped topping. Spoon into crust. Spread remaining pie filling over cream cheese layer. Refrigerate for at least 15 minutes before serving.

1 PIECE: 526 cal., 24g fat (13g sat. fat), 104mg chol., 251mg sod., 72g carb. (61g sugars, 1g fiber), 6g pro.

READER REVIEW

"Added zest of two lemons for more lemon flavor. My dad said all the mothers of the 1950s had this pie in their refrigerators. An easy, delicious, nostalgic icebox pie."
—METROCOOKBOOKDIVANY, TASTEOFHOME.COM

CONTEST-WINNING WHITE CHOCOLATE CHEESECAKE

This is my all-time favorite cheesecake recipe...and I have a lot of them! I've made this delicious cake so many times over the years.
—Janet Gill, Taneytown, MD

- -

Prep: 40 min. • **Bake:** 45 min. + chilling
Makes: 12 servings

- 7 whole cinnamon graham crackers, crushed
- ¼ cup sugar
- ⅓ cup butter, melted

FILLING
- 4 pkg. (8 oz. each) cream cheese, softened
- ½ cup plus 2 Tbsp. sugar
- 1 Tbsp. all-purpose flour
- 1 tsp. vanilla extract
- 4 large eggs, room temperature, lightly beaten
- 2 large egg yolks, room temperature, lightly beaten
- 8 oz. white baking chocolate, melted and cooled

STRAWBERRY SAUCE
- ½ cup sugar
- 2 Tbsp. cornstarch
- ½ cup water
- 1½ cups chopped fresh strawberries
  Red food coloring, optional
  Melted white chocolate

1. In a small bowl, combine cracker crumbs and sugar; stir in butter. Press onto the bottom and 1 in. up the side of a greased 10-in. springform pan.
2. In a large bowl, beat the cream cheese, sugar, flour and vanilla until well blended. Add eggs and yolks; beat on low speed just until combined. Stir in white chocolate. Pour over crust. Place pan on a baking sheet.
3. Bake at 350° for 45-50 minutes or until center is just set. Cool on a wire rack for 10 minutes. Carefully run a knife around edge of pan to loosen; cool 1 hour longer. Refrigerate overnight.
4. For sauce, in a large saucepan, combine the sugar, cornstarch and water until smooth. Add strawberries. Bring to a boil; cook and stir until thickened. Remove from the heat; stir in a few drops of food coloring if desired. Cool.
5. Spread strawberry sauce over top of cheesecake; drizzle with melted white chocolate. Refrigerate leftovers.

1 PIECE: 572 cal., 41g fat (25g sat. fat), 205mg chol., 348mg sod., 46g carb. (38g sugars, 1g fiber), 10g pro.

CRANBERRY ORANGE
CHEESECAKE

HOMEMADE FROZEN CUSTARD

My siblings and I had a hard time finding room for dessert after Mom's meals. But when we were ready, we could always count on some creamy frozen custard.
—*Judy Clark, Elkhart, IN*

Prep: 20 min. + chilling
Process: 20 min./batch + freezing
Makes: 1½ qt.

- 4 cups whole milk
- 1¼ cups sugar
- ⅓ cup cornstarch
- ⅛ tsp. salt
- 4 large eggs
- 1 can (14 oz.) sweetened condensed milk
- 2 Tbsp. vanilla extract

1. In a large saucepan, heat milk to 175°; stir in the sugar, cornstarch and salt until dissolved. Whisk a small amount of the hot mixture into the eggs. Return all to the pan, whisking constantly. Cook and stir over low heat until mixture reaches at least 160° and coats the back of a metal spoon.
2. Remove from the heat. Cool quickly by placing pan in a bowl of ice water; stir for 2 minutes. Stir in condensed milk and vanilla. Press waxed paper onto surface of custard. Refrigerate for several hours or overnight.
3. Fill cylinder of ice cream maker two-thirds full; freeze according to the manufacturer's directions. Refrigerate remaining mixture until ready to freeze. When ice cream is frozen, transfer to a freezer container; freeze for 2-4 hours before serving.
½ CUP: 280 cal., 7g fat (4g sat. fat), 81mg chol., 126mg sod., 47g carb. (43g sugars, 0 fiber), 7g pro.

CRANBERRY ORANGE CHEESECAKE

I can't go to any Christmas gathering without this showstopping dessert in tow. The combination of cranberries, chocolate and orange is a winner.
—*Laurie Lufkin, Essex, MA*

Prep: 45 min. • **Bake:** 1 hour + chilling
Makes: 12 servings

- 1 cup finely chopped pecans
- ⅔ cup chocolate wafer crumbs
- ¼ cup butter, melted
- 3 Tbsp. brown sugar
- 2 pkg. (8 oz. each) cream cheese, softened
- 2 cartons (8 oz. each) mascarpone cheese
- 1¼ cups sugar
- 2 Tbsp. cornstarch
- 2 tsp. orange juice
- 1 tsp. orange extract
- 4 large eggs, room temperature, lightly beaten
- ¾ cup whole-berry cranberry sauce
- ¼ cup dried cranberries
- 1 Tbsp. water
- ¼ cup chocolate ice cream topping, warmed
  Sugared cranberries and orange slices, optional

1. Place a greased 9-in. springform pan on a double thickness of heavy-duty foil (about 18 in. square). Securely wrap foil around pan.
2. Combine the pecans, wafer crumbs, butter and brown sugar. Press onto the bottom and 1 in. up the side of prepared pan. Place on a baking sheet. Bake at 325° 8-10 minutes or until lightly browned. Cool on a wire rack.
3. In a large bowl, beat the cheeses, sugar, cornstarch, orange juice and extract until smooth. Add eggs; beat on low speed just until combined. Pour half of the batter over crust.
4. Place the cranberry sauce, cranberries and water in a food processor; cover and process until blended. Gently spread over batter in pan; top with remaining batter.
5. Place springform pan in a large baking pan; add 1 in. of hot water to larger pan. Bake at 325° until center is just set and top appears dull, 60-70 minutes.
6. Remove pan from water bath. Cool on a wire rack for 10 minutes. Carefully run a knife around edge of pan to loosen; cool 1 hour longer. Refrigerate overnight. Just before serving, top with chocolate topping. If desired, garnish with sugared cranberries and orange slices.
SUGARED CRANBERRY GARNISH: Heat 3 Tbsp. light corn syrup in microwave until warm; gently toss with 1 cup fresh or frozen cranberries, allowing excess syrup to drip off. Toss in ⅓ cup sugar to coat. Place on waxed paper; let stand until set, about 1 hour.
1 PIECE: 599 cal., 44g fat (22g sat. fat), 169mg chol., 229mg sod., 45g carb. (36g sugars, 2g fiber), 9g pro.

MINI CHERRY CHEESECAKES

These little cheesecakes make a fun dessert that's just right for cooks who don't have a lot of time for fussy recipes. Plus, you get to eat a whole mini cheesecake yourself!
—*Kay Keller, Morenci, MI*

Prep: 20 min. + chilling
Bake: 15 min. + cooling
Makes: 12 servings

- 1 cup crushed vanilla wafers (about 30 wafers)
- 3 Tbsp. butter, melted
- 1 pkg. (8 oz.) cream cheese, softened
- ⅓ cup sugar
- 2 tsp. lemon juice
- 1½ tsp. vanilla extract
- 1 large egg, room temperature, lightly beaten

TOPPING
- 1 lb. pitted canned or frozen tart red cherries
- ½ cup sugar
- 1 Tbsp. cornstarch
  Red food coloring, optional

1. Preheat oven to 350°. Combine crumbs and butter; press gently onto bottoms of 12 foil-lined muffin cups. In another bowl, combine cream cheese, sugar, lemon juice and vanilla. Add egg; beat on low speed just until combined. Spoon over crusts.
2. Bake until centers are almost set, 12-15 minutes. Cool completely.
3. For topping, drain cherries, reserving ½ cup juice in a saucepan; discard remaining juice. To reserved juice, add cherries, sugar, cornstarch and, if desired, food coloring. Bring to a boil; cook until thickened, about 1 minute. Cool; spoon over cheesecakes. Refrigerate, covered, at least 2 hours.

1 MINI CHEESECAKE: 213 cal., 12g fat (6g sat. fat), 44mg chol., 127mg sod., 26g carb. (21g sugars, 1g fiber), 2g pro.

CLASSIC CREME BRULEE

My favorite dessert is creme brulee, so I quickly learned how to successfully make this on my own. Recently I was at a party where the guests finished off their own desserts broiling the sugar on their portions with a small torch. What a clever idea!
—*Joylyn Trickel, Helendale, CA*

Prep: 30 min. • **Bake:** 25 min. + chilling
Makes: 8 servings

- 4 cups heavy whipping cream
- 9 large egg yolks
- ¾ cup sugar
- 1 tsp. vanilla extract
  Brown sugar

1. Preheat oven to 325°. In a small saucepan, heat cream until bubbles form around side of pan; remove from heat. In a large bowl, whisk egg yolks and sugar until blended but not foamy. Slowly stir in hot cream. Stir in vanilla.
2. Place eight 6-oz. broiler-safe ramekins in a baking pan large enough to hold them without touching. Pour egg mixture into ramekins. Place pan on oven rack; add very hot water to pan to within ½ in. of top of ramekins. Bake until centers are just set (egg mixture will jiggle), 25-30 minutes. Immediately remove ramekins from water bath to a wire rack; cool 10 minutes. Refrigerate until cold.
3. Place ramekins on a baking sheet; let stand at room temperature 15 minutes. Preheat broiler. Sprinkle custards evenly with 1-2 tsp. brown sugar each. Broil 8 in. from heat until sugar is caramelized, 4-7 minutes.

1 SERVING: 551 cal., 50g fat (29g sat. fat), 402mg chol., 53mg sod., 22g carb. (22g sugars, 0 fiber), 6g pro.

CREME BRULEE TIPS

Can you use a blowtorch instead of the broiler to caramelize the sugar? Of course! We suggest working slowly, as well as keeping the ramekins on a baking sheet to protect your countertops.

Can you make this creme brulee recipe ahead of time? Yes! Keep baked, cooled ramekins covered in the refrigerator for 1-3 days. Top with sugar and caramelize the custards right before serving.

CREAMY CARAMEL FLAN

A small slice of this impressively rich, creamy treat goes a long way. What a delightful finish for a special meal or holiday celebration.
—*Pat Forete, Miami, FL*

Prep: 25 min. + standing
Bake: 50 min. + chilling
Makes: 10 servings

- ¾ cup sugar
- ¼ cup water
- 1 pkg. (8 oz.) cream cheese, softened
- 5 large eggs, room temperature
- 1 can (14 oz.) sweetened condensed milk
- 1 can (12 oz.) evaporated milk
- 1 tsp. vanilla extract

1. In a heavy saucepan, cook sugar and water over medium-low heat until melted and golden, about 15 minutes. Brush down crystals on the side of the pan with additional water as necessary. Quickly pour into an ungreased 2-qt. round baking or souffle dish, tilting to coat the bottom; let stand for 10 minutes.

2. Preheat oven to 350°. In a bowl, beat the cream cheese until smooth. Beat in eggs, 1 at a time, until thoroughly combined. Add remaining ingredients; mix well. Pour over caramelized sugar.

3. Place the dish in a larger baking pan. Pour boiling water into larger pan to a depth of 1 in. Bake custard until the center is just set (mixture will jiggle), 50-60 minutes.

4. Remove dish from a larger pan to a wire rack; cool for 1 hour. Refrigerate overnight.

5. To unmold, run a knife around edge and invert onto a large rimmed serving platter. Cut into wedges or spoon onto dessert plates; spoon additional sauce over each serving.

1 PIECE: 345 cal., 16g fat (9g sat. fat), 140mg chol., 189mg sod., 41g carb. (41g sugars, 0 fiber), 10g pro.

CHEESECAKE POPS

Customize these cute cheesecake bites for any occasion by using different toppings.
—*Evelyn Moore, Elk Grove, CA*

Prep: 2 hours + freezing
Makes: 45 cheesecake pops

- 3 pkg. (8 oz. each) cream cheese, softened
- 1 cup sugar
- 1 cup sour cream
- 1 tsp. vanilla extract
- 3 large eggs, room temperature, lightly beaten
- 1 cup graham cracker crumbs
- 45 lollipop sticks (4 in. long)
   3 pkg. (10 to 12 oz. each) white baking chips
- 3 Tbsp. shortening
   Toppings: Grated coconut, grated chocolate and assorted sprinkles

1. Line the bottom of a 9-in. springform pan with parchment; coat paper and side of pan with cooking spray.

2. In a large bowl, beat cream cheese and sugar until smooth. Beat in sour cream and vanilla extract until blended. Add eggs; beat on low speed just until combined. Pour into the prepared pan.

3. Place pan on a baking sheet. Bake at 350° until center is almost set, 45-50 minutes. Cool on a wire rack for 10 minutes. Carefully run a knife around edge of pan to loosen; cool 1 hour longer. Cover and freeze overnight.

4. Remove from the freezer and let stand for 30 minutes. Place cracker crumbs in a shallow bowl. Working quickly, scoop out 1-in. balls of cheesecake; roll each in cracker crumbs and insert a lollipop stick. Place on waxed paper-lined baking sheets. Freeze for 1 hour or until firm.

5. In a microwave, melt white chips and shortening at 70% power; stir until smooth. Place toppings in shallow bowls. Dip cheesecake pops in white chip mixture; allow excess to drip off. Roll in toppings. Place on waxed paper; let stand until set. Store in the refrigerator.

1 CAKE POP: 203 cal., 14g fat (8g sat. fat), 37mg chol., 80mg sod., 18g carb. (16g sugars, 0 fiber), 3g pro.

PINEAPPLE CHEESECAKE

A co-worker shared the recipe for this easy yet elegant dessert years ago, and our family has enjoyed it many times since then.
—*Phoebe Carre, Mullica Hill, NJ*

Prep: 15 min. + chilling
Makes: 10 servings

- 2 pkg. (8 oz. each) cream cheese, softened
- ½ cup sugar
- 1 can (20 oz.) crushed pineapple, drained
- 1 carton (8 oz.) frozen whipped topping, thawed
- 2 pkg. (3 oz. each) ladyfingers (about 48)
- 1 pint fresh strawberries, sliced

1. In a large bowl, beat cream cheese and sugar until smooth. Stir in pineapple. Fold in whipped topping.
2. Place ladyfingers around the side and on the bottom of a greased 9-in. springform pan. Pour filling into pan. Cover and refrigerate for 8 hours or overnight. Carefully remove side of pan. Top with strawberries.
1 PIECE: 366 cal., 20g fat (13g sat. fat), 82mg chol., 263mg sod., 41g carb. (33g sugars, 1g fiber), 5g pro.

OTHER GARNISH IDEAS

Fresh strawberries are always a tasty choice to top desserts, but don't stop there. You can also top this cheesecake with toasted shaved coconut, sprigs of fresh mint, raspberries, diced fresh mango, sliced star fruit and kiwi or drained mandarin orange segments. A dollop of whipped cream would also be welcome.

DOUBLE CHOCOLATE ALMOND CHEESECAKE

This cheesecake is easy to make—but it's definitely not easy to wait till the next day to eat it! The recipe came from a friend and former co-worker.
—*Darlene Brenden, Salem, OR*

Prep: 25 min. + chilling
Bake: 50 min. + chilling
Makes: 16 servings

CRUST
- 1 pkg. (9 oz.) chocolate wafer cookies, crushed (about 2 cups)
- ¼ cup sugar
- ¼ tsp. ground cinnamon
- ¼ cup butter, melted

FILLING
- 2 pkg. (8 oz. each) cream cheese, softened
- 1 cup sugar
- 1 cup sour cream
- 8 oz. semisweet chocolate, melted and cooled
- ½ tsp. almond extract
- 2 large eggs, room temperature, lightly beaten

TOPPING
- 1 cup sour cream
- ¼ tsp. baking cocoa
- 2 Tbsp. sugar
- ½ tsp. almond extract
   Sliced almonds, toasted, optional

1. In a small bowl, combine crust ingredients; reserve 2 Tbsp. for garnish. Press remaining crumbs evenly onto the bottom and 2 in. up the side of a 9-in. springform pan. Chill.
2. For filling, in a large bowl, beat cream cheese and sugar until smooth. Beat in the sour cream, chocolate and extract. Add eggs; beat on low speed just until combined. Pour into crust.
3. Place pan on a baking sheet. Bake at 350° for 40 minutes (filling will not be set). Remove from oven and let stand for 5 minutes.
4. Meanwhile, combine the 4 topping ingredients. Gently spread over filling. Sprinkle with reserved crumbs. Bake 10 minutes longer.
5. Cool on a wire rack for 10 minutes. Carefully run a knife around edge of pan to loosen; cool 1 hour longer. Refrigerate overnight. Garnish with sliced, toasted almonds if desired.
1 PIECE: 315 cal., 19g fat (11g sat. fat), 78mg chol., 215mg sod., 31g carb. (19g sugars, 1g fiber), 4g pro.

RICH & CREAMY TIRAMISU

Tiramisu is Italian for pick-me-up, and this one is definitely true to its name! My version of the classic Tuscan dessert has both coffee and espresso for layers of java flavor.
—*Lauren McAnelly, Des Moines, IA*

Prep: 15 min. + standing
Cook: 10 min. + chilling
Makes: 16 servings

- 2   cartons (8 oz. each) mascarpone cheese
- 5   large egg yolks
- ½   cup plus 2 Tbsp. sugar, divided
- ⅓   cup plus 2 Tbsp. Marsala wine, Kahlua (coffee liqueur) or rum, divided
- ½   tsp. salt
- 1   cup heavy whipping cream
- ¾   cup strong brewed coffee, room temperature
- 2   tsp. instant espresso powder
- 1   pkg. (7 oz.) crisp ladyfinger cookies
- 1   Tbsp. Dutch-processed cocoa

1. Stir mascarpone cheese; let stand at room temperature 30 minutes. Whisk yolks, ½ cup sugar, ⅓ cup Marsala and salt in top of a double boiler until mixture is thickened (ribbon stage) and a thermometer reads 160°. Remove from heat; whisk in mascarpone until almost smooth. Whip cream and remaining sugar until soft peaks form; fold into mascarpone mixture.

2. Combine the coffee, espresso powder and remaining Marsala. Briefly dip 8 ladyfingers into coffee mixture and place in bottom of a 9-in. springform pan. Top with 1½ cups mascarpone mixture. Repeat 2 more times. Refrigerate, covered, 6 hours or overnight. To serve, loosen and remove rim; sprinkle with cocoa powder.
1 SERVING: 280 cal., 21g fat (11g sat. fat), 123mg chol., 115mg sod., 19g carb. (14g sugars, 0 fiber), 5g pro.

SECRETS TO THE BEST TEXTURE

Feel free to vigorously whip the yolk mixture in the double boiler to add volume and to get the desired ribbonlike texture. But work more gently when mixing in the mascarpone cheese. You can even leave it a little lumpy; the carryover warmth from the yolk mixture will soften those lumps while you whip the cream. When you fold in the whipped cream, those lumps will disappear entirely.

POTS DE CREME

Looking for an easy dessert recipe that's still guaranteed to impress? Served in pretty stemmed glasses, this classic chocolate custard really sets the tone.
—*Connie Dreyfoos, Cincinnati, OH*

Prep: 15 min. + chilling
Makes: 5 servings

- 1 large egg
- 2 Tbsp. sugar
  Dash salt
- ¾ cup half-and-half cream
- 1 cup semisweet chocolate chips
- 1 tsp. vanilla extract
  Optional: Whipped cream and assorted fresh fruit

1. In a small saucepan, combine the egg, sugar and salt. Whisk in cream. Cook and stir over medium heat until mixture reaches 160° and coats the back of a metal spoon.
2. Remove from the heat; whisk in chocolate chips and vanilla until smooth. Pour into small dessert dishes. Cover and refrigerate 8 hours or overnight. If desired, garnish with whipped cream and fruit.
⅓ CUP: 246 cal., 15g fat (9g sat. fat), 55mg chol., 66mg sod., 28g carb. (25g sugars, 2g fiber), 4g pro.

LEMON DREAM CHEESECAKE

This cheesecake bakes like a dream with no cracks. Plus it cuts well and everyone loves the light lemon flavor—a refreshing treat any time of year.
—*Bonnie Jost, Manitowoc, WI*

Prep: 30 min. • **Bake:** 55 min. + chilling
Makes: 16 servings

- 2 cups graham cracker crumbs
- 6 Tbsp. butter, melted
- ¼ cup sugar

FILLING
- 4 pkg. (8 oz. each) cream cheese, softened
- 1 cup sugar
- ½ cup heavy whipping cream
- ¼ cup lemon juice
- 2 Tbsp. all-purpose flour
- 1 Tbsp. grated lemon zest
- 2½ tsp. vanilla extract
- 1 tsp. lemon extract
- 10 drops yellow food coloring, optional
- 5 large eggs, room temperature, lightly beaten

1. Preheat oven to 325°. In a small bowl, combine the cracker crumbs, butter and sugar. Press onto bottom and 1-2 in. up the inside of a greased 10-in. springform pan. Place pan on a baking sheet. Bake for 10 minutes. Cool on a wire rack.
2. In a large bowl, beat cream cheese and sugar until smooth. Beat in cream, lemon juice, flour, lemon zest, extracts and, if desired, food coloring. Add the eggs; beat on low speed just until combined. Pour into crust. Return pan to baking sheet.
3. Bake 55-65 minutes or until center is almost set. Cool on a wire rack 10 minutes. Carefully run a knife around edge of pan to loosen; cool 1 hour. Refrigerate overnight. Remove side of pan.
1 PIECE: 396 cal., 29g fat (18g sat. fat), 150mg chol., 286mg sod., 27g carb. (19g sugars, 0 fiber), 7g pro.

GET THE MOST JUICE

Next time you squeeze fresh lemon, warm it in the microwave 7-10 seconds first. Then roll the lemon back and forth under your palm on the counter, giving it firm pressure. You'll get more juice and the lemon will be easier to squeeze. Works for limes too.

JAM-TOPPED MINI CHEESECAKES

Presto! We turned cheesecake into irresistible bite-sized snacks with these cute little treats. Feel free to use your favorite flavor jam.
—Taste of Home *Test Kitchen*

Prep: 20 min. • **Bake:** 15 min. + chilling
Makes: 9 servings

- ⅔ cup graham cracker crumbs
- 2 Tbsp. butter, melted
- 1 pkg. (8 oz.) cream cheese, softened
- ⅓ cup sugar
- 1 tsp. vanilla extract
- 1 large egg, room temperature
- 3 Tbsp. assorted jams, warmed

1. In a small bowl, combine graham cracker crumbs and butter. Press gently onto the bottoms of 9 paper-lined muffin cups. In another small bowl, beat the cream cheese, sugar and vanilla until smooth. Add egg; beat on low speed just until combined. Spoon over crusts.

2. Bake at 350° until centers are set, 15-16 minutes. Cool for 10 minutes before removing from pan to a wire rack to cool completely. Refrigerate for at least 1 hour.

3. Remove paper liners; top each cheesecake with 1 tsp. jam.

1 MINI CHEESECAKE: 198 cal., 13g fat (7g sat. fat), 53mg chol., 141mg sod., 19g carb. (14g sugars, 0 fiber), 3g pro.

WATCH THE TIME

The key to getting the creamiest cheesecake is to not overbake it. It's a good idea to start checking on baked goods a few minutes earlier than the recommended time in case your oven runs hot.

S'MORE CHEESECAKE

This luscious dessert is just as wonderfully tasty as the campfire snack that inspired it. It's a great way to savor a summer classic any time of year.
—*Robin Andrews, Cary, NC*

Prep: 20 min. • **Bake:** 45 min. + chilling
Makes: 12 servings

- 2¼ cups graham cracker crumbs (about 36 squares)
- ⅓ cup sugar
- ½ cup butter, melted

FILLING
- 2 pkg. (8 oz. each) cream cheese, softened
- 1 can (14 oz.) sweetened condensed milk
- 2 tsp. vanilla extract
- 3 large eggs, room temperature, lightly beaten
- 1 cup miniature semisweet chocolate chips
- 1 cup miniature marshmallows

TOPPING
- 1 cup miniature marshmallows
- ½ cup semisweet chocolate chips
- 1 Tbsp. shortening

1. In a small bowl, combine cracker crumbs and sugar; stir in butter. Press onto the bottom and 1¾ in. up the side of a greased 10-in. springform pan.

2. In a large bowl, beat the cream cheese, milk and vanilla until smooth. Add eggs; beat on low just until combined. Stir in chocolate chips and marshmallows. Pour over crust. Place on a baking sheet.

3. Bake cheesecake at 325° until the center is almost set, 40-45 minutes. Sprinkle with marshmallows. Bake until the marshmallows are puffed, 4-6 minutes longer.

4. Meanwhile, melt chocolate chips and shortening in a heavy saucepan or microwave; stir until smooth. Drizzle over marshmallows.

5. Cool on a wire rack for 10 minutes. Carefully run a knife around edge of pan to loosen; cool 1 hour longer. Refrigerate overnight. Remove side of pan. Refrigerate leftovers.

1 PIECE: 486 cal., 27g fat (15g sat. fat), 106mg chol., 292mg sod., 57g carb. (44g sugars, 2g fiber), 8g pro.

WHITE CHOCOLATE CREME BRULEE

If you like classic creme brulee, you have to try this version. Dressed up with white chocolate, it's a special romantic treat.
—Carole Resnick, Cleveland, OH

- -

Prep: 15 min. • **Bake:** 50 min. + chilling
Makes: 2 servings

- 3   large egg yolks
- 6   Tbsp. sugar, divided
- 1   cup heavy whipping cream
- 2   oz. white baking chocolate, finely chopped
- ¼   tsp. vanilla extract

1. In a small bowl, whisk egg yolks and 2 Tbsp. sugar; set aside. In a small saucepan, combine the cream, chocolate and 2 Tbsp. sugar. Heat over medium-low heat until chocolate is melted and mixture is smooth, stirring constantly.
2. Remove from the heat. Stir in vanilla. Stir a small amount of hot mixture into egg yolk mixture; return all to the pan, stirring constantly.
3. Pour into two 10-oz. ramekins. Place in a baking pan. Add 1 in. of boiling water to pan. Bake, uncovered, at 325° for 50-55 minutes or until center is set. Remove from water bath. Cool for 10 minutes. Refrigerate for at least 4 hours.
4. If using a creme brulee torch, sprinkle with remaining sugar. Heat sugar with the torch until caramelized. Serve immediately.
5. If broiling the custards, place ramekins on a baking sheet; let stand at room temperature for 15 minutes. Sprinkle with remaining sugar. Broil 8 in. from the heat for 4-7 minutes or until sugar is caramelized. Refrigerate for 1-2 hours or until firm.

1 SERVING: 854 cal., 62g fat (36g sat. fat), 488mg chol., 86mg sod., 70g carb. (68g sugars, 0 fiber), 9g pro.

CHOCOLATE-COVERED CHEESECAKE SQUARES

Satisfy your cheesecake craving with these bite-size delights! The party favorites are perfect for the holidays when there are so many sweets to choose from.
—Esther Neustaeter, La Crete, AB

- -

Prep: 1½ hours + cooling
Bake: 35 min. + freezing
Makes: 49 squares

- 1   cup graham cracker crumbs
- ¼   cup finely chopped pecans
- ¼   cup butter, melted

FILLING
- 2   pkg. (8 oz. each) cream cheese, softened
- ½   cup sugar
- ¼   cup sour cream
- 2   large eggs, room temperature, lightly beaten
- ½   tsp. vanilla extract

COATING
- 24   oz. semisweet chocolate, chopped
- 3   Tbsp. shortening

1. Preheat oven to 325°. Line a 9-in. square baking pan with foil and grease the foil. In a small bowl, combine graham cracker crumbs, chopped pecans and butter. Press onto bottom of prepared pan.
2. In a large bowl, beat cream cheese, sugar and sour cream until smooth. Add eggs and vanilla; beat on low speed just until combined. Pour over crust. Bake until center is almost set, 35-40 minutes. Cool on a wire rack. Freeze overnight.
3. In a microwave, melt the chocolate and shortening; stir until smooth. Cool slightly.
4. Using foil, lift cheesecake out of pan. Gently peel off foil. Cut cheesecake into 1¼-in. squares; refrigerate. Remove a few squares at a time for dipping, keeping remaining squares refrigerated until ready to dip.
5. Using a toothpick, completely dip squares, 1 at a time, into melted chocolate mixture; allow excess to drip off. Place on waxed paper-lined baking sheets. Spoon additional chocolate over the tops if necessary to coat. (Reheat chocolate if needed to finish dipping.) Let stand for 20 minutes or until set. Store in an airtight container in the refrigerator or freezer.

1 PIECE: 141 cal., 10g fat (6g sat. fat), 22mg chol., 48mg sod., 12g carb. (10g sugars, 1g fiber), 2g pro.

READER REVIEW
"These are delicious! I used Wilton's candy coating instead of melting the chocolate because I find it much easier to work with. But if you like cheesecake and chocolate, you can't really go wrong with these."
—GINAXS, TASTEOFHOME.COM

CHOCOLATE-COVERED
CHEESECAKE SQUARES

WHITE CHOCOLATE
PUMPKIN CHEESECAKE
WITH ALMOND TOPPING

CHERRY CHEESE PIE

When I worked full time and needed a quick dessert to take to a potluck or a friend's home, this pie was always the answer. You can substitute a graham cracker crust or use another type of fruit pie filling for a change of pace. Even the chilling time is flexible if you're in a big hurry.
—Mary Smith, Bradenton, FL

Short & Sweet

Prep: 15 min. + chilling
Makes: 8 servings

- 11 oz. cream cheese, softened
- 1   cup confectioners' sugar
- 1   carton (8 oz.) frozen whipped topping, thawed
- 1   shortbread crust (9 in.) or graham cracker crust (9 in.)
- 1   can (21 oz.) cherry pie filling

In a bowl, beat the cream cheese and sugar until smooth. Fold in whipped topping; spoon into crust. Top with pie filling. Refrigerate until serving.

1 PIECE: 464 cal., 24g fat (14g sat. fat), 43mg chol., 250mg sod., 57g carb. (46g sugars, 1g fiber), 4g pro.

MIX THINGS UP

Use your imagination to make this simple recipe your own. Consider an Oreo cookie crust and strawberry pie filling. Or use mini crusts to create several flavors.

WHITE CHOCOLATE PUMPKIN CHEESECAKE WITH ALMOND TOPPING

You'll want to put this delectable cheesecake on a pedestal! The crunchy almond topping is a delightful finishing touch.
—Phyllis Schmalz, Kansas City, KS

Prep: 30 min. • **Bake:** 1 hour + chilling
Makes: 12 servings

- 1½ cups crushed gingersnap cookies (about 32 cookies)
- ¼   cup butter, melted
- 3   pkg. (8 oz. each) cream cheese, softened
- 1   cup sugar
- 3   large eggs, room temperature, lightly beaten
- 1   tsp. vanilla extract
- 5   oz. white baking chocolate, melted and cooled
- ¾   cup canned pumpkin
- 1   tsp. ground cinnamon
- ¼   tsp. ground nutmeg

ALMOND TOPPING
- ½   cup chopped almonds
- 2   Tbsp. butter, melted
- 1   tsp. sugar

1. Preheat oven to 350°. Place a greased 9-in. springform pan on a double thickness of heavy-duty foil (about 18 in. square). Wrap foil securely around pan. Place on a baking sheet.
2. In a small bowl, combine gingersnap crumbs and butter. Press onto the bottom of prepared pan. Bake until set, 8-10 minutes. Cool on a wire rack.
3. In a large bowl, beat cream cheese and sugar until smooth. Add eggs and vanilla; beat on low speed just until combined. Stir in melted white chocolate. Combine pumpkin and spices; gently fold into cream cheese mixture. Pour over crust.
4. Place springform pan in a large baking pan; add 1 in. of hot water to larger pan. Bake until center is just set and top appears dull, 60-70 minutes. Remove springform pan from water bath. Cool cheesecake on a wire rack 10 minutes. Loosen side from pan with knife; remove foil. Cool 1 hour longer. Refrigerate overnight, covering when completely cool.
5. For topping, combine almonds, butter and sugar; spread in a shallow baking pan. Bake until almonds are golden brown, about 10 minutes, stirring twice. Cool. Transfer topping to an airtight container; store in the refrigerator.
6. Remove side of pan. Just before serving, sprinkle topping over cheesecake.

1 PIECE: 509 cal., 34g fat (19g sat. fat), 119mg chol., 344mg sod., 45g carb. (31g sugars, 2g fiber), 8g pro.

SLOW-COOKER CHOCOLATE POTS DE CREME

Lunch on the go just got a whole lot sweeter. Tuck jars of rich chocolate custard into lunch bags for a midday treat. These portable desserts are fun for picnics too.
—*Nick Iverson, Denver, CO*

- -

Prep: 20 min. • **Cook:** 4 hours + chilling
Makes: 8 servings

- 2 cups heavy whipping cream
- 8 oz. bittersweet chocolate, finely chopped
- 1 Tbsp. instant espresso powder
- 4 large egg yolks
- ¼ cup sugar
- ¼ tsp. salt
- 1 Tbsp. vanilla extract
- 3 cups hot water
  Optional: Whipped cream, grated chocolate and fresh raspberries

1. Place cream, chocolate and espresso in a microwave-safe bowl; microwave on high until chocolate is melted and cream is hot, about 4 minutes. Whisk to combine.
2. In a large bowl, whisk egg yolks, sugar and salt until blended but not foamy. Slowly whisk in cream mixture; stir in vanilla.
3. Ladle egg mixture into eight 4-oz. jars. Center lids on jars and screw on bands until fingertip tight. Add hot water to a 7-qt. slow cooker; place jars in slow cooker. Cook, covered, on low for 4 hours or until set. Remove jars from slow cooker; cool on counter for 30 minutes. Refrigerate until cold, about 2 hours.
4. If desired, top with whipped cream, grated chocolate and raspberries.
1 SERVING: 424 cal., 34g fat (21g sat. fat), 160mg chol., 94mg sod., 13g carb. (11g sugars, 1g fiber), 5g pro.

STRAWBERRY GELATO

You'll love this smooth and creamy gelato with bright strawberry flavor and just a hint of sea salt and honey.
—*Shelly Bevington, Hermiston, OR*

- -

Prep: 10 min. + chilling
Process: 25 min./batch + freezing
Makes: 12 servings

- 2 cups whole milk
- 2 Tbsp. light corn syrup
- 1 Tbsp. honey
- ¾ cup sugar
- ½ tsp. sea salt
- 2½ cups fresh strawberries (about 12 oz.), halved
- ½ cup heavy whipping cream
- 1 tsp. lemon juice

1. Place first 6 ingredients in a blender; cover and blend. While blending, gradually add cream, blending just until combined. Remove to a bowl; stir in lemon juice. Refrigerate, covered, until cold, about 4 hours.
2. Fill cylinder of ice cream maker no more than two-thirds full; freeze according to manufacturer's directions. (Refrigerate any remaining mixture until ready to freeze.)
3. Transfer ice cream to freezer containers, allowing headspace for expansion. Freeze until firm, 3-4 hours.
½ CUP: 160 cal., 6g fat (4g sat. fat), 18mg chol., 124mg sod., 26g carb. (25g sugars, 1g fiber), 2g pro.

GELATO TIPS

Corn syrup and honey contribute to the smoothness of this frozen treat by preventing the formation of ice crystals. Fresh raspberries or blackberries can be substituted for the strawberries. If your berries are tart, you may want to add a touch more sugar or honey.

BRIOCHE, PAGE 167

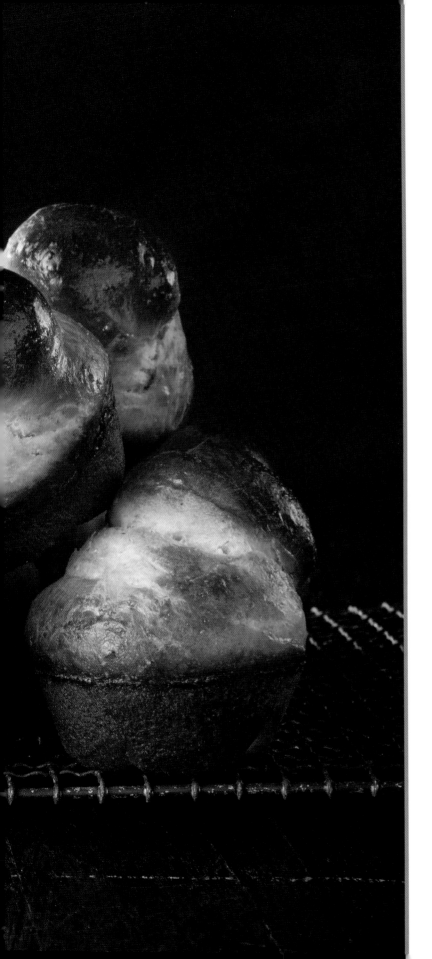

Daily Breads

Nothing warms the heart and makes you feel at home like fragrant oven-fresh bread.

CHOCOLATE BABKA

I love this chocolate babka. It's a rewarding recipe for taking the next step in your bread baking. Even if it's slightly imperfect going into the oven, it turns out gorgeous. Just look at those swirls!

—Lisa Kaminski, Wauwatosa, WI

Prep: 20 min. + chilling
Bake: 35 min. + cooling
Makes: 2 loaves (16 pieces each)

4¼ to 4¾ cups all-purpose flour
½ cup sugar
2½ tsp. quick-rise yeast
¾ tsp. salt
⅔ cup butter
½ cup water
3 large eggs plus 1 large egg yolk, room temperature, beaten
2 Tbsp. grated orange zest

FILLING
½ cup butter, cubed
5 oz. dark chocolate chips
½ cup confectioners' sugar
⅓ cup baking cocoa
¼ tsp. salt

GLAZE
¼ cup sugar
¼ cup water

1. In a large bowl, mix 2 cups flour, sugar, yeast and salt. Cut in butter until crumbly. In a small saucepan, heat water to 120°-130°; stir into dry ingredients. Stir in eggs and yolk, orange zest and enough remaining flour to form a soft dough (dough will be sticky).

2. Turn dough onto a floured surface; knead 6-8 minutes or until smooth and elastic. Place in a greased bowl, turning once to grease the top. Cover and refrigerate 8 hours or overnight.

3. Turn out dough onto a lightly floured surface; divide in half. Roll each half into a 12x10-in. rectangle. For filling, in a microwave, melt the butter and chocolate chips; stir until smooth. Stir in confectioners' sugar, cocoa and salt. Spread filling to within ½ in. of edges. Roll up jelly-roll style, starting with a long side; pinch seam and ends to seal.

4. Using a sharp knife, cut each roll lengthwise in half; carefully turn each half cut side up. Loosely twist strips around each other, keeping cut surfaces facing up; pinch ends together to seal. Place in 2 greased 9x5-in. loaf pans, cut side up. Cover with kitchen towels; let rise in a warm place until almost doubled, about 1 hour. Preheat oven to 375°.

5. Bake 35-45 minutes or until golden brown, tenting with foil halfway through baking. Meanwhile, in a saucepan, combine the sugar and water; bring to a boil. Reduce heat; simmer, uncovered, 10 minutes. Brush over warm babka. Cool for 10 minutes before removing from pans to wire racks.

1 PIECE: 181 cal., 9g fat (5g sat. fat), 41mg chol., 136mg sod., 23g carb. (10g sugars, 1g fiber), 3g pro.

READER REVIEW

"Loved it! Used espresso chips instead of chocolate chips just to give it a different kick."
—APSCHWARTZ, TASTEOFHOME.COM

WATCH US
MAKE IT
Just hover your
camera here.

A BIT NUTTY BOSTON BROWN BREAD

Hearty and dense, my homemade Boston brown bread features chopped hazelnuts for a delightfully nutty taste. Thick slices pair well with just about anything, from soups and stews to roasts and casseroles.
—Lorraine Caland, Shuniah, ON

Prep: 30 min. • **Bake:** 45 min. + cooling
Makes: 2 loaves (12 pieces each)

- 3 cups whole wheat flour
- 1 cup all-purpose flour
- 2½ tsp. baking soda
- 1 tsp. salt
- 2½ cups buttermilk
- 1 cup molasses
- 1 cup golden raisins
- ¾ cup chopped hazelnuts

1. In a large bowl, combine the flours, baking soda and salt. In a small bowl, whisk the buttermilk and molasses. Stir into dry ingredients just until moistened. Fold in raisins and nuts. Transfer to 2 greased 8x4-in. loaf pans.
2. Bake at 350° for 45-50 minutes or until a toothpick inserted in the center comes out clean. Cool for 10 minutes before removing from pans to wire racks.

NOTE: To substitute for each cup of buttermilk, use 1 Tbsp. white vinegar or lemon juice plus enough milk to measure 1 cup. Stir, then let stand 5 min. Or, use 1 cup plain yogurt or 1¾ tsp. cream of tartar plus 1 cup milk.

1 PIECE: 159 cal., 3g fat (0 sat. fat), 1mg chol., 263mg sod., 31g carb. (13g sugars, 3g fiber), 4g pro.

BRIOCHE

These classic French rolls (pronounced BREE-osh) are rich in butter and eggs. The unique shape resembles a muffin.
—Wanda Kristoffersen, Owatonna, MN

Prep: 30 min. + rising • **Bake:** 15 min.
Makes: 1 dozen

- 3½ cups all-purpose flour
- ½ cup sugar
- 2 pkg. (¼ oz. each) active dry yeast
- 1 tsp. grated lemon zest
- ½ tsp. salt
- ⅔ cup butter, cubed
- ½ cup 2% milk
- 5 large eggs, divided use

1. In a large bowl, combine 1½ cups flour, sugar, yeast, lemon zest and salt. In a small saucepan, heat the butter and milk to 120°-130°. Add to dry ingredients; beat until moistened. Add 4 eggs; beat on medium speed for 2 minutes. Add 1 cup flour. Beat until smooth. Stir in the remaining flour. Do not knead.
2. Spoon into a greased bowl, turning once to grease the top. Cover and let rise in a warm place until doubled, about 1 hour. Stir dough down. Cover and refrigerate overnight.
3. Preheat oven to 375°. Punch dough down. Turn onto a lightly floured surface. Cover; let rest for 15 minutes. Cut one-sixth from the dough; set aside. Shape remaining dough into 12 balls (about 2½ in); place in well-greased muffin cups.
4. Divide reserved dough into 12 small balls. Make an indentation in the top of each large ball; place a small ball in each indentation. Cover and let rise in a warm place until doubled, about 1 hour.
5. Beat remaining egg; brush over rolls. Bake until golden brown, 15-20 minutes. Remove from pan to a wire rack to cool.

1 ROLL: 295 cal., 13g fat (7g sat. fat), 117mg chol., 234mg sod., 37g carb. (9g sugars, 1g fiber), 7g pro.

WARM EGGS FOR BETTER BAKING
Many recipes benefit from room-temperature eggs, and it's an easy thing to do. Just place eggs in hot water while you prep your recipe. They'll be ready when it's time to get cracking.

CRUSTY FRENCH BREAD

I love to treat guests to these crusty loaves. Don't hesitate to try this recipe even if you are not an accomplished bread baker. It's so easy because there's no kneading required!
—*Christy Freeman, Central Point, OR*

Prep: 30 min. + rising • **Bake:** 20 min.
Makes: 2 loaves (10 pieces each)

    1   pkg. (¼ oz.) active dry yeast
    1½ cups warm water (110° to 115°),
        divided
    1   Tbsp. sugar
    2   tsp. salt
    1   Tbsp. shortening, melted
    4   to 5 cups all-purpose flour
        Cornmeal

1. In a large bowl, dissolve yeast in ½ cup water. Add the sugar, salt, shortening, remaining 1 cup water and 3½ cups flour. Beat until smooth. Stir in enough remaining flour to form a soft dough. Do not knead. Cover and let rise in a warm place until doubled, about 1 hour.

2. Turn onto a floured surface. Divide in half; let rest for 10 minutes. Roll each half into a 10x8-in. rectangle. Roll up from a long side; pinch to seal. Place seam side down on 2 greased baking sheets sprinkled with cornmeal. Sprinkle the tops with cornmeal. Cover and let rise until doubled, about 45 minutes.

3. With a very sharp knife, make 5 diagonal cuts across the top of each loaf. Bake at 400° until lightly browned, 20-30 minutes. Remove from pans to wire racks to cool.

1 PIECE: 100 cal., 1g fat (0 sat. fat), 0 chol., 237mg sod., 20g carb. (1g sugars, 1g fiber), 3g pro.

RUSTIC RYE BREAD

This gorgeous rye bread has just a touch of sweetness and the perfect amount of caraway seeds. With a crusty top and firm texture, it holds up well for sandwiches.
—*Holly Wade, Harrisonburg, VA*

Prep: 25 min. + rising • **Bake:** 30 min.
Makes: 2 loaves (12 pieces each)

    1   pkg. (¼ oz.) active dry yeast
    1¾   cups warm water (110° to 115°),
         divided
    ¼   cup packed brown sugar
    ¼   cup light molasses
    3   Tbsp. caraway seeds
    2   Tbsp. canola oil
    1   Tbsp. salt
    1¾   cups rye flour
    ¾   cup whole wheat flour
    2½   to 3 cups all-purpose flour

1. In a large bowl, dissolve yeast in ¼ cup warm water. Stir in brown sugar, molasses, caraway seeds, oil, salt and remaining water. Add rye flour, whole wheat flour and 1 cup all-purpose flour; beat on medium speed until smooth. Stir in enough remaining all-purpose flour to form a firm dough.

2. Turn dough onto a floured surface; knead 6-8 minutes or until smooth and elastic. Place in a greased bowl, turning once to grease the top. Cover and let rise in a warm place until doubled, about 1½ hours.

3. Punch down dough. Turn onto a lightly floured surface; divide in half. Shape each into a round loaf; place on a baking sheet coated with cooking spray. Cover with kitchen towels; let rise in a warm place until almost doubled, about 1½ hours. Preheat oven to 350°.

4. Bake 30-35 minutes or until golden brown. Remove from pan to wire racks to cool.

1 PIECE: 118 cal., 2g fat (0 sat. fat), 0 chol., 298mg sod., 24g carb. (5g sugars, 2g fiber), 3g pro.

ADD A TRADITIONAL TOPPING

Before baking, brush loaves with an egg white beaten lightly with water; sprinkle with caraway seeds.

CHALLAH

Eggs lend to the richness of this traditional challah bread recipe. The attractive golden color and delicious flavor make it hard to resist.
—Taste of Home *Test Kitchen*

Prep: 30 min. + rising • **Bake:** 30 min.
Makes: 2 loaves (16 pieces each)

2 pkg. (¼ oz. each) active dry yeast
1 cup warm water (110° to 115°)
½ cup canola oil
⅓ cup sugar
1 Tbsp. salt
4 large eggs, room temperature
6 to 6½ cups all-purpose flour
TOPPING
1 large egg
1 tsp. cold water
1 Tbsp. sesame or poppy seeds, optional

1. In a large bowl, dissolve yeast in warm water. Add the oil, sugar, salt, eggs and 4 cups flour. Beat until smooth. Stir in enough remaining flour to form a firm dough. Turn onto a floured surface; knead until smooth and elastic, 6-8 minutes. Place in a greased bowl, turning once to grease top. Cover and let rise in a warm place until doubled, about 1 hour.

2. Punch dough down. Turn onto a lightly floured surface; divide in half. Divide each portion into thirds. Shape each piece into a 15-in. rope.

3. Place 3 ropes on a greased baking sheet and braid; pinch ends to seal and tuck under. Repeat with remaining dough. Cover and let rise until doubled, about 1 hour.

4. Preheat oven to 350°. Beat egg and cold water; brush over braids. Sprinkle with sesame or poppy seeds if desired. Bake 30-40 minutes or until golden brown. Remove to wire racks to cool.

1 PIECE: 139 cal., 5g fat (1g sat. fat), 29mg chol., 233mg sod., 20g carb. (2g sugars, 1g fiber), 4g pro.

CHALLAH TIPS

How do you make challah with more braids? This recipe makes a braided loaf with 3 strands, but you can create a more intricate braid with 6 strands, if you wish. There are different methods for making a loaf with 6 strands. To braid the 6 strands, start by dividing the dough and rolling it into 6 even ropes. Pinch the ropes together at one end, then tuck the end under. To braid, start with the far-right rope and weave toward the left in this pattern: over 2 strands, under 1 strand, over 2 strands. Start again at the new far-right rope and weave toward the left in the same pattern. Keep repeating until the whole loaf is braided. Pinch the ends together, then tuck under.

How do you make a round challah? Although elongated loaves of challah are a year-round treat, round challahs are traditional for Rosh Hashanah because they represent continuity and the cyclical nature of the world. To create a round loaf, first create the braid, then wrap it around itself in a coil and tuck the end under. It's a good idea to make the individual ropes a little longer so the braid is long enough to shape into a full coil.

How do you store challah? Store a completely cooled challah in an airtight container at room temperature. It will keep fresh for a few days. Another option is to freeze it for up to 6 months. To freeze challah, wrap it tightly in foil or freezer paper.

What can you make with leftover challah? If you haven't yet tried french toast or bread pudding made with a loaf of challah, you're in for a treat! The egg in the challah gives these dishes a rich, custardy texture. You can also use challah in any recipe that calls for brioche.

SWEET ONION FLATBREAD

Because there are just a few ingredients in this recipe, you'll get the best results if you use the finest-quality foods, like a fresh Vidalia onion and aged Parmesan cheese.
—*Lisa Speer, Palm Beach, FL*

Prep: 25 min. • **Bake:** 10 min.
Makes: 4 servings

- 1 large sweet onion, thinly sliced
- 2 Tbsp. butter
- 2 Tbsp. olive oil, divided
- 1 can (13.8 oz.) refrigerated pizza crust
- ¼ cup grated Parmesan cheese

1. In a large cast-iron or other ovenproof skillet, saute onion in butter and 1 Tbsp. oil until softened. Reduce heat to medium-low; cook, stirring occasionally, until golden brown, 15-20 minutes. Set aside.
2. Brush bottom and side of skillet with remaining oil. Unroll crust into skillet; flatten crust and build up edge slightly. Top with onion mixture and cheese. Bake at 450° until golden brown, 10-12 minutes. Cut into 4 wedges.
1 WEDGE: 415 cal., 17g fat (5g sat. fat), 19mg chol., 776mg sod., 53g carb. (9g sugars, 2g fiber), 11g pro.

BUTTERY CROISSANTS

A traditional roll like this is always a welcome addition to dinner. The recipe makes a big batch, so it's great for entertaining.
—*Loraine Meyer, Bend, OR*

Prep: 1 hour + chilling
Bake: 15 min./batch
Makes: about 3 dozen

- 1½ cups butter, softened
- ⅓ cup all-purpose flour
- DOUGH
- 1 pkg. (¼ oz.) active dry yeast
- ¼ cup warm water (110° to 115°)
- 1 cup warm 2% milk (110° to 115°)
- ¼ cup sugar
- 1 large egg, room temperature
- 1 tsp. salt
- 3½ to 3¾ cups all-purpose flour

1. In a small bowl, beat butter and flour until combined; spread into a 12x6-in. rectangle on a piece of waxed paper. Cover with another piece of waxed paper; refrigerate for at least 1 hour.
2. In a large bowl, dissolve yeast in warm water. Add the milk, sugar, egg, salt and 2 cups flour; beat until smooth. Stir in enough remaining flour to form a soft dough. Turn onto a floured surface; knead until smooth and elastic, 6-8 minutes.
3. Roll dough into a 14-in. square. Remove top sheet of waxed paper from butter; invert onto half of dough. Remove waxed paper. Fold dough over butter; seal edges.
4. Roll into a 20x12-in. rectangle. Fold into thirds. Repeat rolling and folding twice. (If butter softens, chill after folding.) Wrap dough and refrigerate overnight.

5. Unwrap dough. On a lightly floured surface, roll into a 25x20-in. rectangle. Cut into 5-in. squares. Cut each square diagonally in half, forming 2 triangles.
6. Roll up triangles from the wide end; place 2 in. apart with point down on ungreased baking sheets. Curve ends down to form crescent shape. Cover and let rise until doubled, about 45 minutes.
7. Bake at 375° until golden brown, 12-14 minutes. Remove to wire racks. Serve warm.
1 CROISSANT: 115 cal., 7g fat (4g sat. fat), 25mg chol., 133mg sod., 11g carb. (2g sugars, 0 fiber), 2g pro.

CUSTOMIZED CROISSANTS

You can make homemade croissants your own by adding a filling such as Nutella, almond paste or chocolate chips.

WONDERFUL ENGLISH MUFFINS

When I was growing up on a farm, my mom always seemed to be making homemade bread—nothing tasted so good! Now I like to make these simple, delicious muffins for my own family.
—Linda Rasmussen, Twin Falls, ID

- -

Prep: 30 min. + rising • **Cook:** 25 min.
Makes: 12 muffins

- 1 cup whole milk
- ¼ cup butter, cubed
- 2 Tbsp. sugar
- 1 tsp. salt
- 2 pkg. (¼ oz. each) active dry yeast
- 1 cup warm water (110° to 115°)
- 2 cups all-purpose flour
- 3 to 3½ cups whole wheat flour
- 1 Tbsp. sesame seeds
- 1 Tbsp. poppy seeds
   Cornmeal

1. Scald milk in a saucepan; add butter, sugar and salt. Stir until butter melts; cool to lukewarm. In a small bowl, dissolve yeast in warm water; add to milk mixture. Stir in all-purpose flour and 1 cup whole wheat flour until smooth. Add sesame seeds, poppy seeds and enough remaining whole wheat flour to make a soft dough.
2. Turn onto a floured surface; knead until smooth and elastic, 8-10 minutes. Place in a greased bowl, turning once to grease top. Cover and let rise until doubled, about 1 hour.
3. Punch dough down. Roll to ⅓-in. thickness on a cornmeal-covered surface. Cut into circles with a 3½-in. or 4-in. cutter; cover with a towel and let rise until nearly doubled, about 30 minutes.
4. Place muffins, cornmeal side down, in a greased skillet; cook over medium-low heat until bottoms are browned, 12-14 minutes. Turn and cook until other sides are browned, 12-14 minutes. Cool on wire racks; split and toast to serve.

1 MUFFIN: 240 cal., 6g fat (3g sat. fat), 13mg chol., 248mg sod., 41g carb. (4g sugars, 4g fiber), 7g pro.

SUNFLOWER SEED & HONEY WHEAT BREAD

I've tried other bread recipes, but this one is a staple in our home. I won $50 in a baking contest with a loaf that I had stored in the freezer.
—Mickey Turner, Grants Pass, OR

- -

Prep: 40 min. + rising • **Bake:** 35 min.
Makes: 3 loaves (12 pieces each)

- 2 pkg. (¼ oz. each) active dry yeast
- 3¼ cups warm water (110° to 115°)
- ¼ cup bread flour
- ⅓ cup canola oil
- ⅓ cup honey
- 3 tsp. salt
- 6½ to 7½ cups whole wheat flour
- ½ cup sunflower kernels
- 3 Tbsp. butter, melted

1. In a large bowl, dissolve yeast in warm water. Add the bread flour, oil, honey, salt and 4 cups whole wheat flour. Beat until smooth. Stir in the sunflower kernels and enough of the remaining flour to form a firm dough.
2. Turn onto a floured surface; knead until smooth and elastic, 6-8 minutes. Place in a greased bowl, turning once to grease the top. Cover and let rise in a warm place until doubled, about 1 hour.
3. Punch dough down; divide into 3 portions. Shape into loaves; place in 3 greased 8x4-in. loaf pans. Cover and let rise until doubled, about 30 minutes.
4. Bake at 350° until golden brown, 35-40 minutes. Brush with melted butter. Remove from pans to wire racks to cool.

FREEZE OPTION: Securely wrap cooled loaves in foil and then freeze. To use, thaw loaves at room temperature.

1 PIECE: 125 cal., 4g fat (1g sat. fat), 3mg chol., 212mg sod., 19g carb. (3g sugars, 3g fiber), 4g pro. **DIABETIC EXCHANGES:** 1 starch, 1 fat.

FOCACCIA

Focaccia is one of my favorite breads and is one of the least labor intensive since there isn't all the kneading as with other breads. I've been adjusting the quantities over the years and am happy where this recipe is at. The dough is very wet, which is perfect for a tender yet chewy bread with a very distinct salt bite.

—*James Schend, Pleasant Prairie, WI*

- -

Prep: 30 min. + rising • **Bake:** 20 min.
Makes: 1 loaf (24 pieces)

- 1 pkg. (¼ oz.) active dry yeast
- 1¼ cups warm water (110° to 115°)
- 1 Tbsp. honey
- 3 cups all-purpose flour
- ¼ cup plus 3 Tbsp. olive oil, divided
- ¾ tsp. kosher salt
- 1 tsp. flaky sea salt, optional

1. In a large bowl, dissolve yeast in ½ cup warm water and the honey; let stand for 5 minutes. Add flour, ¼ cup oil, the kosher salt and remaining ¾ cup warm water; mix until smooth (dough will be wet). Scrape the side of the bowl clean; cover and let rise in a warm place until doubled, about 45 minutes.

2. Preheat oven to 425°. Brush a 13x9-in. baking dish or 12-in. cast-iron skillet with 1 Tbsp. oil. Gently scrape dough directly into pan. With oiled hands, gently spread dough. If dough springs back, wait 10 minutes and stretch again. Make indentations in the dough with your fingers. Drizzle with remaining 2 Tbsp. oil; let rise until doubled in size, 30-40 minutes.

3. If desired, sprinkle with sea salt. Bake 20-25 minutes or until golden brown. Cut into squares; serve warm.

1 PIECE: 95 cal., 4g fat (1g sat. fat), 0 chol., 61mg sod., 13g carb. (1g sugars, 1g fiber), 2g pro.

FOCACCIA TIPS

What makes focaccia different from other breads? Unlike a lot of recipes for homemade bread, focaccia is a no-knead bread—making it great for beginner bread bakers. It's also customizable. You can adjust a focaccia recipe to make it thick and fluffy (perfect for sandwiches!) or thin and crispy and add different toppings.

What variations can you make on this focaccia recipe? There are many ingredient variations you can make on focaccia. Arrange sliced vegetables on top for a gorgeous garden focaccia or add fresh herbs to create a rosemary focaccia. Try experimenting with different cheeses, vegetables, and fresh or dried herbs.

How do you store focaccia? Focaccia is best eaten the same day you bake it. You can store it at room temperature, tightly covered, for up to 2 days.

CONCHAS (SEASHELLS)

SWIRLED CINNAMON RAISIN BREAD

My mother received this recipe from a friend in West Virginia. We have found that slices of this warm cinnamon bread and a cup of hot tea work wonders for holiday visitors in our home.
—*Joan Ort, Milford, NJ*

Prep: 25 min. + rising • **Bake:** 45 min.
Makes: 2 loaves (16 slices each)

- 2 pkg. (¼ oz. each) active dry yeast
- 2 cups warm water (110° to 115°)
- 1 cup sugar, divided
- ¼ cup canola oil
- 2 tsp. salt
- 2 large eggs
- 6 to 6½ cups all-purpose flour
- 1 cup raisins
  Additional canola oil
- 3 tsp. ground cinnamon

1. In a large bowl, dissolve yeast in warm water. Add ½ cup sugar, oil, salt, eggs and 4 cups flour. Beat until smooth. Stir in enough remaining flour to form a soft dough.
2. Turn onto a floured surface; knead dough 6-8 minutes or until smooth and elastic. Place in a greased bowl, turning once to grease top. Cover and let rise in a warm place or until doubled, about 1 hour.
3. Punch dough down. Turn onto a lightly floured surface; divide in half. Knead ½ cup raisins into each; roll each portion into a 15x9-in. rectangle. Brush with additional oil. Combine cinnamon and remaining sugar; sprinkle to within ½ in. of edges.
4. Tightly roll dough up, jelly-roll style, starting with a short side; pinch seam to seal. Place, seam side down, in two greased 9x5-in. loaf pans. Cover and let rise 30 minutes or until doubled.
5. Preheat oven to 375°. Brush with oil. Bake 45-50 minutes or until golden brown. Remove from pans to wire racks to cool.
1 PIECE: 145 cal., 2g fat (0 sat. fat), 12mg chol., 153mg sod., 28g carb. (9g sugars, 1g fiber), 3g pro.

CONCHAS (SEASHELLS)

Concha (Mexican sweet bread) is a sweet breakfast or snack bread found all over Mexico. It has a fluffy brioche-like dough with a crispy streusel topping, scored to resemble a shell. The pastry can come in a variety of colors and other shapes, but I prefer the plain and chocolate streusel.
—*Johnna Johnson, Scottsdale, AZ*

Prep: 45 min. + rising
Bake: 15 min. + cooling
Makes: 1 dozen

- ⅓ cup sugar
- 1 pkg. (¼ oz.) active dry yeast
- 1 tsp. salt
- 1 tsp. ground cinnamon
- 5 to 5½ cups all-purpose flour
- 1 cup 2% milk
- ½ cup unsalted butter, cubed
- 2 large eggs, room temperature
  STREUSEL
- ½ cup unsalted butter, softened
- 1 cup all-purpose flour
- ⅔ cup sugar
- 1 tsp. vanilla extract
- 1 oz. semisweet chocolate, ground
- 1 large egg
- 2 Tbsp. 2% milk

1. In a large bowl, mix sugar, yeast, salt, cinnamon and 2 cups flour. In a small saucepan, heat milk and butter to 120°-130°. Add to dry ingredients; beat 2 minutes on medium speed. Add eggs; beat on high 2 minutes. Stir in enough remaining flour to form a stiff dough (dough will be sticky).
2. Turn dough onto a floured surface; knead until smooth and elastic, 6-8 minutes. Place in a greased bowl, turning once to grease the top. Cover and let rise in a warm place until doubled, about 1 hour.
3. Meanwhile, to make streusel, in a large bowl, beat butter, flour, sugar and vanilla until combined. Divide in half. Mix chocolate into 1 half; set aside.
4. Punch down dough. Divide dough into 12 portions; form each into a 3-in. oval. Place 2 in. apart on parchment-lined baking sheets. In a small bowl, whisk egg with milk; brush over dough. Divide plain streusel into 6 portions; roll each into a 3-in. circle. Place over half the rolls. Repeat with chocolate streusel and remaining rolls. Using a sharp knife, cut through streusel on top of rolls to resemble a clamshell.
5. Cover with kitchen towels; let rise in a warm place until almost doubled, about 30 minutes. Preheat oven to 375°. Brush rolls with remaining egg wash. Bake until the tops are lightly browned, 15-20 minutes. Remove to a wire rack to cool completely.
1 ROLL: 475 cal., 19g fat (11g sat. fat), 89mg chol., 229mg sod., 67g carb. (19g sugars, 2g fiber), 9g pro.

PRETTY TOPPINGS

You can add a little food coloring to color the plain streusel topping for different occasions.

ASIAGO BAGELS

Discover a cheesy alternative to the usual sweet bread brunch offerings. There's no need to stop by a bakery when you can make bagels at home.
—*Tami Kuehl, Loup City, NE*

Prep: 30 min. + resting • **Bake:** 15 min.
Makes: 1 dozen

- 1 cup water (70° to 80°)
- 2 large eggs
- ¼ cup plus 1 Tbsp. olive oil
- 2 Tbsp. honey
- ¾ cup shredded Asiago cheese, divided
- ⅓ cup nonfat dry milk powder
- 1½ tsp. salt
- 1 tsp. dried basil
- 2 cups whole wheat flour
- 1½ cups plus 2 Tbsp. all-purpose flour
- 4 tsp. active dry yeast
- 1 large egg white
- 1 Tbsp. water

1. In bread machine pan, place the water, eggs, oil, honey, ½ cup cheese, milk powder, salt, basil, flours and yeast in order suggested by manufacturer. Select dough setting (check dough after 5 minutes of mixing; add 1 to 2 Tbsp. of water or flour if needed).

2. When cycle is completed, turn dough onto a lightly floured surface. Shape into 12 balls. Push thumb through centers to form a 1½-in. hole. Stretch and shape dough to form an even ring. Cover and let rest for 10 minutes; flatten bagels slightly.

3. Fill a Dutch oven two-thirds full with water; bring to a boil. Drop bagels, 2 at a time, into boiling water. Cook for 45 seconds; turn and cook 45 seconds longer. Remove with a slotted spoon; drain well on paper towels.

4. In a small bowl, combine egg white and water; brush over bagels. Sprinkle with remaining cheese. Place 2 in. apart on greased baking sheets. Bake at 400° for 15-20 minutes or until golden brown. Remove to wire racks to cool.

NOTE: We recommend you do not use a bread machine's time-delay feature for this recipe.

1 BAGEL: 239 cal., 9g fat (2g sat. fat), 42mg chol., 342mg sod., 32g carb. (5g sugars, 3g fiber), 9g pro.

GARLIC KNOTS

Here's a handy bread that can be made in no time flat. Refrigerated biscuits make preparation simple. The classic Italian flavors complement a variety of meals.
—*Jane Paschke, University Park, FL*

Takes: 30 min. • **Makes:** 2½ dozen

- 1 tube (12 oz.) refrigerated buttermilk biscuits
- ¼ cup canola oil
- 3 Tbsp. grated Parmesan cheese
- 1 tsp. garlic powder
- 1 tsp. dried oregano
- 1 tsp. dried parsley flakes

1. Preheat oven to 400°. Cut each biscuit into thirds. Roll each piece into a 4-in. rope and tie into a knot; tuck ends under. Place 2 in. apart on a greased baking sheet. Bake until golden brown, 8-10 minutes.

2. In a large bowl, combine oil, cheese, garlic powder, oregano and parsley; add the warm knots and gently toss to coat.

1 ROLL: 46 cal., 2g fat (0 sat. fat), 0 chol., 105mg sod., 6g carb. (0 sugars, 0 fiber), 1g pro.

GARLIC KNOTS TIPS

Can you use other kinds of dough to make garlic knots? Pizza dough is great for these garlic knots. Whether you opt for homemade or store-bought, pizza dough will require a slightly longer baking time. Allow them to bake for 13-15 minutes or until golden brown.

How can you make garlic knots your own? These knots can be tossed in any spice mixture. Add red pepper flakes for a little heat or go for sweet with cinnamon and sugar. You can also use melted butter in place of the canola oil for a richer flavor.

GARLIC KNOTS

BAKER'S DOZEN YEAST ROLLS

A yummy honey-garlic topping turns these easy dinner rolls into something extra special.
—Taste of Home *Test Kitchen*

Prep: 25 min. + rising • **Bake:** 15 min.
Makes: 13 rolls

- 2 to 2½ cups all-purpose flour
- 2 Tbsp. sugar
- 1 pkg. (¼ oz.) quick-rise yeast
- ½ tsp. salt
- ¾ cup warm water (120° to 130°)
- 2 Tbsp. plus 4 tsp. butter, melted, divided
- ¾ cup shredded sharp cheddar cheese
- 2 tsp. honey
- ⅛ tsp. garlic salt

1. In a large bowl, combine 1½ cups flour, sugar, yeast and salt. Add water and 2 Tbsp. butter; beat on medium speed for 3 minutes or until smooth. Stir in cheese and enough remaining flour to form a soft dough.
2. Turn onto a lightly floured surface; knead dough until smooth and elastic, 4-6 minutes. Cover and let rest for 10 minutes. Divide into 13 pieces. Shape each into a ball. Place in a greased 9-in. round baking pan. Cover and let rise in a warm place until doubled, about 30 minutes.
3. Preheat oven to 375°. Bake rolls until lightly browned, 11-14 minutes. Combine honey, garlic salt and remaining butter; brush over rolls. Remove from pan to a wire rack.
1 ROLL: 131 cal., 5g fat (3g sat. fat), 15mg chol., 169mg sod., 18g carb. (3g sugars, 1g fiber), 4g pro.

ROSEMARY FOCACCIA

The savory aroma of rosemary as this classic bread bakes is irresistible. Try this bread as a side with any meal or as a snack or pizza crust.
—*Debrah Peoples, Calgary, AB*

Prep: 30 min. + rising • **Bake:** 25 min.
Makes: 2 loaves (8 pieces each)

- ¼ cup plus 3 Tbsp. olive oil, divided
- 2 medium onions, chopped
- 1½ tsp. active dry yeast
- 1½ cups warm water (110° to 115°), divided
- ½ tsp. sugar
- ½ tsp. salt
- 3 to 4 cups all-purpose flour
- 2 Tbsp. snipped fresh rosemary or 2 tsp. dried rosemary, crushed, divided
  - Cornmeal
  - Coarse salt

1. In a large skillet, heat ¼ cup oil over medium heat. Add onions; cook and stir until tender, 6-8 minutes. In a large bowl, dissolve yeast in ¼ cup warm water. Add sugar; let stand 5 minutes. Add 2 Tbsp. oil, salt and remaining water. Add 2 cups flour. Beat until smooth. Stir in enough remaining flour to form a soft dough.
2. Turn onto a floured surface; knead until smooth and elastic, 6-8 minutes. Add onions and 1 Tbsp. rosemary. Knead 1 minute longer. Place in a greased bowl, turning once to grease top. Cover and let rise in a warm place until doubled, about 40 minutes.
3. Punch dough down. Turn onto a lightly floured surface; divide in half. Pat each piece flat. Let rest 5 minutes. Grease two baking sheets and sprinkle with cornmeal. Stretch each portion of dough into a 10-in. circle on prepared pans. Cover and let rise until doubled, about 40 minutes. Preheat oven to 375°.
4. Brush with remaining 1 Tbsp. oil. Sprinkle with coarse salt and remaining 1 Tbsp. rosemary. Bake until golden brown, 25-30 minutes. Remove from pans to wire racks. Serve warm.
1 PIECE: 147 cal., 6g fat (1g sat. fat), 0 chol., 75mg sod., 20g carb. (2g sugars, 1g fiber), 3g pro.
PARMESAN ROSEMARY FOCACCIA: Sprinkle 1 Tbsp. Parmesan cheese over each focaccia before baking.
ROSEMARY OLIVE FOCACCIA: Prepare dough as directed, omitting sauteed onions. Knead as directed, adding ⅓ cup well-drained sliced ripe olives along with half of the rosemary. Sprinkle 1 Tbsp. Parmesan cheese over each focaccia before baking.

OLD-FASHIONED
BLUEBERRY MUFFINS,
PAGE 197

Muffins & Scones

Your coffee or tea's new BFF is tucked away in this tempting chapter. You'll also find savory versions to round out any meal.

BLUEBERRY SCONES

You'll want to stash a few of these homemade morsels in the freezer to serve to visitors who drop in unexpectedly. Just pop a frozen scone in the microwave for 20 seconds or so, and you have a warm treat.
—*Joan Francis, Spring Lake, NJ*

Prep: 20 min. • **Bake:** 15 min.
Makes: 16 scones

- 4 cups all-purpose flour
- 6 Tbsp. sugar
- 4½ tsp. baking powder
- ½ tsp. salt
- ½ cup plus 2 Tbsp. cold butter
- 2 large eggs
- ¾ cup plus 2 Tbsp. whole milk, divided
- 1½ cups fresh or frozen blueberries

1. In a bowl, combine the flour, sugar, baking powder and salt; cut in butter until mixture resembles coarse crumbs. In a bowl, whisk eggs and ¾ cup milk; add to dry ingredients just until moistened. Turn onto a lightly floured surface; gently knead in the blueberries.
2. Divide the dough in half. Pat each portion into an 8-in. circle; cut each into 8 wedges. Place on greased baking sheets. Brush with remaining milk. Bake at 375° for 15-20 minutes or until the tops are golden brown. Serve warm.
1 SCONE: 220 cal., 9g fat (5g sat. fat), 48mg chol., 274mg sod., 31g carb. (7g sugars, 1g fiber), 5g pro.

SPARKLE & SHINE

To add a sheen to your scones, brush them with beaten egg before baking. Sprinkle with coarse sugar to give them a satisfying crunch plus a bit of sparkle.

APPLE STREUSEL MUFFINS

These muffins remind us of coffee cake, and my husband and kids love them as a quick breakfast or snack on the run. The drizzle of glaze makes them pretty enough for company.
—*Dulcy Grace, Roaring Spring, PA*

Prep: 20 min. • **Bake:** 15 min.
Makes: 1 dozen

- 2 cups all-purpose flour
- 1 cup sugar
- 1 tsp. baking powder
- ½ tsp. baking soda
- ½ tsp. salt
- 2 large eggs, room temperature
- ½ cup butter, melted
- 1¼ tsp. vanilla extract
- 1½ cups peeled chopped tart apples

STREUSEL TOPPING
- ⅓ cup packed brown sugar
- 1 Tbsp. all-purpose flour
- ⅛ tsp. ground cinnamon
- 1 Tbsp. cold butter

GLAZE
- ¾ cup confectioners' sugar
- 2 to 3 tsp. 2% milk
- 1 tsp. butter, melted
- ⅛ tsp. vanilla extract
  Dash salt

1. Preheat oven to 375°. Whisk together first 5 ingredients. In another bowl, whisk together eggs, melted butter and vanilla; add to flour mixture, stirring just until moistened (batter will be stiff). Fold in apples.
2. Fill 12 greased or paper-lined muffin cups three-fourths full. For topping, mix brown sugar, flour and cinnamon; cut in butter until crumbly. Sprinkle over batter.
3. Bake until a toothpick inserted in center comes out clean, 15-20 minutes. Cool 5 minutes before removing from pan to a wire rack to cool. Mix glaze ingredients; drizzle over tops.
1 MUFFIN: 295 cal., 10g fat (6g sat. fat), 55mg chol., 398mg sod., 49g carb. (32g sugars, 1g fiber), 3g pro.

CREAM CHEESE CRANBERRY MUFFINS

Moist and packed with colorful berries, these marvelous muffins are a seasonal specialty. They are light and tasty, and they freeze very well.
—*Leonard Keszler, Bismarck, ND*

Prep: 15 min. • **Bake:** 20 min.
Makes: 2 dozen

- 1 cup butter, softened
- 1 pkg. (8 oz.) cream cheese, softened
- 1½ cups sugar
- 4 eggs, room temperature
- 1½ tsp. vanilla extract
- 2 cups all-purpose flour
- 1½ tsp. baking powder
- ½ tsp. salt
- 2 cups fresh or frozen cranberries
- ½ cup chopped pecans

DRIZZLE

- 2 cups confectioners' sugar
- 3 Tbsp. 2% milk

1. Preheat oven to 350°. In a large bowl, cream butter, cream cheese and sugar until light and fluffy, 5-7 minutes. Add eggs, 1 at a time, beating well after each addition. Beat in vanilla. Combine flour, baking powder and salt; stir into creamed mixture just until moistened. Fold in cranberries and pecans.
2. Fill greased or paper-lined muffin cups three-fourths full. Bake until a toothpick inserted in the muffins comes out clean, 20-25 minutes. Cool 5 minutes before removing from pans to wire racks.
3. Combine confectioners' sugar and milk; drizzle over muffins.
1 MUFFIN: 105 cal., 6g fat (3g sat. fat), 46mg chol., 113mg sod., 10g carb. (1g sugars, 1g fiber), 3g pro.

BEST BRAN MUFFINS

Having these muffins for breakfast provides a good start to a busy day. My husband loves pineapple, which makes these muffins moist and delicious!
—*Suzanne Smith, Framingham, MA*

Takes: 30 min. • **Makes:** 18 muffins

- ½ cup old-fashioned oats
- 1 cup all-purpose flour
- 1 cup whole wheat flour
- ½ cup All-Bran cereal
- ½ tsp. salt
- 1 tsp. baking powder
- 1 tsp. baking soda
- 1 large egg, beaten
- ¼ cup vegetable oil
- ½ cup molasses
- ¾ cup buttermilk
- 1 can (8 oz.) crushed pineapple in natural juice, undrained
- ½ cup chopped nuts, dates or raisins

1. In a bowl, combine the first 7 ingredients. Make a well in the center. Combine egg, vegetable oil, molasses, buttermilk and pineapple with juice. Pour into well; mix just until dry ingredients are moistened. Stir in the nuts, dates or raisins.
2. Fill 18 greased muffin cups two-thirds full. Bake at 400° until golden brown, 12 minutes.
NOTE: To substitute for each cup of buttermilk, use 1 Tbsp. white vinegar or lemon juice plus enough milk to measure 1 cup. Stir, then let stand for 5 minutes. Or, use 1 cup plain yogurt or 1¾ tsp. cream of tartar plus 1 cup milk.

1 MUFFIN: 151 cal., 6g fat (1g sat. fat), 11mg chol., 194mg sod., 22g carb. (9g sugars, 2g fiber), 4g pro. **DIABETIC EXCHANGES:** 1½ starch, 1 fat.

BEST BRAN MUFFINS TIPS

- **How should you store bran muffins?** Bran muffins (as well as most biscuits and scones) should be stored in an airtight container at room temperature. Muffins stay fresh for three days.

- **Can you freeze bran muffins?** Yes! Freeze muffins in an airtight container for up to 1 month.

PUMPKIN CHIP MUFFINS

My sisters, brothers and I started cooking and baking when we were young. Mom was a very good teacher—she told us we would learn our way around the kitchen. Now, I tell my kids the same thing!
—*Cindy Middleton, Champion, AB*

Prep: 20 min. • **Bake:** 15 min. + cooling
Makes: 2 dozen

- 4 large eggs
- 2 cups sugar
- 1 can (15 oz.) pumpkin
- 1½ cups canola oil
- 3 cups all-purpose flour
- 2 tsp. baking soda
- 1 tsp. baking powder
- 1 tsp. ground cinnamon
- 1 tsp. salt
- 2 cups semisweet chocolate chips

1. In a large bowl, beat the eggs, sugar, pumpkin and oil until smooth. Combine the flour, baking soda, baking powder, cinnamon and salt; gradually add to pumpkin mixture and mix well. Fold in chocolate chips. Fill greased or paper-lined muffin cups three-fourths full.
2. Bake at 400° for 15-18 minutes or until a toothpick inserted in the center comes out clean. Cool in pan 10 minutes before removing to wire racks.

1 MUFFIN: 328 cal., 19g fat (4g sat. fat), 35mg chol., 250mg sod., 39g carb. (25g sugars, 2g fiber), 4g pro.

SWEET POTATO SPICE MUFFINS

This is my own recipe, and I make it often. My five grandchildren think these are a delicious treat.
—*Christine Johnson, Ricetown, KY*

Takes: 25 min. • **Makes:** 2 dozen

- 2 cups self-rising flour
- 2 cups sugar
- 2 tsp. ground cinnamon
- 1 large egg
- 2 cups cold mashed sweet potatoes (without added butter or milk)
- 1 cup canola oil

GLAZE
- 1 cup confectioners' sugar
- 2 Tbsp. plus 1½ tsp. 2% milk
- 1½ tsp. butter, melted
- 1 tsp. vanilla extract
- ½ tsp. ground cinnamon

1. Preheat oven to 375°. In a small bowl, combine flour, sugar and cinnamon. In another bowl, whisk egg, sweet potatoes and oil. Stir into dry ingredients just until moistened.
2. Fill greased muffin cups or muffin liners two-thirds full. Bake until a toothpick inserted in muffin comes out clean, 15-18 minutes. Cool 5 minutes before removing from pans to wire racks.
3. In a small bowl, combine the glaze ingredients; drizzle over warm muffins.
NOTE: As a substitute for each cup of self-rising flour, place 1½ tsp. baking powder and ½ tsp. salt in a measuring cup. Add all-purpose flour to measure 1 cup.

1 MUFFIN: 225 cal., 10g fat (1g sat. fat), 10mg chol., 133mg sod., 34g carb. (23g sugars, 1g fiber), 2g pro.

SWEET POTATO MUFFINS TIPS

- **How do you cook sweet potatoes for these muffins?** Boiling is the simplest method for cooking sweet potatoes. Cut potatoes into 1-in. cubes and boil for 12-15 minutes. Since you'll be mashing the potatoes, be sure you can pierce them easily with a fork. For 2 cups mashed, start with 3 medium-sized sweet potatoes.

- **Can I use canned sweet potatoes instead?** You can use canned sweet potatoes for this recipe, but make sure they're not sweetened. Also, note that you may need 2 cans—a standard 15-oz. can yields about 1¾ cups mashed sweet potatoes. Or you could use just 1 can and decrease the other batter ingredients accordingly (1¾ cups each of flour and sugar, 1¾ tsp. cinnamon, 1 egg and 14 Tbsp. oil).

CHOCOLATE CHIP MUFFINS

Both of my daughters love these chocolate chip muffins! I usually double this recipe so I have extras to keep in the freezer for a quick breakfast or snack.
—*Lori Thompson, New London, TX*

- -

Prep: 15 min. • **Bake:** 20 min.
Makes: 1 dozen

- 2 cups all-purpose flour
- ½ cup sugar
- 1 Tbsp. baking powder
- ½ tsp. salt
- 1 large egg
- ¾ cup 2% milk
- ⅓ cup canola oil
- ¾ cup miniature semisweet chocolate chips

1. Preheat oven to 400°. In a large bowl, combine the first 4 ingredients. In a small bowl, beat egg, milk and oil. Stir into dry ingredients just until moistened. Fold in chocolate chips.
2. Fill 12 greased or paper-lined muffin cups three-fourths full. Bake muffins 18-20 minutes or until a toothpick comes out clean. Cool for 5 minutes before removing to a wire rack.

1 MUFFIN: 229 cal., 10g fat (3g sat. fat), 20mg chol., 213mg sod., 32g carb. (15g sugars, 1g fiber), 4g pro.

Short & Sweet

LEMON SCONES

These delicate scones are the perfect lightly sweet treat to serve with coffee or tea at any holiday get-together. It's a simple bread since, like biscuits, it doesn't require much kneading and there's no need to let the dough rise.
—*Maureen DeGarmo, Martinez, CA*

- -

Prep: 15 min. • **Bake:** 20 min.
Makes: 1 dozen

- 2 cups all-purpose flour
- ¼ cup sugar
- 1 tsp. baking powder
- 1 tsp. baking soda
- ¼ tsp. salt
- ½ cup cold butter
- ½ cup buttermilk
- 1½ tsp. grated lemon zest
   Additional sugar

1. Preheat oven to 350°. In a large bowl, combine flour, sugar, baking powder, baking soda and salt. Cut in butter until mixture resembles coarse crumbs. Add buttermilk and lemon zest, stirring just until moistened.
2. Turn onto a floured surface; knead gently 6 times. Transfer dough to a greased baking sheet. Pat dough into an 8½- in. circle. Cut into wedges, but do not separate. Sprinkle with sugar. Bake until edges are lightly browned, 20-25 minutes. Serve warm.

NOTE: To substitute for each cup of buttermilk, use 1 Tbsp. white vinegar or lemon juice plus enough milk to measure 1 cup. Stir, then let stand for 5 minutes. Or, use 1 cup plain yogurt or 1¾ tsp. cream of tartar plus 1 cup milk.

1 SCONE: 198 cal., 10g fat (6g sat. fat), 26mg chol., 324mg sod., 25g carb. (6g sugars, 1g fiber), 3g pro.

LEMON SCONES TIPS

- **How can you make sure your lemon scones are fluffy?** It's important to not overwork the dough. The more you handle the dough, the tougher and flatter your scones will be. Also, use very cold butter to ensure that when the scones bake, the butter melts and creates airy pockets inside the scones. Sticking the dough in the freezer for a few minutes before baking will ensure the butter is cold.

- **Can you put a glaze on top of lemon scones?** Nothing is easier or tastier than a simple glaze of confectioners' sugar, milk and vanilla on these scones. If you really want to brighten up the lemon flavor, add a few drops of lemon extract to the glaze.

GLUTEN-FREE BANANA MUFFINS

I've been cooking gluten-free since 2003, when my husband was diagnosed with celiac disease. Over the years, I've managed to perfect some recipes so that when family and friends join us, they can't tell they're eating gluten-free. This is one of those recipes, and it's excellent!
—*Trish Pannell, College Station, TX*

Prep: 20 min.
Bake: 20 min. + cooling
Makes: 16 muffins

- 1 cup mashed ripe bananas (2 medium)
- ¾ cup sugar
- 2 large eggs
- ½ cup unsweetened applesauce
- ¼ cup canola oil
- ¼ cup orange juice
- 1 tsp. vanilla extract
- 1½ cups gluten-free all-purpose baking flour (without xanthan gum)
- ¾ tsp. baking soda
- ¾ tsp. xanthan gum
- ½ tsp. salt
- ½ tsp. ground cinnamon
- ⅓ cup finely chopped walnuts

1. Preheat oven to 350°. In a large bowl, beat the first 7 ingredients until well blended. In a second large bowl, combine the flour, baking soda, xanthan gum, salt and cinnamon; gradually beat into banana mixture until blended.

2. Coat muffin cups with cooking spray or use paper liners; fill three-fourths full with batter. Sprinkle with walnuts. Bake 20-25 minutes or until a toothpick inserted in the center comes out clean. Cool muffins in pans 5 minutes before removing from pans to cool completely on wire racks.

NOTE: Read all ingredient labels for possible gluten content prior to use. Ingredient formulas can change, and production facilities vary among brands. If you're concerned that your brand may contain gluten, contact the company.

1 MUFFIN: 149 cal., 6g fat (1g sat. fat), 23mg chol., 144mg sod., 23g carb. (13g sugars, 2g fiber), 2g pro. **DIABETIC EXCHANGES:** 1½ starch, 1 fat.

GLUTEN-FREE BANANA MUFFINS TIPS

- **What else can you add to gluten-free banana muffins?** Chocolate chips, nuts, dried fruits (such as dates or cranberries), are great additions.

- **How should you store gluten-free banana muffins?** Store these gluten-free muffins as you would any others. Store in a covered airtight container for 3-5 days. You can also freeze them in an airtight container for 3-6 months.

SAVE THOSE BUTTER WRAPPERS
When you're finished with a stick of butter, don't toss its paper in the trash! Save them in a freezer bag. Next time you're baking, grab one to wipe across your pans to grease them with ease.

TRADITIONAL SCONES

Making scones is very simple; I learned when my wife and I hosted an English tea. These simple favorites are light and delicious.
—*Chuck Hinz, Parma, OH*

Prep: 20 min. • **Bake:** 25 min.
Makes: 1 dozen

- 2 cups all-purpose flour
- 2 Tbsp. sugar
- 3 tsp. baking powder
- ⅛ tsp. baking soda
- 6 Tbsp. cold butter, cubed
- 1 large egg
- ½ cup buttermilk

1. Preheat oven to 350°. In a large bowl, combine flour, sugar, baking powder and baking soda. Cut in butter until mixture resembles coarse crumbs. In a small bowl, whisk egg and buttermilk until blended; add to crumb mixture just until moistened.
2. Turn dough onto a lightly floured surface; gently knead 10 times. Divide dough in half; pat each portion into a 5-in. circle. Cut each circle into 6 wedges.
3. Separate wedges and place 1 in. apart on an ungreased baking sheet. Bake 25-30 minutes or until golden brown. Serve scones warm.

NOTE: To substitute for each cup of buttermilk, use 1 Tbsp. white vinegar or lemon juice plus enough milk to measure 1 cup. Stir, then let stand for 5 minutes. Or, use 1 cup plain yogurt or 1-¾ tsp. cream of tartar plus 1 cup milk.

1 SCONE: 144 cal., 6g fat (4g sat. fat), 33mg chol., 170mg sod., 19g carb. (3g sugars, 1g fiber), 3g pro.

OLD-FASHIONED BLUEBERRY MUFFINS

At the end of the summer years ago, our family often gathered to pick wild blueberries. Mother canned them and saved them for special treats during the holidays. If there were any left over, she made them into these delicious blueberry muffins.
—*June Morris, Water Mill, NY*

Takes: 30 min. • **Makes:** 6 muffins

- 1 cup all-purpose flour
- ⅓ cup sugar
- 1 tsp. baking powder
- ¼ tsp. salt
- 1 large egg, room temperature
- ¼ cup milk
- 2 Tbsp. butter, melted
- ½ tsp. vanilla extract
- ¾ cup fresh or frozen blueberries

1. Preheat oven to 400°. In a small bowl, combine the flour, sugar, baking powder and salt. In another bowl, whisk the egg, milk, butter and vanilla; stir into dry ingredients just until moistened. Fold in blueberries.
2. Fill greased or paper-lined muffin cups three-fourths full. Bake until a toothpick inserted in the center comes out clean, 18-22 minutes. Cool for 5 minutes before removing from pan to a wire rack. Serve warm.

NOTE: If using frozen blueberries, use without thawing to avoid discoloring the batter.

1 MUFFIN: 192 cal., 5g fat (3g sat. fat), 42mg chol., 226mg sod., 33g carb. (15g sugars, 2g fiber), 4g pro.

OLD-FASHIONED BLUEBERRY MUFFINS TIPS

- **What are some variations for this recipe?** You can adapt this recipe to practically any fruit—raspberries or diced strawberries, for example. Or, create a mix! Blueberries pair beautifully with chopped peaches. If you like, you can add an icing, glaze or streusel topping.

- **How should you store blueberry muffins?** These homemade muffins lose moisture the longer they sit. To prevent that, place a paper towel underneath a single layer of muffins in an airtight container. Then add another paper towel on top. You can use this technique to stack larger batches of muffins too. Separate each layer with paper towels. Keep muffins at room temperature for up to 3 days.

SWEET CORN MUFFINS

I love to make cornbread and corn muffins, but often the results are not moist or sweet enough for my taste. I experimented until I came up with these light, pleasantly sweet muffins. They ended up winning a blue ribbon at our county fair.
—*Patty Bourne, Owings, MD*

Prep: 10 min. • **Bake:** 25 min.
Makes: 1 dozen

- 1½ cups all-purpose flour
- 1 cup sugar
- ¾ cup cornmeal
- 1 Tbsp. baking powder
- ½ tsp. salt
- 2 large eggs, room temperature
- ½ cup shortening
- 1 cup 2% milk, divided

Short & Sweet

In a bowl, combine the dry ingredients. Add eggs, shortening and ½ cup milk; beat for 1 minute. Add remaining milk; beat just until blended. Fill 12 paper-lined muffin cups three-fourths full. Bake at 350° until a toothpick inserted in muffin comes out clean, 25-30 minutes.

1 MUFFIN: 254 cal., 10g fat (3g sat. fat), 33mg chol., 241mg sod., 38g carb. (18g sugars, 1g fiber), 4g pro.

READER REVIEW
"These are such a hit in our house; so easy to make and come out beautiful every time! Now we have the neighbors hooked on them, especially during the winter—they go great with homemade soup!"
—TAMARACHRONISTER, TASTEOFHOME.COM

MINI SWEET POTATO SCONES WITH ROSEMARY & BACON

I grow my own sweet potatoes, so I'm always trying to think of new ways to use them. I created this recipe on a whim and am thrilled with the results—everyone who tries these scones thinks they're delicious! To save a little time in the morning, I like to combine the dry ingredients and cut in the butter the night before. I usually stir in the crumbled bacon at that time too. I cover and refrigerate overnight, proceeding with the recipe the next morning. In addition to saving time, this also allows the rosemary and bacon flavor to develop, and chilling the butter (in the mix) results in tender scones.
—*Sue Gronholz, Beaver Dam, WI*

Prep: 30 min. • **Bake:** 15 min.
Makes: 16 scones

- 2½ cups all-purpose flour
- ½ cup sugar
- 2½ tsp. baking powder
- 1½ tsp. pumpkin pie spice or ground cinnamon
- 1½ tsp. minced fresh rosemary or ½ tsp. dried rosemary, crushed
- ½ tsp. salt
- ¼ tsp. baking soda
- ½ cup cold butter
- 4 bacon strips, cooked and crumbled
- ½ cup mashed sweet potatoes
- ¼ cup plain Greek yogurt
- 1 large egg
- 2 Tbsp. maple syrup

TOPPING
- 1 Tbsp. 2% milk
- 1 Tbsp. sugar

1. Preheat oven to 425°. In a large bowl, whisk the first 7 ingredients. Cut in butter until mixture resembles coarse crumbs. Stir in bacon. In another bowl, whisk sweet potatoes, yogurt, egg and maple syrup until blended; stir into crumb mixture just until combined.

2. Turn onto a floured surface; knead gently 10 times. Divide dough in half. Pat each half into a 6-in. circle. Cut each into 8 wedges. Place wedges on a greased baking sheet. Brush with milk; sprinkle with sugar. Bake until golden brown, 12-14 minutes. Serve warm.

FREEZE OPTION: Freeze cooled scones in freezer containers. To use, thaw before serving or, if desired, reheat on a baking sheet in a preheated 350° oven until warmed, 3-4 minutes.

1 SCONE: 184 cal., 7g fat (4g sat. fat), 30mg chol., 261mg sod., 26g carb. (9g sugars, 1g fiber), 3g pro.

FOLLOW THE
STEP-BY-
STEP VIDEO
Just hover your
camera here.

JUMBO PUMPKIN PECAN MUFFINS

Perk up an autumn morning with one of these hearty muffins. You'll really enjoy the pumpkin-spice flavor and crumbly nut topping—and so will everyone else!
—*Janice Christofferson, Eagle River, WI*

Prep: 25 min. • **Bake:** 25 min.
Makes: 6 muffins

- 2½ cups all-purpose flour
- ½ cup sugar
- ¼ cup packed brown sugar
- 2 tsp. pumpkin pie spice
- 1 tsp. baking powder
- 1 tsp. baking soda
- ½ tsp. salt
- 2 large eggs, room temperature
- 1 cup canned pumpkin
- ½ cup buttermilk
- ¼ cup canola oil
- 1 tsp. vanilla extract
- ½ cup chopped pecans

TOPPING
- ⅓ cup packed brown sugar
- ⅓ cup finely chopped pecans
- ¼ cup all-purpose flour
- ¼ cup cold butter, cubed

1. In a large bowl, combine the first 7 ingredients. In another bowl, combine the eggs, pumpkin, buttermilk, oil and vanilla. Stir into dry ingredients just until moistened. Fold in pecans. Fill 6 greased or paper-lined jumbo muffin cups three-fourths full.
2. In a small bowl, combine the brown sugar, pecans and flour; cut in butter until crumbly. Sprinkle over batter.
3. Bake at 375° for 25-30 minutes or until a toothpick inserted in the center comes out clean. Cool for 5 minutes before removing from pan to a wire rack. Serve warm.
1 MUFFIN: 660 cal., 30g fat (7g sat. fat), 83mg chol., 619mg sod., 89g carb. (41g sugars, 4g fiber), 11g pro.

LEMON POUND CAKE MUFFINS

I make these lemony muffins for all kinds of occasions. My family is always asking for them. They have a rich cakelike taste and a sweet, tangy flavor. All I can say is: They're so unbelievably good!
—*Lola Baxter, Winnebago, MN*

Prep: 15 min. • **Bake:** 20 min.
Makes: 1 dozen

- ½ cup butter, softened
- 1 cup sugar
- 2 large eggs, room temperature
- ½ cup sour cream
- 1 tsp. vanilla extract
- ½ tsp. lemon extract
- 1¾ cups all-purpose flour
- ½ tsp. salt
- ¼ tsp. baking soda

GLAZE
- 2 cups confectioners' sugar
- 3 Tbsp. lemon juice

1. In a large bowl, cream the butter and sugar until light and fluffy, 5-7 minutes. Add eggs, 1 at a time, beating well after each addition. Beat in the sour cream and extracts. Combine the flour, salt and baking soda; add to creamed mixture just until moistened.
2. Fill 12 greased or paper-lined muffin cups three-fourths full. Bake at 400° until a toothpick inserted in the center comes out clean, 18-20 minutes. Cool for 5 minutes before removing from pan to a wire rack.
3. Combine the glaze ingredients; drizzle over muffins. Serve warm.
1 MUFFIN: 311 cal., 10g fat (6g sat. fat), 63mg chol., 218mg sod., 51g carb. (36g sugars, 1g fiber), 3g pro.

READER REVIEW
"I added lemon zest to the muffin batter. I only used 1 cup of confectioners' sugar and the juice from a large lemon for the glaze, and it was plenty to cover all 12 muffins. Perfect recipe to beat the winter blahs!"
—JMARTINELLI13, TASTEOFHOME.COM

HALVA & NUTELLA
BABKA BUNS, PAGE 208

Coffee Cakes & Sweet Rolls

Find the perfect pick-me-up for your next celebratory brunch or afternoon coffee klatch. Classic handhelds and stunning cakes to share are on the menu.

PULL-APART CARAMEL COFFEE CAKE

The first time I made this delightful breakfast treat for a brunch party, it was a huge hit. Now I get requests every time my family or friends do anything around the breakfast hour! I always keep the four simple ingredients on hand.

—Jaime Keeling, Keizer, OR

Short & Sweet

Prep: 10 min. • Bake: 25 min.
Makes: 16 servings

- 2 tubes (12 oz. each) refrigerated buttermilk biscuits
- 1 cup packed brown sugar
- ½ cup heavy whipping cream
- 1 tsp. ground cinnamon

1. Preheat oven to 350°. Cut each biscuit into 4 pieces; arrange evenly in a 10-in. fluted tube pan coated with cooking spray. In a small bowl, mix remaining ingredients until blended; pour over biscuits.
2. Bake 25-30 minutes or until golden brown. Cool in pan 5 minutes before inverting onto a serving plate.

5 PIECES: 204 cal., 8g fat (3g sat. fat), 10mg chol., 457mg sod., 31g carb. (16g sugars, 0 fiber), 3g pro.

HEAVENLY CHEESE DANISH

This tempting cheese Danish is baked to flaky perfection and made to shine with a simple egg wash. It tastes just as decadent as any breakfast pastry you'd find in a bakery or coffee shop.

—Josephine Triton, Lakewood, OH

Prep: 50 min. + chilling • Bake: 15 min.
Makes: 16 rolls

- 2 pkg. (¼ oz. each) active dry yeast
- ½ cup warm water (110° to 115°)
- 4 cups all-purpose flour
- ⅓ cup sugar
- 2 tsp. salt
- 1 cup cold butter, cubed
- 1 cup 2% milk
- 4 large egg yolks, room temperature

ASSEMBLY
- 3 tsp. ground cinnamon
- 12 oz. cream cheese, softened
- ⅓ cup sugar
- 1 large egg, separated
- 1 Tbsp. water
- 2 Tbsp. maple syrup

1. Dissolve yeast in warm water. In another bowl, mix flour, sugar and salt; cut in butter until crumbly. Add milk, egg yolks and yeast mixture; stir to form a soft dough (dough will be sticky). Cover and refrigerate 8-24 hours.
2. To assemble, punch down dough; divide into 4 portions. On a lightly floured surface, pat each portion into a 9x4-in. rectangle; sprinkle each with ¾ tsp. cinnamon. Cut each rectangle lengthwise into four 9x1-in. strips. Twist each strip, then loosely wrap strip around itself to form a coil; tuck the end under and pinch to seal. Place 3 in. apart on greased baking sheets.
3. Beat cream cheese, sugar and egg yolk until smooth. Press an indentation in the center of each roll; fill with 1 rounded Tbsp. cream cheese mixture. Cover; let rise in a warm place until doubled, about 45 minutes. Preheat oven to 350°.
4. Whisk egg white with water; brush over rolls. Bake until golden brown, 15-20 minutes. Remove to wire racks; brush with syrup. Serve warm. Refrigerate leftovers.

1 DANISH: 359 cal., 21g fat (12g sat. fat), 111mg chol., 468mg sod., 37g carb. (12g sugars, 1g fiber), 7g pro.

FROSTED PUMPKIN DOUGHNUTS

Our three children grew pumpkins to sell. During harvest, it was time to make these scrumptious doughnuts. The frosting with a hint of orange is super.
—*Connie Simon, Jensen Beach, FL*

Prep: 20 min. • **Cook:** 30 min.
Makes: about 3 dozen

- 2 large eggs
- 1 cup sugar
- 2 Tbsp. butter, softened
- 1 cup canned pumpkin
- 1 Tbsp. lemon juice
- 4½ cups all-purpose flour
- 2 tsp. baking powder
- 1 tsp. baking soda
- ½ tsp. salt
- ½ tsp. ground cinnamon
- ½ tsp. ground nutmeg
- 1 cup evaporated milk
   Oil for deep-fat frying

FROSTING

- 3 cups confectioners' sugar
- 2 to 3 Tbsp. orange juice
- 1 Tbsp. evaporated milk
- 1 tsp. grated orange zest

1. In a large bowl, beat eggs, sugar and butter until smooth. Beat in pumpkin and lemon juice. Combine flour, baking powder, baking soda, salt, cinnamon and nutmeg; gradually add to pumpkin mixture alternately with milk. Cover and refrigerate for 2 hours.
2. Turn onto a lightly floured surface; knead 5-6 times. Roll to ⅜-in. thickness. Cut with a lightly floured 2½-in. doughnut cutter.
3. In an electric skillet or deep-fat fryer, heat oil to 375°. Fry, a few at a time, until golden brown on both sides. Drain on paper towels. Combine frosting ingredients; dip tops of warm doughnuts into frosting.
1 DOUGHNUT: 184 cal., 7g fat (1g sat. fat), 14mg chol., 111mg sod., 29g carb. (16g sugars, 1g fiber), 3g pro.

FRESH PLUM KUCHEN

In summer when plums are in season, this tender fruit-topped cake is delectable! For variety, you can use fresh pears or apples instead.
—*Anna Daley, Montague, PE*

Prep: 20 min. • **Bake:** 40 min. + cooling
Makes: 12 servings

- ¼ cup butter, softened
- ¾ cup sugar
- 2 large eggs, room temperature
- 1 cup all-purpose flour
- 1 tsp. baking powder
- ¼ cup 2% milk
- 1 tsp. grated lemon zest
- 2 cups sliced fresh plums (about 4 medium)
- ½ cup packed brown sugar
- 1 tsp. ground cinnamon
   Confectioners' sugar, optional

1. Preheat oven to 350°. In a small bowl, cream butter and sugar until light and fluffy, 5-7 minutes. Beat in eggs. Combine flour and baking powder; add to the creamed mixture alternately with milk, beating well after each addition. Add lemon zest. Pour into a greased 10-in. springform pan. Arrange plums on top; gently press into batter. Sprinkle the top with brown sugar and cinnamon.
2. Place pan on a baking sheet. Bake until top is golden and a toothpick inserted in the center comes out clean, 40-50 minutes. Cool 10 minutes. Run a knife around edge of pan; remove rim. Cool on a wire rack. If desired, dust with confectioners' sugar just before serving.
1 PIECE: 185 cal., 5g fat (3g sat. fat), 46mg chol., 89mg sod., 33g carb. (24g sugars, 1g fiber), 3g pro.

PLUM POINTERS

Choose fresh in-season plums that yield slightly when pressed gently with your thumb. Hard plums are not as juicy and are tougher to cut—but you can ripen them by leaving on the counter for a few days. While color choice is completely up to you, red-skinned plums with golden interiors make especially pretty plum desserts.

HALVA & NUTELLA BABKA BUNS

This recipe is the result of many years of tweaking and perfecting. It is a favorite that visitors often request when they come to my farm.
—Dawn Lamoureux-Crocker, Machiasport, ME

Prep: 1 hour + rising • **Bake:** 15 min.
Makes: 8 buns

3¾ to 4¼ cups all-purpose flour
⅓ cup sugar
¼ tsp. salt
1 Tbsp. active dry yeast
6 Tbsp. butter, softened
¾ cup warm 2% milk (110° to 115°)
½ tsp. vanilla extract
2 tsp. grated lemon zest
2 large eggs, room temperature
1 jar (13 oz.) Nutella
6 oz. halva with pistachio, crumbled (about 1 cup)
½ cup semisweet chocolate chips
GLAZE (OPTIONAL)
½ cup sugar
½ cup water
2 Tbsp. butter

1. In a large bowl, combine 1½ cups flour, sugar, salt and yeast. Cut in butter until crumbly. Add warm milk, vanilla and lemon zest to dry ingredients; beat just until moistened. Add eggs; beat on medium for 2 minutes. Stir in enough remaining flour to form a firm dough. Turn onto a floured surface; knead until smooth and elastic, 5-7 minutes. Place in a greased bowl, turning once to grease top. Cover and let rise in a warm place until doubled, about 1 hour.
2. Turn out dough onto a lightly floured surface; divide into 8 pieces. Roll each piece into a 10x5-in. rectangle about ⅛ in. thick. For each, spread Nutella to within ½ in. of edges, sprinkle with 2 Tbsp. halva and 1 Tbsp. chocolate chips, and roll up jelly-roll style, starting with a long side; pinch seam and ends to seal.
3. Using a sharp knife, cut each roll lengthwise in half; carefully turn each half cut side up. Loosely twist strips around each other, keeping cut surfaces facing up; pinch ends together to seal. Repeat for remaining buns. Place cut side up on parchment-lined baking sheets. Cover with kitchen towels; let rise in a warm place until almost doubled, about 30 minutes. Preheat oven to 375°.
4. Bake 15-20 minutes or until golden brown. If desired, in a small saucepan, bring sugar and water to a boil; reduce heat and simmer until the sugar is dissolved, 1-2 minutes. Remove from heat and add butter, stirring until melted. Brush over buns. Serve buns warm.

1 BUN: 748 cal., 34g fat (11g sat. fat), 72mg chol., 196mg sod., 102g carb. (52g sugars, 5g fiber), 14g pro.

NUTELLA BABKA BUNS TIPS

- **What does brushing the sugar syrup on at the end do for the Nutella babka?** These buns look beautiful before glazing, but adding that last touch makes these pastries fit for a spot in a bakery window. Not only does the sugar syrup give a nice finish and added sweetness, but it also helps seal the buns so you can enjoy them longer.

- **How do you store Nutella babka?** Store these buns in a sealed container and eat within 2 or 3 days. Reheat them in the microwave for a warm, gooey treat. They also freeze well! Freeze in a single layer in airtight containers for up to 3 months.

- **Can you make these Nutella babka buns into traditionally shaped babka instead?** Yes. Divide the dough in half and roll each portion into a 12x10-in. rectangle. Fill, roll and twist dough as directed, but tuck ends under rather than pinching them together. Bake in 2 greased 9x5-in. loaf pans for 35-45 minutes, tenting with foil halfway through baking.

RASPBERRY CHEESE DANISH

Your guests will think you made these yummy rolls from scratch ... or bought them from a specialty bakery. No one needs to know the recipe calls for refrigerated crescent dough!

—*Karen Weir, Litchfield, CT*

- -

Takes: 25 min. • **Makes:** 8 servings

- 4   oz. cream cheese, softened
- ¼   cup plus ½ cup confectioners' sugar, divided
- 1   can (8 oz.) refrigerated crescent rolls
- ½   cup seedless raspberry jam
- 2   tsp. 2% milk

1. In a small bowl, beat cream cheese and ¼ cup confectioners' sugar until smooth. Unroll crescent dough and separate into 4 rectangles; seal perforations. Cut each rectangle in half, making 8 squares.

2. Transfer squares to a parchment-lined baking sheet. Spread 1 Tbsp. cream cheese mixture diagonally across each square. Top with 1 Tbsp. jam. Bring 2 opposite corners of dough over filling; pinch together firmly to seal.

3. Bake at 375° for 10-12 minutes or until golden brown. Combine milk and remaining ½ cup confectioners' sugar; drizzle over pastries. Serve warm. Refrigerate the leftovers.

1 DANISH: 257 cal., 11g fat (5g sat. fat), 16mg chol., 272mg sod., 36g carb. (25g sugars, 0 fiber), 4g pro.

Short & Sweet

OLD-TIME CAKE DOUGHNUTS

This tender cake doughnut is a little piece of heaven at breakfast. For a variation, add a little rum extract or 1 Tbsp. of dark rum.

—*Alissa Stehr, Gau-Odernheim,*

- -

Prep: 30 min. + chilling
Cook: 5 min./batch
Makes: about 2 dozen

- 2   Tbsp. unsalted butter, softened
- 1½ cups sugar, divided
- 3   large eggs, room temperature
- 4   cups all-purpose flour
- 1   Tbsp. baking powder
- 3   tsp. ground cinnamon, divided
- ½   tsp. salt
- ⅛   tsp. ground nutmeg
- ¾   cup 2% milk
     Oil for deep-fat frying

1. In a large bowl, beat butter and 1 cup sugar until crumbly, about 2 minutes. Add eggs, 1 at a time, beating well after each addition.

2. Combine the flour, baking powder, 1 tsp. cinnamon, salt and nutmeg; add to butter mixture alternately with milk, beating well after each addition. Cover and refrigerate 2 hours.

3. Turn onto a heavily floured surface; pat dough to ¼-in. thickness. Cut with a floured 2½-in. doughnut cutter. In an electric skillet or deep fryer, heat oil to 375°.

4. Fry doughnuts, a few at a time, until golden brown on both sides, about 2 minutes per side. Drain on paper towels.

5. Combine remaining ½ cup sugar and 2 tsp. cinnamon; roll warm doughnuts in mixture.

FREEZE OPTION: After frying, cool doughnuts. Wrap in foil and transfer to a resealable freezer container. May be frozen for up to 3 months. To use, remove foil. Thaw doughnuts at room temperature. Warm if desired. Combine ½ cup sugar and 2 tsp. cinnamon; roll doughnuts in mixture.

1 DOUGHNUT: 198 cal., 8g fat (1g sat. fat), 30mg chol., 112mg sod., 29g carb. (13g sugars, 1g fiber), 3g pro.

GLAZED CAKE DOUGHNUTS: Omit cinnamon-sugar. Combine 2 cups confectioners' sugar, 1-2 Tbsp. orange juice, and 1 tsp. grated orange peel. Spread over cooled doughnuts.

STRAWBERRY DOUGHNUTS

These summery doughnuts have pale pink interiors. For a whimsical garnish, sprinkle with freeze-dried strawberry bits, pink jimmies and/or pearl sugar.
—Taste of Home *Test Kitchen*

Prep: 20 min. • **Bake:** 15 min. + cooling
Makes: 1 dozen

- 1 cup all-purpose flour
- ½ cup sugar
- ½ tsp. baking powder
- ½ tsp. baking soda
- ¼ tsp. salt
- 1 large egg
- ¼ cup sour cream
- ¼ cup 2% milk
- 1 Tbsp. canola oil
- ½ tsp. vanilla extract
- ½ cup finely chopped fresh strawberries

STRAWBERRY GLAZE
- 1½ cups confectioners' sugar
- 3 Tbsp. pureed strawberries
- ½ tsp. grated lemon zest, optional

1. Preheat oven to 350°. In a small bowl, combine the first 5 ingredients. Combine egg, sour cream, milk, oil and vanilla; stir into dry ingredients just until moistened.
2. Transfer batter to a pastry bag fitted with a round tip. Pipe the batter into 2 greased 6-cavity doughnut pans, filling the cavities half full.
3. Bake until a toothpick inserted in the center comes out clean, 12-15 minutes. Cool doughnuts for 5 minutes before removing from pans to wire racks to cool completely.
4. In a small bowl, combine glaze ingredients. Dip each doughnut halfway, allowing excess to drip off. Place on wire rack; let stand until set.
1 DOUGHNUT: 161 cal., 3g fat (1g sat. fat), 19mg chol., 132mg sod., 33g carb. (24g sugars, 0 fiber), 2g pro.

CLASSIC LONG JOHNS

I came across the recipe for these wonderful raised doughnuts many years ago. I remember Mom making some similar to these. You can frost them with maple or chocolate glaze, then top with chopped nuts, jimmies, toasted coconut or sprinkles.
—Ann Sorgent, Fond du Lac, WI

Prep: 30 min. + rising
Cook: 5 min./batch + cooling
Makes: 2 dozen

- 2 pkg. (¼ oz. each) active dry yeast
- ½ cup warm water (110° to 115°)
- ½ cup half-and-half cream
- ¼ cup sugar
- ¼ cup shortening
- 1 large egg, room temperature
- 1 tsp. salt
- ½ tsp. ground nutmeg
- 3 to 3½ cups all-purpose flour
  Oil for deep-fat frying

MAPLE FROSTING
- ¼ cup packed brown sugar
- 2 Tbsp. butter
- 1 Tbsp. half-and-half cream
- ⅛ tsp. maple flavoring
- ½ cup confectioners' sugar

CHOCOLATE FROSTING
- 2 oz. semisweet chocolate, chopped
- 2 Tbsp. butter
- ½ cup confectioners' sugar
- 2 Tbsp. boiling water
- 1 tsp. vanilla extract

1. In a large bowl, dissolve yeast in warm water. Add cream, sugar, shortening, egg, salt, nutmeg and 3 cups flour. Beat until smooth. Stir in enough remaining flour to form a soft dough (dough will be sticky).
2. Turn onto a floured surface; knead until smooth and elastic, 6-8 minutes. Place in a greased bowl, turning once to grease the top. Cover and let rise in a warm place until doubled, about 1 hour.
3. Punch down dough; divide in half. Turn onto a lightly floured surface; roll each half into a 12x6-in. rectangle. Cut each portion into twelve 3x2-in. rectangles. Place on greased baking sheets. Cover and let rise in a warm place until doubled, about 30 minutes.
4. In an electric skillet or deep fryer, heat oil to 375°. Fry long johns, a few at a time, until golden brown on both sides. Drain on paper towels; cool completely.
5. For the maple frosting, combine brown sugar and butter in a small saucepan. Bring to a boil, stirring to dissolve sugar. Remove from heat; stir in cream and maple flavoring. Add the confectioners' sugar; beat for 1 minute or until smooth. Frost cooled long johns.
6. For the chocolate frosting, in a microwave, melt chocolate and butter; stir until smooth. Stir in remaining ingredients. Spread over cooled long johns; let stand until set.
1 LONG JOHN: 186 cal., 9g fat (3g sat. fat), 16mg chol., 121mg sod., 22g carb. (10g sugars, 1g fiber), 3g pro.

CLASSIC LONG JOHNS

GLUTEN-FREE APPLE CIDER DOUGHNUTS

I wanted to make a cider doughnut that tasted amazing; the fact that it's gluten-free is beside the point!
—*Kathryn Conrad, Milwaukee, WI*

Prep: 20 min. + standing
Bake: 15 min.
Makes: 10 doughnuts

- 2 cups gluten-free biscuit/baking mix
- ¾ cup sugar
- 1 pkg. (¼ oz.) quick-rise yeast
- 1½ tsp. baking powder
- ½ tsp. salt
- ½ tsp. apple pie spice
- ¼ tsp. ground cinnamon
- ⅛ tsp. baking soda
- ½ cup warm water (110° to 115°)
- 6 Tbsp. butter, melted
- ¼ cup unsweetened applesauce, room temperature
- 1 Tbsp. vanilla extract

GLAZE
- 1 cup apple cider or juice
- 1 Tbsp. butter, softened
- ⅔ to ¾ cup confectioners' sugar

1. In a large bowl, mix together the first 8 ingredients. In another bowl, whisk the water, butter, applesauce and vanilla until blended. Add to the dry ingredients; stir until blended. Cover and let rest for 10 minutes.
2. Transfer batter to a pastry bag fitted with a round tip. Pipe batter into a 6-cavity doughnut pan coated with cooking spray, filling cavities three-fourths full.
3. Bake at 325° for 11-14 minutes or until golden brown. Cool for 5 minutes before removing from pan to a wire rack. Repeat with remaining batter.
4. For glaze, in a small saucepan, bring apple cider to a boil; cook until liquid is reduced to 3 Tbsp.. Transfer to a small bowl; stir in butter until melted. Stir in enough confectioners' sugar to reach glaze consistency. Dip each doughnut halfway, allowing excess to drip off. Place on wire rack; let stand until set.

1 DOUGHNUT: 273 cal., 8g fat (4g sat. fat), 18mg chol., 565mg sod., 47g carb. (27g sugars, 4g fiber), 4g pro.

GET OUR GUIDE TO GLUTEN-FREE BAKING
Just hover your camera here.

BRUNCH BEIGNETS

Enjoy breakfast the New Orleans way with these warm and crispy bites. Topped with powdered sugar, they are a delight!
—*Lois Rutherford, Elkton, FL*

Prep: 20 min. + standing
Cook: 5 min./batch
Makes: about 2 dozen

- 2 large eggs, separated
- 1¼ cups all-purpose flour
- 1 tsp. baking powder
- ⅛ tsp. salt
- ½ cup sugar
- ¼ cup water
- 1 Tbsp. butter, melted
- 2 tsp. grated lemon zest
- 1 tsp. vanilla extract
- 1 tsp. brandy, optional
  - Oil for deep-fat frying
  - Confectioners' sugar

1. Place egg whites in a small bowl; let stand at room temperature for 30 minutes.
2. Meanwhile, in a large bowl, combine the flour, baking powder and salt. Combine the egg yolks, sugar, water, butter, lemon zest, vanilla and, if desired, brandy; stir into dry ingredients just until combined. Beat egg whites on medium speed until soft peaks form; fold into batter.
3. In a cast-iron or electric skillet, heat oil to 375°. Drop batter by teaspoonfuls, a few at a time, into hot oil. Fry until golden brown, about 1½ minutes on each side. Drain on paper towels. Dust with confectioners' sugar. Serve warm.

1 BEIGNET: 66 cal., 3g fat (1g sat. fat), 17mg chol., 42mg sod., 9g carb. (4g sugars, 0 fiber), 1g pro.

GLAZED OLD-FASHIONED DOUGHNUTS

These finger-licking-good delicacies are so light and luscious, my family has always referred to them as angel food doughnuts! They're lovely at Christmastime.

—*Darlene Brenden, Salem, OR*

Prep: 35 min. + chilling
Cook: 15 min.
Makes: About 1½ dozen doughnuts plus doughnut holes

- ½ cup sour cream
- ½ cup buttermilk
- 1 cup sugar
- 3 eggs
- 1 tsp. vanilla extract
- 4 cups all-purpose flour
- 2 tsp. baking powder
- ½ tsp. baking soda
- ¼ tsp. salt
  Oil for deep-fat frying

GLAZE
- 1⅓ cups confectioners' sugar
- 5 to 6 tsp. water
- ½ tsp. vanilla extract

1. In a large bowl, beat sour cream and buttermilk until smooth. Beat in sugar until smooth. Beat in eggs and vanilla just until combined. Combine flour, baking powder, baking soda and salt. Gradually add the flour mixture to the buttermilk mixture just until combined (dough will be sticky). Cover and refrigerate for 2-3 hours.

2. Turn dough onto a well-floured surface; knead until smooth, 2-3 minutes. Roll out to ½-in. thickness. Cut with a floured 2½-in. doughnut cutter.

3. In an electric skillet or deep-fat fryer, heat oil to 375°. Fry doughnuts, a few at a time, until golden brown, about 3 minutes on each side. Fry doughnut holes until golden brown. Drain on paper towels. For glaze, in a large bowl, combine confectioners' sugar, water and vanilla until smooth. Dip warm doughnuts in glaze. Cool on wire racks.

1 DOUGHNUT WITH 1 DOUGHNUT HOLE: 262 cal., 9g fat (2g sat. fat), 36mg chol., 149mg sod., 42g carb. (21g sugars, 1g fiber), 4g pro.

GERMAN
APPLE CAKE

BONUTS

A from-scratch doughnut ready to devour in 20 minutes—simply amazing! People always love this biscuit-meets-doughnut hybrid.
—*Jaclyn Bell, Logan, UT*

Prep: 15 min. • **Cook:** 5 min./batch
Makes: about 2½ dozen

- ¼ cup sugar
- ¼ cup 2% milk
- ¼ cup buttermilk
- 3 Tbsp. butter, melted
- 1¼ cups all-purpose flour
- 2 tsp. baking powder
- ¼ tsp. salt
  Oil for frying
  Cinnamon sugar, confectioners' sugar and additional sugar

1. In a large bowl, beat sugar, milk, buttermilk and melted butter until smooth. Combine flour, baking powder and salt. Gradually add flour mixture to buttermilk mixture just until moistened (dough will be sticky).
2. In a deep skillet or electric skillet, heat 1 in. of oil to 375°. Gently roll 1½ teaspoonfuls of dough into balls. Drop, a few at a time, into hot oil. Fry until golden brown, 1-2 minutes on each side. Drain on paper towels. While warm, roll each bonut in either cinnamon sugar, confectioners' sugar or additional sugar.

1 BONUT: 52 cal., 3g fat (1g sat. fat), 4mg chol., 70mg sod., 6g carb. (2g sugars, 0 fiber), 1g pro.

BONUTS MADE EASY

This recipe uses drop biscuit dough, so it's quick to make (with no rolling pin or biscuit cutters required).

GERMAN APPLE CAKE

With the long, cold winters we have here, this German apple cake recipe has warmed many a kitchen. The cake is perfect for breakfast, dessert or an evening snack. I've made it for many parties, and I've always received compliments on it.
—*Grace Reynolds, Bethlehem, PA*

Prep: 15 min. • **Bake:** 70 min. + cooling
Makes: 16 servings

- 3 cups all-purpose flour
- 3 tsp. baking powder
- 1 tsp. salt
- 4 large eggs, room temperature
- 2 cups sugar
- 1 cup canola oil
- ½ cup orange juice
- 2½ tsp. vanilla extract
- 4 cups thinly sliced peeled apples (about 4 to 5 apples)
- 2 tsp. ground cinnamon
- 3 Tbsp. sugar
  Confectioners' sugar, optional

1. Preheat oven to 350°. Grease and flour a 10-in. tube pan. Combine the flour, baking powder and salt; set aside.
2. In a large bowl, beat eggs and sugar. Combine oil and orange juice and add alternately with dry ingredients to egg mixture. Beat until smooth; add vanilla and beat well.
3. Pour half of the batter into prepared pan. Arrange half the apples over the batter. Combine cinnamon and sugar and sprinkle half over the apples. Top with remaining batter, apples and cinnamon mixture.
4. Bake until a toothpick inserted in the center comes out clean, about 70 minutes. Cool 1 hour before removing from pan. Cool, apple side up, on a wire rack. If desired, sprinkle with confectioners' sugar.

1 PIECE: 353 cal., 15g fat (1g sat. fat), 47mg chol., 256mg sod., 50g carb. (31g sugars, 1g fiber), 4g pro.

READER REVIEW
"Very pretty—looks like it took a lot of work when the hardest part was peeling and slicing the apples—and so tasty. Not too sweet. I can't wait to have another slice at breakfast."
—REBECCA967, TASTEOFHOME.COM

SUGARED DOUGHNUT HOLES

These tasty, tender doughnut bites are easy to make. Serve them warm in a small paper bag, as is done at the fair, or tuck them into a small gift box and wrap with ribbon as a party favor. No matter how they arrive, they make any day special.
—Judy Jungwirth, Athol, SD

- -

Takes: 20 min. • **Makes:** about 3 dozen

 1½ cups all-purpose flour
 ⅓ cup sugar
 2 tsp. baking powder
 ½ tsp. salt
 ½ tsp. ground nutmeg
 1 large egg, room temperature
 ½ cup 2% milk
 2 Tbsp. butter, melted
  Oil for deep-fat frying
  Confectioners' sugar

1. In a large bowl, combine flour, sugar, baking powder, salt and nutmeg. In a small bowl, combine egg, milk and butter. Add to dry ingredients and mix well.

2. In an electric skillet or deep-fat fryer, heat oil to 375°. Drop dough by heaping teaspoonfuls, 5 or 6 at a time, into oil. Fry until browned, 1-2 minutes, turning once. Drain on paper towels. Roll warm doughnut holes in confectioners' sugar.

1 DOUGHNUT HOLE: 47 cal., 2g fat (1g sat. fat), 7mg chol., 68mg sod., 6g carb. (2g sugars, 0 fiber), 1g pro.

OVERNIGHT CHERRY DANISH

These rolls with their cherry-filled centers melt in your mouth and store well unfrosted in the freezer.
—Leann Sauder, Tremont, IL

- -

Prep: 1½ hours + chilling • **Bake:** 15 min.
Makes: 3 dozen

 2 pkg. (¼ oz. each) active dry yeast
 ½ cup warm 2% milk (110° to 115°)
 6 cups all-purpose flour
 ⅓ cup sugar
 2 tsp. salt
 1 cup cold butter, cubed
 1½ cups warm half-and-half cream (70° to 80°)
 6 large egg yolks, room temperature
 1 can (21 oz.) cherry pie filling

ICING
 3 cups confectioners' sugar
 2 Tbsp. butter, softened
 ¼ tsp. vanilla extract
  Dash salt
 4 to 5 Tbsp. half-and-half cream

1. In a small bowl, dissolve yeast in warm milk. In a large bowl, combine flour, sugar and salt. Cut in butter until crumbly. Add yeast mixture, cream and egg yolks; stir until mixture forms a soft dough (dough will be sticky). Refrigerate, covered, overnight.

2. Punch down dough. Turn onto a lightly floured surface; divide into 4 portions. Roll each portion into an 18x4-in. rectangle; cut into 4x1-in. strips.

3. Place 2 strips side by side; twist together. Shape into a ring and pinch ends together. Place 2 in. apart on greased baking sheets. Repeat with remaining strips. Cover with kitchen towels; let rise in a warm place until doubled, about 45 minutes.

4. Preheat oven to 350°. Using the end of a wooden spoon handle, make a ½-in.-deep indentation in the center of each Danish. Fill each with about 1 Tbsp. pie filling. Bake 14-16 minutes or until lightly browned. Remove from pans to wire racks to cool.

5. For icing, in a large bowl, beat the confectioners' sugar, butter, vanilla, salt and enough cream to reach desired consistency. Drizzle over Danish.

1 DANISH: 218 cal., 8g fat (5g sat. fat), 55mg chol., 188mg sod., 33g carb. (16g sugars, 1g fiber), 3g pro.

BERRY NECTARINE BUCKLE

I found this recipe in a magazine a long time ago, but modified it over the years. The combination of blueberries, raspberries, blackberries and nectarines is heavenly, particularly when the cake is served warm with low-fat frozen yogurt.
—*Lisa Sjursen-Darling, Scottsville, NY*

Prep: 25 min. • **Bake:** 35 min.
Makes: 20 servings

- ⅓ cup all-purpose flour
- ⅓ cup packed brown sugar
- 1 tsp. ground cinnamon
- 3 Tbsp. cold butter

BATTER

- 6 Tbsp. butter, softened
- ¾ cup plus 1 Tbsp. sugar, divided
- 2 large eggs, room temperature
- 1½ tsp. vanilla extract
- 2¼ cups all-purpose flour
- 2½ tsp. baking powder
- ½ tsp. salt
- ½ cup 2% milk
- 1 cup fresh blueberries
- 1 lb. nectarines, peeled, sliced and patted dry or 1 pkg. (16 oz.) frozen unsweetened sliced peaches, thawed and patted dry
- ½ cup fresh raspberries
- ½ cup fresh blackberries

1. For topping, in a small bowl, combine the flour, brown sugar and cinnamon; cut in butter until crumbly. Set aside.

2. For batter, in a large bowl, cream the butter and ¾ cup sugar until light and fluffy, 5-7 minutes. Add eggs, 1 at a time, beating well after each addition. Beat in vanilla. Combine the flour, baking powder and salt; add to creamed mixture alternately with milk, beating well after each addition. Set aside ¾ cup batter. Fold blueberries into remaining batter.

3. Spoon batter with blueberries into a 13x9-in. baking dish coated with cooking spray. Arrange nectarines on top; sprinkle with remaining 1 Tbsp. sugar. Drop the reserved batter by teaspoonfuls over nectarines. Sprinkle with raspberries, blackberries and reserved topping.

4. Bake at 350° for 35-40 minutes or until a toothpick inserted in the center comes out clean. Serve warm.

1 PIECE: 177 cal., 6g fat (3g sat. fat), 35mg chol., 172mg sod., 28g carb. (15g sugars, 1g fiber), 3g pro.

MAPLE BUTTER TWISTS

My stepmother passed along the recipe for this delicious yeast coffee cake that's shaped into pretty rings. When I make it for friends, they always ask for seconds.
—*June Gilliland, Hope, IN*

Prep: 35 min. + rising
Bake: 25 min. + cooling
Makes: 2 coffee cakes (16 pieces each)

- 3¼ to 3½ cups all-purpose flour
- 3 Tbsp. sugar
- 1½ tsp. salt
- 1 pkg. (¼ oz.) active dry yeast
- ¾ cup 2% milk
- ¼ cup butter
- 2 large eggs, room temperature

FILLING

- ⅓ cup packed brown sugar
- ¼ cup sugar
- 3 Tbsp. butter, softened
- 3 Tbsp. maple syrup
- 4½ tsp. all-purpose flour
- ¾ tsp. ground cinnamon
- ¾ tsp. maple flavoring
- ⅓ cup chopped walnuts

GLAZE

- ½ cup confectioners' sugar
- ¼ tsp. maple flavoring
- 2 to 3 tsp. 2% milk

1. In a large bowl, combine 1½ cups flour, sugar, salt and yeast. In a small saucepan, heat the milk and butter to 120°-130°. Add to dry ingredients; beat just until moistened. Add eggs; beat on medium for 2 minutes. Stir in enough remaining flour to form a firm dough. Turn onto a floured surface; knead until smooth and elastic, 5-7 minutes. Place in a greased bowl, turning once to grease top. Cover and let rise in a warm place until doubled, about 70 minutes.

2. In a small bowl, combine the first 7 filling ingredients; beat for 2 minutes. Punch dough down; turn onto a lightly floured surface. Divide in half; roll each into a 16x8-in. rectangle. Spread filling to within ½ in. of edges. Sprinkle with walnuts. Roll up jelly-roll style, starting with a long side.

3. With a sharp knife, cut each roll in half lengthwise. Open halves so cut side is up; gently twist ropes together. Transfer to 2 greased 9-in. round baking pans. Coil into a circle. Tuck ends under; pinch to seal. Cover and let rise in a warm place until doubled, about 45 minutes.

4. Bake at 350° for 25-30 minutes or until golden brown. Cool for 10 minutes; remove from pans to wire racks. For the glaze, combine the confectioners' sugar, maple flavoring and enough milk to reach desired consistency; drizzle over warm coffee cakes.

1 PIECE: 119 cal., 4g fat (2g sat. fat), 21mg chol., 144mg sod., 19g carb. (8g sugars, 0 fiber), 2g pro.

MAPLE BUTTER
TWISTS

CHOCOLATE COFFEE
PAGE 233

Cafe Beverages

Indulge in signature coffees, artisan teas and old-time floats. Our coffee-house classics help you treat yourself, save money and dazzle your friends.

TRES LECHES COFFEE CREAMER

Tres leches cake is one of my family's favorite cakes. I decided to make it into a coffee creamer, so I could enjoy the tres leches flavor in my morning coffee! To make coconut tres leches coffee creamer, substitute 1 cup of the whipping cream with coconut cream, and instead of the vanilla extract add ½ to 1 teaspoon coconut extract.
—*Marina Castle Kelley,*
Canyon Country, CA

Takes: 10 min. • **Makes:** 5 cups

- 2 cups heavy whipping cream
- 1 can (14 oz.) sweetened condensed milk
- 1 can (12 oz.) evaporated milk
- 1½ tsp. vanilla extract
- ½ to 1 tsp. rum extrac

In a small pitcher, whisk all ingredients until blended. Cover and refrigerate up to 4 days. Stir before using.
1 TBSP.: 43 cal., 3g fat (2g sat. fat), 10mg chol., 12mg sod., 3g carb. (3g sugars, 0 fiber), 1g pro.

FROSTY CARAMEL CAPPUCCINO

This frothy, frosty beverage is positively delicious for breakfast, a mid-afternoon snack or even an after-dinner dessert. It's also a great quick treat to serve with a plate of cookies when friends come to call during the holidays.
—*Carol Mann, Summerfield, FL*

Takes: 10 min. • **Makes:** 2 servings

- 1 cup half-and-half cream
- 1 cup 2% milk
- 3 Tbsp. plus 2 tsp. caramel ice cream topping, divided
- 2 tsp. instant coffee granules
- 8 to 10 ice cubes
- 4 Tbsp. whipped cream in a can

1. In a blender, combine the cream, milk, 3 Tbsp. caramel topping, coffee and ice cubes; cover and process until smooth.
2. Pour into 2 chilled glasses. Top with whipped cream and drizzle with remaining caramel topping. Serve immediately.
1 SERVING: 324 cal., 16g fat (11g sat. fat), 75mg chol., 246mg sod., 33g carb. (32g sugars, 0 fiber), 9g pro.

READER REVIEW
"Very tasty! I changed the recipe based on what I had already at home, which was 2% milk and coffee that was already brewed. I used just 1 cup of milk and 2 cups of coffee. This had the perfect amount of sweetness and caramel flavor. Next time, I will add the half-and-half to make it a little more creamy. It was a nice treat!"
—GREATWITHOUTGLUTEN, TASTEOFHOME.COM

CHOCOLATE PEANUT BUTTER MILKSHAKES

These rich chocolate peanut butter shakes will make you feel as if you're sitting at a 1950s soda fountain. Make it modern with an over-the-top garnish like skewered doughnut holes, chocolate-dipped cookies or fluffernutter sandwich squares.
—Taste of Home *Test Kitchen*

Takes: 10 min. • **Makes:** 2 servings

- ¾ cup 2% milk
- 1½ cups chocolate ice cream
- ¼ cup creamy peanut butter
- 2 Tbsp. chocolate syrup
  Optional toppings: Sweetened whipped cream, quartered miniature peanut butter cups and additional chocolate syrup

In a blender, combine the milk, ice cream, peanut butter and syrup; cover and process until smooth. If desired, garnish shakes with whipped cream, peanut butter cups and additional chocolate syrup.

1 CUP: 501 cal., 29g fat (11g sat. fat), 41mg chol., 262mg sod., 51g carb. (43g sugars, 3g fiber), 14g pro.

SPICED APPLE TEA

I love to try new recipes for my husband and our friends. This spiced tea is one of our favorites. I like to serve it warm, but it's also nice served chilled over ice.
—*Sharon Delaney-Chronis, South Milwaukee, WI*

Takes: 25 min. • **Makes:** 5 servings

- 2 cups unsweetened apple juice
- 6 whole cloves
- 1 cinnamon stick (3 in.)
- 3 cups water
- 5 tea bags
  Optional: Apple slices and additional cinnamon sticks (3 in.)

1. In a small saucepan, combine apple juice, cloves and cinnamon stick. Bring to a boil. Reduce heat; simmer, uncovered, 10-15 minutes.
2. Meanwhile, in a large saucepan, bring water to a boil. Remove from the heat; add tea bags. Cover and steep 5 minutes. Discard tea bags. Strain juice mixture, discarding cloves and cinnamon. Stir into tea. Serve hot. If desired, serve with apple slices and additional cinnamon sticks.

1 CUP: 48 cal., 0 fat (0 sat. fat), 0 chol., 11mg sod., 12g carb. (10g sugars, 0 fiber), 0 pro.

SPICED APPLE TEA TIPS

What kind of tea should you use to make spiced apple tea? We recommend using either black or green tea for this spiced apple tea.

Does this spiced apple tea have caffeine? The caffeine content of this tea depends on the amount of caffeine in your tea bags. Choose decaffeinated tea if you prefer.

What can you use to sweeten this spiced apple tea? You can sweeten this tea with sugar, honey or maple syrup. Adding cinnamon will help the tea taste sweeter without adding calories.

SIMPLE ICED COFFEE

My husband came up with this recipe to replace the soda he was drinking every morning. It's a delicious alternative to expensive iced coffees from the local cafe.
—*Sarah Lange, Watertown, WI*

Takes: 5 min. • **Makes:** 8 servings

2   cups water
¼   cup instant coffee granules
¼   to ½ cup sugar
4   cups 2% milk
2   cups half-and-half cream
2   tsp. vanilla extract or hazelnut flavoring syrup, optional

1. Microwave water 90 seconds. Stir in instant coffee. Add sugar.
2. Stir in milk, cream and, if desired, extract or flavoring until combined. Serve over ice.
1 CUP: 174 cal., g fat (6g sat. fat), 40mg chol., 88mg sod., 15g carb. (14g sugars, 0 fiber), 6g pr

CHOCOLATE-CARAMEL RUM COFFEE

This decadent coffee drink can stand alone as a final course or can be a delightful complement to any chocolate or caramel dessert. Our family loves it after a special dinner or just for sipping in front of the fireplace.
—*Joyce Conway, Westerville, OH*

Takes: 25 min. • **Makes:** 8 servings

2   cans (12 oz. each) evaporated milk
¾   cup rum
½   cup chocolate syrup
½   cup caramel sundae syrup
¼   cup packed brown sugar
4   cups hot brewed coffee
2   Tbsp. coffee liqueur

COFFEE WHIPPED CREAM
1   cup heavy whipping cream
6   Tbsp. confectioners' sugar
2   Tbsp. coffee liqueur
    Instant espresso powder, optional

1. In a large saucepan, combine the milk, rum, syrups and brown sugar. Cook over medium heat until hot (do not boil). Stir in coffee and liqueur.
2. Meanwhile, in a small bowl, beat cream until it begins to thicken. Add confectioners' sugar; beat until stiff peaks form. Fold in liqueur until combined.
3. Pour coffee mixture into mugs. Garnish with a dollop of coffee whipped cream and, if desired, sprinkle with espresso powder.
1 CUP COFFEE WITH ¼ CUP COFFEE WHIPPED CREAM: 437 cal., 16g fat (11g sat. fat), 68mg chol., 166mg sod., 50g carb. (43g sugars, 0 fiber), 7g pro.

GO DARK

Choose a dark rum (such as Myers's Original Dark Rum) for richer flavor and body in your dessert and coffee drink recipes that call for rum. Dark rum has been aged to create more depth of flavor and color, while white rum (popular in daiquiris and other cocktails) is bottled right away and has a fresher, lighter taste and appearance.

OLD-FASHIONED ORANGE FLOATS

This treat is a hit with kids and adults alike. Serve it on National Creamsicle Day—August 14—or whenever the temperature calls for frosty flavor.
—*Lillian Weir, Dartmouth, NS*

Takes: 10 min. • **Makes:** 4 servings

- 8 scoops vanilla ice cream (¼ cup each)
- 4 cups orange soda, chilled
- ¼ tsp. orange extract

Place 2 scoops ice cream in each of 4 chilled 16-oz. glasses. In a pitcher, combine the soda and extract. Pour over ice cream.

1½ CUPS: 576 cal., 25g fat (15g sat. fat), 100mg chol., 211mg sod., 84g carb. (70g sugars, 0 fiber), 8g pro.

READER REVIEW
"Tastes just like a Creamsicle. I really enjoyed this easy-to-make drink."
—PAJAMAANGEL, TASTEOFHOME.COM

CHOCOLATE COFFEE

This rich whipped chocolate mixture from our Test Kitchen is used to flavor coffee and to make hot chocolate. Set out a small serving bowl, spoon some of the mixture into mugs and add hot coffee or milk. Yum!
—*Taste of Home Test Kitchen*

Prep: 20 min. • **Cook:** 40 min. + chilling
Makes: 12 servings

- 1 cup sugar
- 1 cup baking cocoa
- 1 cup boiling water
- 1 tsp. vanilla extract
- ¼ tsp. salt
- 4 cups heavy whipping cream, whipped
- 8 cups hot strong brewed coffee or whole milk
  Optional: Whipped cream and finely chopped chocolate

1. In a large heavy saucepan, whisk sugar, cocoa and water until smooth. Cook and whisk over medium-low heat until mixture forms soft peaks when whisk is lifted and resembles thick hot fudge sauce, about 35 minutes.
2. Remove from the heat; stir in vanilla and salt. Transfer to a bowl; refrigerate for at least 2 hours.
3. Just before serving, beat the chilled chocolate mixture. Add 2 cups whipped cream; mix well. Fold in remaining whipped cream. For each serving, place about ½ cup chocolate cream in ⅔ cup coffee or milk; stir to blend. If desired, top with whipped cream and chocolate. Refrigerate leftovers up to 1 day.

1 CUP: 360 cal., 30g fat (18g sat. fat), 90mg chol., 74mg sod., 23g carb. (19g sugars, 1g fiber), 4g pro.

SERVING IDEAS

Top this drink with a seasonal garnish, such as crushed peppermint candies, ground cinnamon or snowflake sprinkles. You could also swap the vanilla extract for your favorite flavor, such as hazelnut or almond.

CARAMEL FRAPPUCCINO

I love Frappuccinos from Starbucks, but they get too expensive. I now make my own, and they are just as good. If you blend the milk with all the other ingredients, it gets too foamy. Instead, you can stir it in with a spoon after all the ice is crushed.
—*Heather Egger, Davenport, IA*

- -

Prep: 10 min. + chilling
Makes: 2 servings

2 Tbsp. ground dark coffee
1 cup water
3 Tbsp. sugar
2 Tbsp. caramel ice cream topping
2 cups ice cubes
1 cup fat-free milk
   Optional: Whipped cream and additional caramel ice cream topping

Place ground coffee in the coffee filter of a drip coffeemaker. Add the water; brew according to manufacturer's directions. Refrigerate coffee until cold. In a blender, combine cold coffee, sugar, caramel topping and ice cubes; process until smooth. Add milk and pulse to combine. Pour into glasses. If desired, top with whipped cream and additional caramel topping.

1 SERVING: 159 cal., 0 fat (0 sat. fat), 2mg chol., 122mg sod., 37g carb. (37g sugars, 0 fiber), 4g pro.

FRAPPUCCINO ORIGIN

Made popular by Starbucks in the 1990s, the Frappuccino is a riff on Italy's froth-topped cappuccino drink. The "frap" portion of the name is inspired by the frappe, a chilled coffee drink.

MANGO LASSI

Learn how to make a mango lassi, the perfect summer drink any mango lover will love. This sweet and refreshing treat only needs a few ingredients!
—*Namrata Telugu, Terre Haute, IN*

Takes: 10 min. • **Makes:** 2 servings

- 1 cup fat-free plain yogurt
- 1 medium mango, peeled and cubed
- 2 cups ice cubes
- 3 Tbsp. sugar
- 5 fresh mint leaves
- 2 crushed cardamom pods, optional

In a blender, combine the yogurt, mango, ice, sugar, mint leaves and, if desired, cardamom pods. Cover and process for 30-60 seconds or until blended. Pour into 2 chilled glasses; serve immediately.

1½ CUPS: 226 cal., 1g fat (0 sat. fat), 3mg chol., 73mg sod., 54g carb. (48g sugars, 3g fiber), 6g pro.

MANGO LASSI RECIPE TIPS

- **Can you make a vegan mango lassi?** Yes! To make a vegan version, switch the yogurt for a dairy-free option. We recommend using a coconut-based yogurt.

- **What other variations can I make to this recipe?** Not a huge fan of mango? You can swap it out for other fruits like banana, strawberry, pineapple, peach or cantaloupe.

SWEET KAHLUA COFFEE

Want to perk up your java? With Kahlua, creme de cacao and a dollop of whipped cream, this chocolaty coffee makes the perfect after-dinner treat at Christmas or anytime.
—*Ruth Gruchow, Yorba Linda, CA*

Prep: 10 min. + cooling • **Cook:** 3 hours
Makes: 9 servings (2¼ qt.)

- 2 qt. hot water
- ½ cup Kahlua (coffee liqueur)
- ¼ cup creme de cacao
- 3 Tbsp. instant coffee granules
- 2 cups heavy whipping cream
- ¼ cup sugar
- 1 tsp. vanilla extract
- 2 Tbsp. grated semisweet chocolate

1. In a 4-qt. slow cooker, mix the water, Kahlua, creme de cacao and coffee granules. Cook, covered, on low for 3-4 hours or until heated through.
2. In a large bowl, beat cream until it begins to thicken. Add sugar and vanilla; beat until soft peaks form. Serve warm coffee with whipped cream and grated chocolate.

1 CUP: 337 cal., 23g fat (15g sat. fat), 68mg chol., 19mg sod., 21g carb. (18g sugars, 0 fiber), 2g pro.

HOMEMADE KAHLUA

This coffee liqueur is an amazing way to elevate your hot chocolate or favorite coffee drink.
—*Susan Stetzel, Gainesville, NY*

Prep: 10 min. • **Cook:** 5 min. + cooling
Makes: 2½ qt.

- 4 cups brewed espresso or strong brewed coffee
- 4 cups sugar
- 4 cups dark rum
- 3 Tbsp. vanilla extract

1. In a large saucepan, bring espresso and sugar to a boil. Reduce heat; simmer, uncovered, for 5 minutes. Cool completely.
2. Stir rum and vanilla into cooled espresso mixture until combined. Pour into glass bottles; seal tightly. Store in a cool, dry place. Shake well before serving.

1½ OZ.: 101 cal., 0 fat (0 sat. fat), 0 chol., 3mg sod., 16g carb. (15g sugars, 0 fiber), 0 pro.

SUNBURST SPICED TEA

Our culinary experts use oranges and lemon to lend a lovely citrus flavor to ordinary black tea.
—Taste of Home *Test Kitchen*

Takes: 25 min. • **Makes:** 4 servings

- 2   medium oranges
- 1   medium lemon
- 4   cardamom pods
- 4   whole cloves
- 4   tsp. English breakfast or other black tea leaves
- 4   cups boiling water
      Lemon slices, optional

1. Using a citrus zester or a vegetable peeler, remove peels from the oranges and lemon in long narrow strips. (Save fruit for another use.) Place the peel strips, cardamom and cloves in a large bowl. With the end of a wooden spoon handle, crush the mixture until aromas are released.

2. Add tea leaves and boiling water. Cover and steep for 6 minutes. Strain the tea, discarding the peel mixture. Add lemon slices if desired. Serve immediately.

1 CUP: 2 cal., 0 fat (0 sat. fat), 0 chol., 7mg sod., 1g carb. (0 sugars, 0 fiber), 0 pro. **DIABETIC EXCHANGES:** 1 free food.

PUMPKIN PIE LATTE

We can't wait for fall to arrive so our favorite coffee shops will bring back pumpkin lattes. The rest of the year, we have to make our own version. With just the right amount of spice, it tastes just like the popular version found at gourmet coffee shops.
—Taste of Home *Test Kitchen*

Takes: 15 min. • **Makes:** 2 servings

- 2   cups whole milk
- 2   Tbsp. canned pumpkin
- 2   Tbsp. sugar
- 2   Tbsp. vanilla extract
- ½   tsp. pumpkin pie spice
- ½   cup hot brewed espresso
      Optional: Whipped cream, pumpkin pie spice and ground nutmeg

1. In a small saucepan, combine the milk, pumpkin and sugar. Cook and stir over medium heat until steaming. Remove from the heat; stir in vanilla and pie spice. Transfer to a blender; cover and process for 15 seconds or until foamy.

2. Pour into 2 mugs; add espresso. If desired, garnish with whipped cream and spices.

1¼ CUPS: 234 cal., 8g fat (5g sat. fat), 33mg chol., 122mg sod., 26g carb. (24g sugars, 1g fiber), 8g pro.

MAKE YOUR OWN PUMPKIN PIE SPICE

Mix 4 tsp. ground cinnamon, 2 tsp. ground ginger, 1 tsp. ground cloves and ½ tsp. ground nutmeg. Store in an airtight container in a cool, dry place for up to 6 months.

ICED COFFEE

When my sister introduced me to iced coffee, I wasn't sure I'd like it. Not only did I love it, but I decided to start making my own. This easy version is a refreshing alternative to hot coffee.
—*Jenny Reece, Lowry, MN*

- -

Takes: 5 min. • **Makes:** 2 servings

    4   tsp. instant coffee granules
    1   cup boiling water
        Sugar substitute equivalent to
        4 tsp. sugar, optional
    1   cup fat-free milk
    4   tsp. chocolate syrup
    ⅛   tsp. vanilla extract
        Ice cubes

In a large bowl, dissolve coffee in the boiling water. Add sweetener if desired. Stir in milk, chocolate syrup and vanilla; mix well. Serve over ice.
1 CUP: 83 cal., 0 fat (0 sat. fat), 2mg chol., 57mg sod., 16g carb. (13g sugars, 0 fiber), 5g pro. **DIABETIC EXCHANGES:** ½ starch, ½ fat-free milk.

ICED COFFEE TIPS

- **How else can you make iced coffee at home?** You can make a simple iced coffee by pouring cooled regular coffee over ice. The key is to brew your coffee stronger because it will be diluted by the melting ice. Use about twice as much ground coffee as you would for regular hot coffee. You can also freeze leftover coffee in an ice cube tray to avoid diluting your cold cup of joe.

- **What's the difference between an iced coffee and an iced latte?** Iced coffee is regular coffee poured over ice. An iced latte is espresso and milk poured over ice.

PINK DRINK

Whether you've seen it at the beach or on your favorite Instagram account, the Starbucks Pink Drink is still one of the most beautiful beverages we know of. Create your own version of the strawberry refresher at home.
—Taste of Home *Test Kitchen*

- -

Prep: 15 min. + chilling. • **Cook:** 20 min.
Makes: 2 servings

    1   cup frozen unsweetened
        strawberries, thawed
    2   berry-flavored green tea bags
    1   cup boiling water

    1½ cups coconut milk, chilled
    2   Tbsp. simple syrup
    2   cups ice cubes
    ¼   cup freeze-dried strawberries,
        slightly crushed

1. In a saucepan, cook strawberries over low heat until they start to break apart, about 15 minutes, stirring occasionally. Remove from heat; cool. Using an immersion blender, puree strawberries. Chill, covered, until ready to serve.

2. Steep tea 5 minutes in boiling water; discard tea bags. Stir in strawberry mixture, coconut milk and simple syrup. Divide mixture between 2 glasses filled with ice. Garnish with freeze-dried strawberries.
1½ CUPS: 367 cal., 27g fat (27g sat. fat), 0 chol., 47mg sod., 28g carb. (23g sugars, 3g fiber), 4g pro.

PINEAPPLE ICED TEA

I like to garnish this iced tea with some of our sweet Hawaiian pineapple.
—*Beverly Toomey, Honolulu, HI*

Prep: 20 min. + chilling • **Cook:** 10 min.
Makes: 20 servings

- 16 cups water
- 24 tea bags
- 6 fresh mint sprigs
- 3⅓ cups sugar
- 3 cups unsweetened pineapple juice
- 1 cup lemon juice
  Lemon slices, optional

1. In a stockpot, bring water to a boil; remove from heat. Add tea bags; steep, covered, 10 minutes. Discard tea bags. Add mint; steep 5 minutes. Discard mint. Add remaining ingredients, stirring to dissolve sugar.

2. Transfer to pitchers or a large covered container. Refrigerate, covered, until cold. If desired, serve with ice and fresh lemon slices.

1 CUP: 154 cal., 0 fat (0 sat. fat), 0 chol., 7mg sod., 40g carb. (38g sugars, 0 fiber), 0 pro.

CHAI TEA

Warm up a chilly December evening—or any day at all—with this inviting tea. The spices really come through, and it's even more delicious when stirred with a cinnamon stick.
—*Taste of Home Test Kitchen*

Takes: 20 min. • **Makes:** 4 servings

- 4 whole cloves
- 2 whole peppercorns
- 4 tea bags
- 4 tsp. sugar
- ¼ tsp. ground ginger
- 1 cinnamon stick (3 in.)
- 2½ cups boiling water
- 2 cups 2% milk

1. Place cloves and peppercorns in a large bowl. With the end of a wooden spoon handle, crush the spices until their aromas are released.

2. Add the tea bags, sugar, ginger, cinnamon stick and boiling water. Cover; steep for 6 minutes. Meanwhile, in a small saucepan, heat the milk.

3. Strain tea, discarding spices and tea bags. Stir in hot milk. Pour into mugs.

1 CUP: 92 cal., 4g fat (2g sat. fat), 12mg chol., 49mg sod., 10g carb. (10g sugars, 0 fiber), 4g pro.

CHAI TEA RECIPE TIPS

- **How can I make chai tea vegan?** To make this chai tea vegan, swap out the milk for a dairy-free option. We recommend using either an almond or coconut milk alternative. Using a milk alternative will make this chai recipe a little thinner than when using 2% milk.

- **How do you store chai tea?** We recommend serving chai right after making it. However, if you want to enjoy your chai later, you can store it in an airtight jar in the refrigerator for a few days.

Short & Sweet

COCONUT COLD-BREW LATTE

Cold-brew lattes are all the rage at coffee shops, but they're so easy to make at home. This coconut cold-brew latte is ridiculously refreshing—and it's even vegan!
—*Natalie Larsen, Grand Prairie, TX*

Prep: 20 min. + chilling
Makes: 4 servings

½ cup coarsely ground
    medium-roast coffee
½ cup hot water (205°)
3½ cups cold water

COCONUT SIMPLE SYRUP

1 cup water
½ cup sugar
½ cup sweetened shredded coconut

EACH SERVING

   Ice cubes
2 Tbsp. coconut milk

1. Place ground coffee in a clean glass container. Pour hot water over coffee; let stand 10 minutes. Stir in the cold water. Cover and refrigerate for 12-24 hours. (The longer the coffee sits, the stronger the flavor.)
2. Meanwhile, for coconut simple syrup, in a small saucepan, bring water, sugar and coconut to a boil. Reduce heat; simmer 10 minutes. Strain and discard coconut. Cool mixture completely.
3. Strain coffee through a fine-mesh sieve; discard grounds. Strain coffee again through a coffee filter; discard grounds. Store coffee in the refrigerator for up to 2 weeks. For each serving, fill a large glass with ice. Add 1 cup cold-brewed coffee and 4 Tbsp. coconut syrup; stir. Top with 2 Tbsp. coconut milk.

1 CUP: 145 cal., 5g fat (5g sat. fat), 0 chol., 12mg sod., 26g carb. (26g sugars, 0 fiber), 1g pro.

CREAMY IRISH COFFEE

My maternal grandmother usually never drank more than a glass of champagne at Christmas, but she couldn't resist Creamy Irish Coffee.
—*Rebecca Little, Park Ridge, IL*

Takes: 10 min. • **Makes:** 4 servings

3 cups hot strong brewed coffee
4 oz. Irish cream liqueur
   Optional: Sweetened whipped
   cream and chocolate shavings

Divide coffee and liqueur among 4 mugs; stir. If desired, top with whipped cream and chocolate shavings.

1 SERVING: 118 cal., 4g fat (0 sat. fat), 0 chol., 1mg sod., 8g carb. (6g sugars, 0 fiber), 0 pro.

HOMEMADE IRISH CREAM

Add some creamy goodness to your coffee with a splash of this alcohol-free version of Irish cream. Stir in whiskey to taste if you prefer.
—*Marcia Severson, Hallock, MN*

Takes: 10 min. • **Makes:** 3⅓ cups

1 can (12 oz.) evaporated milk
1 cup heavy whipping cream
½ cup 2% milk
¼ cup sugar
2 Tbsp. chocolate syrup
1 Tbsp. instant coffee granules
2 tsp. vanilla extract
¼ tsp. almond extract

EACH SERVING

   Hot brewed coffee
   Irish whiskey, optional

1. In a blender, combine all ingredients except the coffee and whiskey; cover and process until smooth. Store in the refrigerator. Shake well before serving.
2. Stir into hot coffee, adding Irish whiskey if desired.

1 OZ.: 62 cal., 4g fat (3g sat. fat), 16mg chol., 20mg sod., 4g carb. (4g sugars, 0 fiber), 1g pro.

DOUBLE CHOCOLATE HOT COCOA MIX

I gave this away at our neighborhood Christmas party in cutie-patootie gift bags and was thrilled that I was able to give something to everyone. The next week I started getting calls from the neighbors who had tried it, and I was blown away at the response. Everyone loves this! The white chocolate makes it extra creamy.

—Mandy Rivers, Lexington, SC

Takes: 10 min.
Makes: 20 servings
(6⅔ cups hot cocoa mix)

- 4 cups nonfat dry milk powder
- 2 cups white baking chips
- 2 cups baking cocoa
- 1½ cups confectioners' sugar
- ½ tsp. salt
EACH SERVING
- 1 cup hot 2% milk

1. Pulse the first 5 ingredients in a food processor until baking chips are finely ground. Transfer to a large airtight container. Store in a cool, dry place up to 6 months.
2. To prepare hot cocoa: Place ⅓ cup hot cocoa mix in a mug. Stir in 1 cup hot milk until blended.

1 CUP PREPARED HOT COCOA: 321 cal., 11g fat (6g sat. fat), 25mg chol., 264mg sod., 43g carb. (38g sugars, 2g fiber), 15g pro.

HOMEMADE VANILLA MARSHMALLOWS

My husband Dale's grandmother fixed these fluffy marshmallows only for special occasions. Since she had no electric mixer, beating the ingredients by hand for 30 minutes was a labor of love. Now, Dale makes them. They're delicious!

—Nancy Shields, Hillsdale, MI

Prep: 25 min. + cooling • **Cook:** 20 min.
Makes: about 8 dozen

    Confectioners' sugar
- 2 cups cold water, divided
- 4 envelopes unflavored gelatin
- 4 cups sugar
- ⅛ tsp. salt
- 2 tsp. vanilla extract

COATING
- 1 cup confectioners' sugar
- ¼ cup cornstarch

1. Generously dust a 13x9-in. pan with confectioners' sugar. In a large bowl, sprinkle gelatin over ¾ cup cold water.
2. In a large heavy saucepan, combine sugar, salt and remaining 1¼ cup water. Bring to a boil over medium heat, stirring occasionally. Cook, covered, 3 minutes. Uncover; cook, without stirring, over medium-high heat until a candy thermometer reads 248° (firm-ball stage). Remove from heat and slowly add to the gelatin mixture, beating on low speed until incorporated. Add vanilla; beat on medium until thick and doubled in volume, about 10 minutes.

3. Spread into prepared pan. Cover; let stand at room temperature 6 hours or overnight.
4. Using a knife coated with cooking spray, cut into 1-in. squares. In a large bowl, combine confectioners' sugar and cornstarch. Add marshmallows in batches; toss to coat. Store in airtight containers in a cool, dry place.

1 MARSHMALLOW: 35 cal., 0 fat (0 sat. fat), 0 chol., 4mg sod., 9g carb. (8g sugars, 0 fiber), 0 pro.

KEEP THEM FROM STICKING

If you live in a humid area, you may find your marshmallows getting a little sticky after a few days. To prevent sticking, simply dust them with a little more confectioners' sugar or cornstarch.

RAINBOW
BIRTHDAY CAKE,
PAGE 257

Best Birthday Ever

Whether your special somebody is turning 1 or 101, you'll find an irresistible sweet to celebrate them in this festive chapter.

MOIST CHOCOLATE CAKE

The cake reminds me of my grandma because it was her specialty. I bake it for family parties, and the fond memories of her come flooding back for everyone. This layered dessert is light and airy but with a decadent chocolate taste.
—*Patricia Kreitz, Richland, PA*

- -

Prep: 15 min. • **Bake:** 25 min. + cooling
Makes: 16 servings

- 2 cups all-purpose flour
- 2 cups sugar
- 2 tsp. baking soda
- ¾ cup baking cocoa
- 1 tsp. salt
- 1 tsp. baking powder
- 1 cup canola oil
- 1 cup brewed coffee
- 1 cup whole milk
- 2 large eggs
- 1 tsp. vanilla extract

FAVORITE ICING

- 5 Tbsp. all-purpose flour
- 1 cup whole milk
- ½ cup butter, softened
- ½ cup shortening
- 1 cup sugar
- 1 tsp. vanilla extract
- 2 to 4 Tbsp. sprinkles, optional

1. Preheat oven to 325°. Grease and flour two 9-in. round baking pans. Sift dry ingredients together into a large bowl. Add oil, coffee and milk; mix at medium speed 1 minute. Add eggs and vanilla; beat 2 minutes longer. (Batter will be thin.) Pour into prepared pans.
2. Bake 25-30 minutes or until a toothpick inserted in the center comes out clean. Cool in pans 10 minutes before removing to wire racks to cool completely.
3. Meanwhile, for icing, in a small saucepan, whisk flour and milk until smooth. Bring to a boil over medium heat; cook and stir until thickened, 1-2 minutes. Transfer to a small bowl. Cover and refrigerate until chilled.

4. In a large bowl, beat butter, shortening, sugar and vanilla until creamy, 3-4 minutes. Add chilled milk mixture and beat 10 minutes. Stir in sprinkles if desired. Spread frosting between layers and over top and side of cake.

1 PIECE: 482 cal., 28g fat (7g sat. fat), 42mg chol., 404mg sod., 55g carb. (39g sugars, 1g fiber), 4g pro.

MOIST CHOCOLATE CAKE TIPS

- **Can you make this chocolate cake ahead of time?** You can assemble the entire cake 2-3 days ahead of time. Just layer and frost the cake and store it in a cake carrier until you want to serve it. Just be sure to let it come to room temperature before serving for maximum flavor. If you are in a time crunch, this cake freezes beautifully too. Wrap the unfrosted layers well, and keep in your freezer for up to 2 months.

- **Can you make this moist chocolate cake in different baking pans?** You can bake this cake in two 8-in. round pans (with leftover batter in 6 additional muffin cups), or even as three thin 8-in. layers. As these are smaller cake pans, keep an eye on time as they bake and test accordingly with a toothpick; they may not need to bake as long.

- **How should you store leftover chocolate cake?** This cake tastes better, and dries out less, if kept at room temperature.

- **Can you use butter in this recipe instead of oil?** Yes. Most of the time, melted butter can substitute for oil in a 1:1 ratio. Simply melt your butter down and measure to the equivalent of the oil in the recipe. Keep in mind that cakes containing butter as a primary fat are a little drier than those made with oil. You will still have a delicious cake, but it may not have as moist a crumb.

BIRTHDAY CAKE
FUDGE

THICK SUGAR COOKIES,
PAGE 8

YELLOW
CUPCAKES

HOW TO BUILD A... BIRTHDAY BOARD

ITEMS TO INCLUDE

- Thick Sugar Cookies (recipe on page 8)
- Icing writers
- Gummy bears
- Gumballs
- M&M's minis
- Jelly beans
- Lollipops
- Yellow Cupcakes (half with chocolate frosting, half with vanilla)
- Oreos (regular, golden and mini)
- Fudge-striped cookies
- Circus Animal Cookies
- Birthday Cake Fudge
- Kit Kat bars, unwrapped
- Caramel corn
- Hershey's Kisses
- Swedish Fish candies

EASY ASSEMBLY

Step 1: Prepare Thick Sugar Cookies as directed but use a 4- or 6-inch cookie cutter to create 1 larger cookie. Use icing writers to decorate the large cookie with "Happy Birthday."

Step 2: Fan remaining Thick Sugar Cookies in the middle of the board in a circle. Set large cookie on top.

Step 3: Fill small bowls with the gummy bears, gumballs, M&M's and jelly beans. Stand the lollipops in a tall glass. Set all on board.

Step 4: Arrange Yellow Cupcakes on the board in 2 groupings. Add Oreos in like groupings. Set fudge-striped and animal cookies next to the Oreos on opposite sides.

Step 5: Stack Birthday Cake Fudge squares and Kit Kats on opposite sides of the board. Fill in gaps with groupings of the remaining items.

YELLOW CUPCAKES

On any given day, someone needs a gorgeous homemade cupcake. This buttery yellow cake base works with any frosting and decorates beautifully.
—Taste of Home *Test Kitchen*

- -

Prep: 20 min. • **Bake:** 15 min. + cooling
Makes: 2 dozen

⅔	cup butter, softened
1¾	cups sugar
2	large eggs, room temperature
1½	tsp. vanilla extract
2½	cups all-purpose flour
2½	tsp. baking powder
½	tsp. salt
1¼	cups 2% milk
	Frosting of your choice

1. Preheat oven to 350°. Line 24 muffin cups with paper liners.
2. In a large bowl, cream butter and sugar until light and fluffy, 5-7 minutes. Add eggs, 1 at a time, beating well after each addition. Beat in vanilla extract. In another bowl, whisk flour, baking powder and salt; add to the creamed mixture alternately with milk, beating well after each addition.
3. Fill prepared cups three-fourths full. Bake 15-20 minutes or until a toothpick inserted in the center comes out clean. Cool cupcakes in pans for 10 minutes before removing to wire racks to cool completely. Spread with frosting.

1 CUPCAKE: 163 cal., 6g fat (4g sat. fat), 32mg chol., 138mg sod., 25g carb. (15g sugars, 0 fiber), 2g pro.

BIRTHDAY CAKE FUDGE

This decadent treat is the perfect thing to make your birthday special. Or prepare it ahead and package it as a surprise gift for a friend.
—*Rashanda Cobbins, Aurora, CO*

- -

Prep: 10 min. + chilling
Makes: 64 pieces

1	can (14 oz.) sweetened condensed milk
1½	cups white baking chips
3	Tbsp. butter
⅛	tsp. salt
1½	cups unprepared Funfetti cake mix
3	Tbsp. sprinkles

1. Line an 8-in. square pan with foil or parchment; grease foil lightly. In a large heavy saucepan, cook and stir milk, baking chips, butter and salt over low heat until smooth. Remove from heat; stir in cake mix until dissolved. Spread into prepared pan; top with sprinkles. Refrigerate until firm, about 2 hours.
2. Using foil, lift fudge out of pan. Remove foil; cut fudge into 1-in. squares. Store in an airtight container in the refrigerator.

1 PIECE: 59 cal., 2g fat (2g sat. fat), 4mg chol., 47mg sod., 9g carb. (7g sugars, 0 fiber), 1g pro.

VARIATION IDEAS

This birthday fudge recipe is easy to customize. If you're making the recipe as a gift, change up the sprinkles to suit the theme of the party or a person's favorite colors. You can also experiment by adding different chopped nuts or chopped dried fruits into the mix.

ICE CREAM BIRTHDAY CAKE

When we were young, Mom made birthday cakes with a small toy on top, chosen just for us. Now that I'm a parent, I go with sprinkles.
—*Becky Herges, Fargo, ND*

Prep: 50 min. + freezing
Makes: 12 servings

- 4 cups birthday cake-flavored ice cream or flavor of your choice, softened if necessary
- 1 funfetti cake mix (regular size)
- 1 carton (8 oz.) frozen whipped topping, thawed
  Sprinkles

1. Line a 9-in. round pan with plastic wrap. Spread ice cream into pan. Freeze 2 hours or until firm.
2. Prepare and bake cake mix according to package directions, using two 9-in. round baking pans. Cool in pans 10 minutes before removing to wire racks to cool completely.
3. Using a serrated knife, trim tops of cakes if domed. Place 1 cake layer on a serving plate. Invert ice cream onto cake layer; remove plastic wrap. Top with remaining cake layer. Spread whipped topping over top and side of cake. Decorate with sprinkles as desired. Freeze 2 hours longer or until firm.
1 PIECE: 374 cal., 19g fat (8g sat. fat), 66mg chol., 315mg sod., 45g carb. (27g sugars, 1g fiber), 5g pro.

ICE CREAM CAKE-CUTTING TIPS

The secret to cutting an ice cream cake is using a warm knife. Remove the cake from the freezer and let it sit at room temperature 10-15 minutes. Place a large, sharp knife in a glass of hot water. When the cake has softened, remove the knife and wipe it dry on a clean cloth or paper towel. Slice the cake, warming and wiping the knife with each cut.

CONFETTI BIRTHDAY CAKE

This is a moist and fluffy vanilla cake with lots of sprinkles and a whipped vanilla buttercream. It's almost impossible not to feel happy when you see the fun pop of rainbow confetti!
—*Courtney Rich, Highland, UT*

Prep: 30 min. • **Bake:** 35 min. + cooling
Makes: 16 servings

- 1 cup unsalted butter, room temperature
- ⅓ cup vegetable oil
- 1¾ cups sugar
- 3 large eggs, room temperature
- 3 large egg whites, room temperature
- 1 Tbsp. vanilla extract
- 3 cups cake flour
- 2 tsp. baking powder
- 1 tsp. salt
- 1 cup buttermilk, room temperature
- ¼ cup rainbow sprinkles
  BUTTERCREAM
- 1½ cups unsalted butter, softened
- 4½ cups confectioners' sugar, sifted
- 3 Tbsp. heavy whipping cream
- 2 tsp. clear vanilla extract
  Soft pink paste food coloring

1. Preheat oven to 325°. Grease a 13x9-in. baking dish. In a large bowl, cream butter, oil and sugar until light and fluffy, 5-7 minutes. Add eggs, then egg whites, 1 at a time, beating well after each addition. Beat in vanilla. In another bowl, whisk flour, baking powder and salt; add to creamed mixture alternately with buttermilk, beating well after each addition. Fold in sprinkles.
2. Transfer to prepared pan. Bake until a toothpick inserted in center comes out clean, 35-40 minutes. Cool completely on a wire rack.
3. For buttercream, in a large bowl, beat butter until creamy. Gradually beat in confectioners' sugar until smooth. Add cream, vanilla and food coloring. Beat until light and fluffy. Frost top of cake with frosting, and, if desired, top with additional sprinkles.
1 PIECE: 823 cal., 47g fat (26g sat. fat), 138mg chol., 279mg sod., 97g carb. (75g sugars, 0 fiber), 6g pro.

RAINBOW
BIRTHDAY CAKE

PINK VELVET CUPCAKES

My daughter loves all things pink, so this recipe was just right for her birthday. Even my teenage son (not a fan of pink) ate his share too.
—*Paulette Smith, Winston-Salem, NC*

Prep: 30 min. + chilling
Bake: 25 min. + cooling
Makes: 2 dozen

- 1 cup butter, softened
- 1¼ cups sugar
- ⅛ tsp. pink paste food coloring
- 3 large eggs, room temperature
- 1 tsp. vanilla extract
- 2½ cups all-purpose flour
- 1½ tsp. baking powder
- ¼ tsp. baking soda
- ¼ tsp. salt
- 1 cup buttermilk

WHITE CHOCOLATE GANACHE
- 2 cups white baking chips
- ½ cup heavy whipping cream
- 1 Tbsp. butter
  Pink coarse sugar and sugar pearls

1. In a large bowl, cream the butter, sugar and food coloring until light and fluffy, 5-7 minutes. Add eggs, 1 at a time, beating well after each addition. Beat in vanilla. Combine the flour, baking powder, baking soda and salt; add to creamed mixture alternately with buttermilk, beating well after each addition.
2. Fill 24 paper-lined muffin cups two-thirds full. Bake at 350° until a toothpick inserted in the center comes out clean, 23-27 minutes. Cool for 10 minutes before removing from pans to wire racks to cool completely.
3. Meanwhile, place white chips in a small bowl. In a small saucepan, bring cream just to a boil. Pour over chips; whisk until smooth. Stir in butter. Transfer to a large bowl. Chill for 30 minutes, stirring once.
4. Beat on high speed until soft peaks form and frosting is light and fluffy, 2-3 minutes. Frost cupcakes. Top cupcakes with coarse sugar and sugar pearls. Store in the refrigerator.
1 CUPCAKE: 266 cal., 15g fat (9g sat. fat), 57mg chol., 154mg sod., 29g carb. (20g sugars, 0 fiber), 3g pro.

RAINBOW BIRTHDAY CAKE

How fun is this rainbow birthday cake? It will add a festive touch to any celebration. Be sure to use gel food coloring for the most vibrant look.
—*Taste of Home Test Kitchen*

Prep: 1 hour • **Bake:** 30 min. + cooling
Makes: 16 servings

- 1 cup butter, softened
- 2½ cups sugar
- 4 large eggs, room temperature
- 4 cups all-purpose flour
- 3 tsp. baking powder
- 1 tsp. salt
- ½ tsp. baking soda
- 1½ cups sour cream
- 6 different colors gel food coloring

FROSTING
- 2 cups butter, softened
- 6 cups confectioners' sugar, sifted
- 2 tsp. vanilla extract
- ¼ to ⅓ cup heavy whipping cream
  Sprinkles

1. Preheat oven to 350°. Line bottoms of 3 greased and floured 8-in. round baking pans with parchment; grease paper. In a large bowl, cream butter and sugar until light and fluffy, 5-7 minutes. Add eggs, 1 at a time, beating well after each addition. Combine flour, baking powder, salt and baking soda; add to the creamed mixture alternately with sour cream, beating well after each addition. Divide batter into equal portions, with 1¼ cups in 6 separate bowls. Tint each portion a different color with food coloring. Cover and refrigerate 3 portions.
2. Transfer 3 remaining portions to prepared pans. Bake until edges begin to just barely brown, 13-15 minutes. Cool for 10 minutes before removing from pans to wire racks to cool completely. Cool, wash and dry pans. Repeat with remaining batter.
3. In a large bowl, beat butter until fluffy, 5-7 minutes. Gradually beat in confectioners' sugar. Beat in vanilla and enough cream to reach desired consistency. Spread frosting between layers and over top and side of cake. Decorate with sprinkles.
1 PIECE: 793 cal., 42g fat (26g sat. fat), 158mg chol., 579mg sod., 101g carb. (77g sugars, 1g fiber), 6g pro.

LAYER CAKE POINTERS

To make sure each layer is the same thickness, give your filled cake pans a firm rap on the counter before putting them in the oven. This releases any air bubbles and levels out the batter so it's evenly dispersed. If you have a kitchen scale, weigh the batter portions for even more precision.

UNICORN CAKE

This magical unicorn cake tastes as good as it looks. Baking in smaller pans creates impressive height, and a few simple decorating tricks turn it into a showstopping dessert.
—*Lauren McAnelly, Des Moines, IA*

Prep: 1 hour • **Bake:** 25 min. + cooling
Makes: 20 servings

- 2¼ cups cake flour
- 1½ cups sugar
- 3½ tsp. baking powder
- ½ tsp. salt
- ½ cup unsalted butter, cubed
- 4 large egg whites, room temperature
- ¾ cup 2% milk, divided
- 1 tsp. clear vanilla extract
- ½ tsp. almond extract
- ⅓ cup rainbow jimmies

BUTTERCREAM
- 6 oz. white baking chocolate, chopped
- ¼ cup heavy whipping cream
- 6 large egg whites
- 1½ cups sugar
- ½ tsp. cream of tartar
- ½ tsp. salt
- 2 cups unsalted butter, cubed
- 1½ tsp. vanilla extract
  Paste food coloring

1. Preheat oven to 350°. Line bottoms of three 6-in. round baking pans with parchment; grease and flour pans.
2. In a large bowl, whisk flour, sugar, baking powder and salt. Beat in butter until crumbly. Add egg whites, 1 at a time, beating well after each addition. Gradually beat in ¼ cup milk and extracts; beat on medium until light and fluffy, about 2 minutes. Gradually beat in remaining milk. Gently fold in jimmies.

3. Transfer batter to prepared pans. Bake 25-30 minutes or until a toothpick inserted in each center comes out clean. Cool in pans 10 minutes before removing to wire racks; remove parchment. Cool completely.
4. For buttercream, in a microwave, melt chocolate with cream until smooth, stirring every 30 seconds. Set aside to cool slightly. In heatproof bowl of stand mixer, whisk egg whites, sugar, cream of tartar and salt until blended. Place over simmering water in a large saucepan over medium heat. Whisking constantly, heat mixture until a thermometer reads 160°, 8-10 minutes.
5. Remove from heat. With whisk attachment of stand mixer, beat on high speed until cooled to 90°, about 7 minutes. Gradually beat in butter, a few tablespoons at a time, on medium speed until smooth; beat in vanilla and white chocolate mixture.
6. Spread frosting between layers and over top and side of cake. Divide remaining buttercream into smaller portions; stir in food coloring to achieve desired colors. Decorate as desired. Store in refrigerator.
DECORATING TIPS: For ears, combine your favorite cookie dough with jimmies; cut into 2-in. hearts and bake. While still warm, mold onto the curve of a large metal spoon; let stand until cooled. Dip edges in melted white chocolate. For horn, coat sugar cone with edible gold mist. For eyes, pipe melted yellow candy coating disks onto parchment; refrigerate until set. For mane, attach pastel meringue cookies with buttercream; fill in with piped buttercream.
1 PIECE: 460 cal., 28g fat (17g sat. fat), 65mg chol., 245mg sod., 51g carb. (38g sugars, 0 fiber), 4g pro.

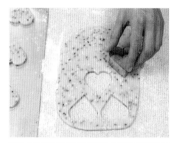

SMASH CAKE

A smash cake is a small, personalized cake given to a baby on their first birthday, allowing them to freely enjoy and "smash" the cake as part of a fun and messy photo opportunity.
—Taste of Home *Test Kitchen*

- -

Prep: 30 min. • **Bake:** 20 min. + cooling
Makes: 6 servings

- ¼ cup butter, softened
- ¾ cup sugar
- 2 large eggs, room temperature
- ¾ tsp. vanilla extract
- 1 cup all-purpose flour
- 1 tsp. baking powder
- ½ tsp. salt
- ½ cup 2% milk

FROSTING
- ½ cup butter, softened
- 2½ cups confectioners' sugar
- ¼ tsp. vanilla extract
- 2 to 3 Tbsp. 2% milk
   Sprinkles of your choice

1. Preheat oven to 350°. Line bottoms of 2 greased and floured 6-in. round baking pans with parchment. In a small bowl, cream butter and sugar until crumbly. Add eggs, 1 at a time, beating well after each addition. Beat in vanilla. In another bowl, whisk flour, baking powder and salt; add to creamed mixture alternately with milk, beating well after each addition.

2. Transfer to prepared pans. Bake until a toothpick inserted in center comes out clean, 20-25 minutes. Cool in pans 10 minutes before removing to a wire rack; remove paper. Cool completely.

3. For frosting, in a small bowl, beat butter and confectioners' sugar until fluffy. Add vanilla and milk; beat until smooth. Spread frosting between layers and over top and side of cake. Decorate as desired. Store in the refrigerator.

1 PIECE: 610 cal., 25g fat (15g sat. fat), 125mg chol., 497mg sod., 92g carb. (76g sugars, 1g fiber), 5g pro.

BIRTHDAY CAKE SHOOTERS

These festive shots are a fun way to get a birthday party started. Use chocolate cake-flavored vodka and chocolate liqueur for a super chocolaty treat.
—Taste of Home *Test Kitchen*

Prep: 5 min. • **Makes:** 2 servings

Ice cubes
2 oz. cake-flavored vodka
1 oz. white chocolate liqueur
Sweetened whipped cream
Sprinkles

Fill shaker three-fourths full with ice. Add vodka and white chocolate liqueur; cover and shake until condensation forms on outside of shaker, 10-15 seconds. Strain into 2 shot glasses. Top with whipped cream and sprinkles.
1½ OZ.: 181 cal., 0 fat (0 sat. fat), 0 chol., 3mg sod., 17g carb. (0 sugars, 0 fiber), 0 pro.

BIRTHDAY CAKE SHOOTERS TIPS

- **Can you use other flavored vodkas in a birthday cake shot?** Cake vodka might be harder to find, especially if you're shopping at smaller stores. If you can't find it, swap in vanilla or whipped cream vodka instead.

- **Can you use frosting and sprinkles to rim the glass?** Absolutely! Before pouring the shots, first dip the rim of each glass in frosting and then in sprinkles.

- **How do you make birthday cake shots for a group?** To make these for a party, mix several batches in advance and leave the shots on a tray in the refrigerator or freezer until ready to enjoy. Top with whipped cream and sprinkles just before serving.

CHOCOLATE VELVET DESSERT

This extra-speical creation is the result of several attempts to duplicate a dessert I enjoyed on vacation. It looks so beautiful on a buffet table that many folks are tempted to forgo the main course in favor of it.
—Molly Seidel, Edgewood, NM

Prep: 20 min. • **Bake:** 45 min. + chilling
Makes: 16 servings

1½ cups chocolate wafer crumbs
2 Tbsp. sugar
¼ cup butter, melted
2 cups semisweet chocolate chips
6 large egg yolks
1¾ cups heavy whipping cream
1 tsp. vanilla extract

CHOCOLATE BUTTERCREAM FROSTING
½ cup butter, softened
3 cups confectioners' sugar
3 Tbsp. baking cocoa
3 to 4 Tbsp. 2% milk

1. In a small bowl, combine wafer crumbs and sugar; stir in butter. Press onto the bottom and 1½ in. up the inside of a greased 9-in. springform pan. Place on a baking sheet. Bake at 350° for 10 minutes. Cool on a wire rack.
2. In a large microwave-safe bowl, melt chocolate chips; stir until smooth. Cool. In a small bowl, combine the egg yolks, cream and vanilla. Gradually stir a small amount of mixture into melted chocolate until blended; gradually stir in remaining mixture. Pour into crust.
3. Place pan on a baking sheet. Bake at 350° until center is almost set, 45-50 minutes. Cool on a wire rack for 10 minutes. Carefully run a knife around edge of pan to loosen; cool 1 hour longer. Refrigerate overnight.
4. In a large bowl, combine the butter, confectioners' sugar, cocoa and enough milk to achieve a piping consistency. Using a large star tip, pipe frosting on dessert.
1 PIECE: 432 cal., 28g fat (16g sat. fat), 139mg chol., 164mg sod., 46g carb. (35g sugars, 2g fiber), 4g pro.

READER REVIEW
"Awesome! Creamy and delicious."
—TJY, TASTEOFHOME.COM

SURPRISE CAKE

We filled our surprise cake with M&Ms, sprinkles and mini chocolate chips, but there are other options. A few mini Oreos would be fun, as would Sixlets or malted milk balls. Get creative, but remember that you want the candies to easily to fall out of the cake. Sour Patch Kids and gummies might not come tumbling out of the cake on their own.
—Taste of Home *Test Kitchen*

Prep: 25 min. + decorating
Bake: 30 min. + cooling
Makes: 16 servings

- 2   pkg. white cake mix (regular size)
- 8   large eggs
- 1   cup buttermilk
- 1   cup vegetable oil
      Blue, green, pink and yellow gel food coloring

FROSTING

- 8   cups confectioners' sugar
- 1½   cups butter, softened
- 2   tsp. vanilla extract
- 4   to 6 Tbsp. heavy whipping cream
- 1¼   cups assorted candies, sprinkles and mini white chips

1. Preheat oven to 350°. Line bottoms of 4 greased 8-in. round baking pans with parchment; grease paper. In a large bowl, combine cake mix, eggs, buttermilk and oil; mix until well combined, about 2 minutes. Divide batter between 4 bowls; tint 1 portion blue, second portion green, third portion pink and remaining portion yellow with food coloring. Transfer batters to prepared pans.

2. Bake cakes for 30-35 minutes or until a toothpick inserted in each center comes out clean. Cool in pans 10 minutes before removing to wire racks; remove paper. Cool completely. Using a serrated knife, trim tops of cake layers to be level (save cake scraps for another use). For frosting, in a large bowl, beat confectioners' sugar, butter, vanilla and enough cream to reach desired consistency.

3. Using a 3-in. round cookie cutter, cut a circle out of the center of the blue cake layer and the pink cake layer (save for another use). Place the green layer on a serving plate; spread with 1 cup frosting. Top with the pink layer and ¾ cup frosting. Repeat with blue layer and frosting. Fill center of cake with assorted candies and sprinkles. Top with the yellow cake layer.

4. Spread remaining frosting over top and side of cake. If desired, use additional frosting and sprinkles to decorate. Store in the refrigerator.

1 PIECE: 574 cal., 27g fat (13g sat. fat), 50mg chol., 353mg sod., 84g carb. (71g sugars, 0 fiber), 2g pro.

FLAG CAKE, PAGE 283

Nostalgic Seasonal Sweets

Relive warm childhood memories and create new family customs of your own when you prepare these beloved vintage classics.

Spring

Bring whimsy and joy to your festivities while you
celebrate enduring traditions at the same time.

· ·

EASTER LAMB CAKE

My grandmother started the tradition
of making this molded Easter lamb
cake when I was little. We continue to
make it every Easter. The memory is so
special that I keep the lamb mold in my
kitchen next to my cookbooks as a
decoration. Make sure to grease and
flour the mold really well so that the
cake does not stick.
—*Debra Waggoner, Grand Island, NE*

- -

Prep: 20 min. + standing
Bake: 45 min. + cooling
Makes: 16 servings

- 3 large egg whites
- ½ cup butter, softened
- 1 cup sugar
- 1 tsp. vanilla extract
- 2 cups all-purpose flour
- 2 tsp. baking powder
- ½ tsp. salt
- ¾ cup 2% milk
- ¼ tsp. cream of tartar
  FROSTING
- 1 pkg. (8 oz.) cream cheese,
    softened
- ½ cup butter, softened
- 3¾ to 4 cups confectioners' sugar
- 1 tsp. vanilla extract
    Assorted decorations: Sweetened
    shredded coconut, sprinkles and
    jelly beans

1. Place egg whites in a small bowl;
let stand at room temperature
30 minutes.
2. Meanwhile, preheat oven to 375°.
Thoroughly grease and flour inside of
a 3D lamb cake pan.
3. In a large bowl, cream butter and
sugar until light and fluffy, 5-7 minutes.
Beat in vanilla. In another bowl, sift
flour, baking powder and salt together
twice; add to creamed mixture
alternately with milk, beating well
after each addition.
4. Add cream of tartar to egg whites;
with clean beaters, beat on high speed
just until stiff but not dry. Fold a fourth
of the whites into batter, then fold in
remaining whites.
5. Gently transfer to bottom half of
mold (the bottom half is the face of
the lamb). Place top mold (back of
lamb) on top, interlocking seams
(make sure half with vent hole is on
top to permit steam to escape). Place
on a baking sheet.
6. Bake 45-50 minutes or until a
toothpick inserted in the vent hole
comes out clean. Let cool 15 minutes
before removing to wire rack to cool
completely.
7. For frosting, in a large bowl, beat
cream cheese and butter until smooth.
Gradually beat in confectioners' sugar
and vanilla. Frost cake. Attach
sprinkles for eyes and nose; sprinkle
body with coconut. If desired, decorate
with additional coconut and jelly beans.
1 PIECE: 377 cal., 17g fat (10g sat. fat),
46mg chol., 286mg sod., 54g carb.
(41g sugars, 0 fiber), 4g pro.

EASTER LAMB CAKE TIPS

- **How should I store Easter lamb
cake?** Because of the cream
cheese frosting, we recommend
storing this Easter cake in a
cake dome or keeper in the
refrigerator—it will last for
3-5 days. If you don't have a
dome or keeper, you can create
one by inverting a large bowl over
the cake on a large plate. For the
best taste and texture, remove
the cake from the refrigerator
30 minutes before serving.

- **What variations can I make to
this Easter lamb cake recipe?** To
change up the flavor, replace the
vanilla extract in the frosting with
a different flavor. Here are 3 fun
extracts to try: Coconut extract
will intensify the coconut flavor of
this cake. Lemon extract will add
a bright citrus flavor to this sweet
cake. Pineapple extract pairs well
with the shredded coconut and
will lend a tasty tropical note to
your cake.

- **How can I make this Easter lamb
cake ahead of time?** To make
this Easter lamb cake ahead of
time, you can make the cake
and frosting and freeze them
separately, tightly wrapped or
covered, for up to 1 month. When
you're ready to assemble and
decorate the cake, you'll just need
to thaw the cake and frosting.

CLASSIC PINEAPPLE UPSIDE-DOWN CAKE

A classic recipe like this never goes out of style! It's delicious with the traditional pineapple, but try it with peaches or a combination of cranberries and orange.
—*Bernardine Melton, Paola, KS*

Prep: 20 min. • **Bake:** 30 min. + standing
Makes: 9 servings

- ⅓ cup butter, melted
- ⅔ cup packed brown sugar
- 1 can (20 oz.) sliced pineapple
- ½ cup chopped pecans
- 3 large eggs, separated, room temperature
- 1 cup sugar
- 1 tsp. vanilla extract
- 1 cup all-purpose flour
- 1 tsp. baking powder
- ¼ tsp. salt
- 9 maraschino cherries
  Whipped topping, optional

1. Preheat oven to 375°. In an ungreased 9-in. square baking pan, combine butter and brown sugar. Drain pineapple, reserving ⅓ cup juice. Arrange 9 pineapple slices in a single layer over sugar (refrigerate any remaining slices for another use). Sprinkle pecans over pineapple; set aside.
2. In a large bowl, beat egg yolks until thick and lemon-colored. Gradually add sugar, beating well. Blend in vanilla and reserved pineapple juice. Combine flour, baking powder and salt; add to batter, beating well.
3. In a small bowl with clean beaters, beat egg whites on high speed until stiff peaks form; fold into batter. Spoon into pan.
4. Bake 30-35 minutes or until a toothpick inserted in center comes out clean. Let stand 10 minutes before inverting onto serving plate. Place a cherry in the center of each pineapple slice. If desired, serve with whipped topping.

1 PIECE: 361 cal., 13g fat (5g sat. fat), 88mg chol., 193mg sod., 58g carb. (46g sugars, 2g fiber), 4g pro.
PEACH UPSIDE-DOWN CAKE: Omit the pineapple, pecans and cherries. Drain 1 can (15 oz.) sliced peaches, reserving ⅓ cup juice. Arrange peaches over brown sugar. Substitute reserved peach juice for the pineapple juice.
CRANBERRY ORANGE UPSIDE-DOWN CAKE: Omit the pineapple, pecans and cherries. Sprinkle 1 cup halved fresh or frozen cranberries and 1 chopped peeled orange over brown sugar. Substitute ⅓ cup orange juice for the pineapple juice.

READER REVIEW
"A big hit at a recent dinner party. The cake has a consistency similar to angel food, which allows the full aroma and flavor of pineapple to shine through."
—JOSEPHMALECKI, TASTEOFHOME.COM

Short & Sweet

CHOCOLATE-DIPPED STRAWBERRIES

Plump berries from our strawberry patch turned into a real treat when I dipped them in chocolate! I like to make these before dinner and put them in the fridge so they're ready when we're finished eating.
—*Valerie Gee, Depew, NY*

Takes: 20 min.
Makes: about 9 strawberries

- 1 pint large strawberries
- 4 oz. semisweet chocolate, chopped
- 1 Tbsp. plus ½ tsp. shortening, divided
- 1 oz. white baking chocolate
- 4 drops food coloring, optional

1. Wash strawberries and gently pat with paper towels until completely dry. In a microwave-safe bowl, melt semisweet chocolate and 1 Tbsp. shortening at 50% power; stir until smooth. Dip each strawberry and place on a waxed paper-lined baking sheet. Freeze strawberries for 5 minutes.
2. Meanwhile, microwave white chocolate and remaining shortening at 30% power until melted; stir until smooth. Stir in food coloring if desired. Drizzle over strawberries. Refrigerate until serving.

1 STRAWBERRY: 57 cal., 4g fat (2g sat. fat), 1mg chol., 4mg sod., 6g carb. (5g sugars, 1g fiber), 1g pro.

TRADITIONAL NEW ORLEANS KING CAKE

Get in on the fun of king cake. Hide a little toy baby in the cake. Whoever finds it has one year of good luck!
—*Rebecca Baird, Salt Lake City, UT*

Prep: 40 min. + rising
Bake: 25 min. + cooling
Makes: 1 cake (12 pieces)

- 2 pkg. (¼ oz. each) active dry yeast
- ½ cup warm water (110° to 115°)
- ¾ cup sugar, divided
- ½ cup butter, softened
- ½ cup warm 2% milk (110° to 115°)
- 2 large egg yolks, room temperature
- 1¼ tsp. salt
- 1 tsp. grated lemon zest
- ¼ tsp. ground nutmeg
- 3¼ to 3¾ cups all-purpose flour
- 1 tsp. ground cinnamon
- 1 large egg, beaten

GLAZE
- 1½ cups confectioners' sugar
- 2 tsp. lemon juice
- 2 to 3 Tbsp. water
  Green, purple and yellow sugars

1. In a large bowl, dissolve yeast in warm water. Add ½ cup sugar, butter, milk, egg yolks, salt, lemon zest, nutmeg and 2 cups flour. Beat until smooth. Stir in enough remaining flour to form a soft dough (dough will be sticky).
2. Turn onto a floured surface; knead until smooth and elastic, 6-8 minutes. Place in a greased bowl, turning once to grease the top. Cover and let rise in a warm place until doubled, about 1 hour.
3. Punch dough down. Turn onto a lightly floured surface. Roll into a 16x10-in. rectangle. Combine cinnamon and remaining sugar; sprinkle over dough to within ½ in. of edges. Roll up jelly-roll style, starting with a long side; pinch seam to seal. Place seam side down on a greased baking sheet; pinch ends together to form a ring. Cover and let rise until doubled, about 1 hour. Brush with egg.
4. Bake at 375° for 25-30 minutes or until golden brown. Cool completely on a wire rack. For glaze, combine the confectioners' sugar, lemon juice and enough water to achieve desired consistency. Spread over cake. Sprinkle with colored sugars.

1 PIECE: 321 cal., 9g fat (5g sat. fat), 73mg chol., 313mg sod., 55g carb. (28g sugars, 1g fiber), 5g pro.

SEE US MAKE,
BAKE &
DECORATE IT
Just hover your
camera here.

HIPPITY HOP BUNNY CAKE

This cute, festive cake will have your guests hopping with happiness! Make the cake ahead and add the decorations close to its debut at your party or special occasion.
—Taste of Home *Test Kitchen*

- -

Prep: 2 hours • **Bake:** 30 min. + cooling
Makes: 20 servings

¼	cup sugar
2	tsp. cornstarch
⅛	tsp. salt
½	cup orange juice
2	large egg yolks, beaten
1	Tbsp. unsalted butter
1	tsp. grated orange zest

CAKE

½	cup unsalted butter, softened
1½	cups sugar
4	large egg whites, room temperature
2	tsp. clear vanilla extract
2	tsp. grated orange zest
2¼	cups cake flour
1	Tbsp. baking powder
½	tsp. salt
1	cup 2% milk

BUTTERCREAM

3	oz. white baking chocolate, chopped
2	Tbsp. heavy whipping cream
3	large egg whites, room temperature
¾	cup sugar
¼	tsp. cream of tartar
¼	tsp. salt
1	cup unsalted butter, cubed
1	tsp. clear vanilla extract
1	cup coarse sugar
	Optional bunny decorations: Bright white candy coating, wooden skewers, light cocoa candy coating, pink coarse sugar, sprinkles, red food coloring, white food color paste and small jelly beans

1. To prepare orange curd, in a small saucepan, combine sugar, cornstarch and salt. Stir in orange juice until smooth. Bring to a boil; cook and stir until thickened, 1 minute. Remove from the heat. Stir a small amount of hot mixture into egg yolks; return all to the pan, stirring constantly. Bring to a gentle boil; cook and stir 1 minute longer. Remove from the heat; gently stir in butter and orange zest. Cool to room temperature without stirring. Refrigerate for 1 hour.

2. Preheat oven to 350°. Line bottoms of three 6-in. round baking pans with parchment; grease pans.

3. Cream butter and sugar until light and fluffy, 5-7 minutes. Add egg whites, 1 at a time, beating well after each addition. Beat in vanilla and zest. Combine flour, baking powder and salt; add to creamed mixture alternately with the milk.

4. Transfer batter to prepared pans. Bake 30-35 minutes or until a toothpick inserted in each center comes out clean. Cool in pans 10 minutes before removing to wire racks; remove parchment. Cool completely.

5. Meanwhile, prepare the buttercream by microwaving chocolate and cream in a small microwave-safe bowl until melted, stirring every 30 seconds until smooth. Set aside to cool slightly. In heatproof bowl of stand mixer, whisk egg whites, sugar, cream of tartar and salt until blended. Place over simmering water in a large saucepan over medium heat. Whisking constantly, heat mixture until a thermometer reads 160°, 5-7 minutes.

6. Remove from heat. With whisk attachment of stand mixer, beat on high speed until cooled to 90°, about 5 minutes. Gradually beat in butter, a few Tbsp. at a time, on medium speed until smooth; beat in vanilla and white chocolate mixture.

7. Spread curd between layers. Spread buttercream over top and side of cake; sprinkle coarse sugar over top and side of cake. Decorate with candies to look like a bunny as desired. Store in the refrigerator.

DECORATING TIPS: For ears and bow, pipe melted white candy coating over skewers onto parchment. Sprinkle with plain and pink coarse sugar; refrigerate until set. For eyes and mouth, pipe melted chocolate onto parchment; refrigerate until set. Place on cake. Use pink frosting for cheeks, pink jellybean for nose and sprinkles for freckles. Attach ears and bow, using skewers as picks into the cake.

1 PIECE: 479 cal., 28g fat (17g sat. fat), 93mg chol., 261mg sod., 55g carb. (42g sugars, 0 fiber), 5g pro.

CITRUS CURD

Citrus curd (such as the orange one used in this recipe) became popular in England in the 1800s as a sweet spread for scones and filling for desserts. Made from citrus juice, sugar, eggs, and butter, this smooth and tangy condiment has become a beloved addition to tarts, cakes and tea trays, where it adds a burst of bright flavor.

PACZKI

My mom used to make these when I was growing up. She filled them with raspberry or apricot jam, but prune filling is pretty traditional in Polish and Czech households.
—*Lisa Kaminski, Wauwatosa, WI*

- -

Prep: 35 min. + rising
Cook: 5 min./batch
Makes: 2 dozen

- 1¼ cups sugar, divided
- 1 pkg. (¼ oz.) active dry yeast
- 1 tsp. salt
- 3¼ to 3¾ cups all-purpose flour
- ¾ cup 2% milk
- ¼ cup shortening
- ¼ cup water
- 1 large egg, room temperature
  Oil for deep-fat frying
- 1 cup seedless raspberry jam

1. In a large bowl, mix ¼ cup sugar, yeast, salt and 2 cups flour. In a small saucepan, heat milk, shortening and water to 120°-130°. Add to dry ingredients; beat on medium speed 2 minutes. Add egg; beat on high 2 minutes. Stir in enough remaining flour to form a soft dough (dough will be sticky).

2. Turn the dough onto a floured surface; knead until smooth and elastic, 6-8 minutes. Place in a greased bowl, turning once to grease the top. Cover and let rise in a warm place until doubled, about 1 hour.

3. Punch down dough. Turn onto a lightly floured surface; roll to ½-in. thickness. Cut with a floured 3-in. round cutter. Place 2 in. apart on greased baking sheets. Cover and let rise in a warm place until nearly doubled, about 1 hour.

4. In an electric skillet or deep fryer, heat oil to 375°. Fry doughnuts, a few at a time, until golden brown, 2-3 minutes on each side. Drain on paper towels. Cool slightly; roll in remaining 1 cup sugar.

5. Cut a small hole in the tip of a pastry bag; insert a small pastry tip. Fill bag with jam. With a small knife, pierce a hole into the side of each doughnut; fill with jam.

1 DOUGHNUT: 183 cal., 6g fat (1g sat. fat), 8mg chol., 105mg sod., 30g carb. (17g sugars, 1g fiber), 2g pro.

PICK YOUR PACZKI

Although raspberry is the classic filling flavor, you can mix up the fillings by using blueberry, plum or strawberry jam. Also consider vanilla pastry cream and lemon pie filling. Just be sure your filling doesn't have large bits of fruit, which can clog the pastry tip.

Summertime

And the livin' is easy. Celebrate that school's-out feeling with frosty ice cream creations, star-spangled treats and sweets that pop.

JUICY CHERRY PIE

Cherry season is in the heart of summer. For this pie, choose fresh tart cherries that are bright in color, shiny and plump. They also should feel relatively firm when pressed lightly.
—*Karen Berner, New Canaan, CT*

Prep: 35 min. + chilling
Bake: 55 min. + cooling
Makes: 8 servings

2½ cups all-purpose flour
½ tsp. salt
⅔ cup cold unsalted butter, cubed
⅓ cup shortening
6 to 10 Tbsp. ice water
FILLING
5 cups fresh tart cherries, pitted
2 tsp. lemon juice
¼ tsp. almond extract
1 cup sugar
⅓ cup all-purpose flour
1 tsp. ground cinnamon

SUGAR TOPPING
1 Tbsp. 2% milk
1 tsp. sugar

1. n a large bowl, mix flour and salt; cut in butter and shortening until crumbly. Gradually add ice water, tossing with a fork until dough holds together when pressed. Divide dough in half. Shape each into a disk; wrap. Refrigerate 1 hour or overnight.
2. Preheat oven to 375°. For filling, place cherries in a large bowl; drizzle with lemon juice and almond extract. In a small bowl, mix sugar, flour and cinnamon. Sprinkle over cherries and toss gently to coat.
3. On a lightly floured surface, roll 1 dough portion into a ⅛-in.-thick circle; transfer to a 9-in. pie plate. Trim crust even with rim. Add filling.

4. Roll remaining dough into a ⅛-in.-thick circle; cut out stars or other shapes using cookie cutters. Place top crust over filling. Trim, seal and flute edge. If desired, decorate top with cutouts.
5. Bake 40 minutes. For the topping, brush top of pie with milk; sprinkle with sugar. Bake 15-20 minutes longer or until crust is golden brown and filling is bubbly. Cool on a wire rack.
1 PIECE: 521 cal., 24g fat (12g sat. fat), 41mg chol., 155mg sod., 72g carb. (34g sugars, 3g fiber), 6g pro.

CHOCOLATE-RASPBERRY FONDUE

You don't need a fancy fondue pot to make this melt-in-your-mouth concoction. I serve the dip in my small slow cooker. Folks of all ages love the chocolate-raspberry combination.
—*Heather Maxwell, Fort Riley, KS*

- -

Takes: 20 min. • **Makes:** 5 cups

- 1   pkg. (14 oz.) caramels
- 2   cups semisweet chocolate chips
- 1   can (12 oz.) evaporated milk
- ½   cup butter
- ½   cup seedless raspberry jam
       Frozen pound cake, thawed
       Assorted fresh fruit

1. In a large saucepan, combine the first 5 ingredients. Cook over low heat until the caramels, chips and butter are melted, about 15 minutes. Stir until smooth.
2. Transfer to a 1½-qt. slow cooker or fondue pot. Serve warm with pound cake and fruit.

2 TBSP.: 120 cal., 6g fat (4g sat. fat), 10mg chol., 57mg sod., 16g carb. (15g sugars, 1g fiber), 1g pro.

S'MORE POPS

My daughters and I came up with this treat when planning a candy-making party. The pops also make adorable hostess gifts, are perfect for potlucks, and they would sell out quickly at a bake sale.
—*Lisa Haboush, Geneva, IL*

- -

Takes: 20 min. • **Makes:** 2 dozen

- 4   whole graham crackers, coarsely crushed
- 24   lollipop sticks
- 24   large marshmallows
- 4   oz. milk chocolate candy coating, melted

1. Place crushed crackers in a shallow bowl. Insert 1 lollipop stick into each marshmallow. Dip two-thirds of each marshmallow in melted candy coating; allow excess to drip off. Dip marshmallow in cracker crumbs, covering about half of the chocolate.
2. Place on waxed paper; let stand until set. Store in an airtight container.

1 POP: 42 cal., 1g fat (0 sat. fat), 0 chol., 15mg sod., 8g carb. (6g sugars, 0 fiber), 0 pro.

GO DOTTY

Use your imagination (and what's on hand) to decorate these simple mallow pops. Think about rainbow sprinkles, red, white and blue stars or colored nonpareils (as shown at right).

READER REVIEW

"I am a teacher, and we used this recipe for a camping theme day in my classroom today! I heated up the coating in a small slow cooker at school. We dipped the marshmallows in the chocolate. Next, we rolled them in the crushed graham crackers that I put into cupcake wrappers so that each student had their own. Wow! What a fun activity and a super way to end the school year."
—CMALINOW, TASTEOFHOME.COM

FLAG CAKE
(PICTURED ON PAGE 266)

Get ready to hear oohs and aahs! This stars-and-stripes cake is sure to light up your Fourth of July party or other patriotic celebration.
—Taste of Home *Test Kitchen*

- -

Prep: 1½ hours + chilling
Bake: 35 min. + cooling
Makes: 15 servings

- 1   pkg. French vanilla cake mix (regular size)
- 1   cup buttermilk
- ⅓   cup canola oil
- 4   large eggs

FILLING
- 1   pkg. (3 oz.) berry blue gelatin
- 1½ cups boiling water, divided
- 1   cup cold water, divided
  Ice cubes
- 1   pkg. (3 oz.) strawberry gelatin
- ⅔   cup finely chopped fresh strawberries
- ¼   cup fresh blueberries

FROSTING
- ¾   cup butter, softened
- 2   cups confectioners' sugar
- 1   Tbsp. 2% milk
- 1   jar (7 oz.) marshmallow creme

1. Preheat oven to 350°. Line a 13x9-in. baking pan with parchment paper and grease the paper; set aside. In a large bowl, combine cake mix, buttermilk, oil and eggs; beat on low speed for 30 seconds. Beat on medium for 2 minutes. Pour into prepared pan.
2. Bake cake 35-40 minutes or until a toothpick inserted in the center comes out clean. Cool 10 minutes before removing from pan to a wire rack to cool completely.
3. Transfer cake to a covered cake board. Using a small knife, cut out a 5x4-in. rectangle (½ in. deep) in the top left corner of cake, leaving a ½-in. border along edges of cake. For red stripes, cut out ¾-in. wide rows (½ in. deep), leaving a ½-in. border between stripes and around edges of cake. Using a fork, carefully remove cut-out cake pieces.
4. In a small bowl, dissolve the berry blue gelatin in ¾ cup boiling water. Pour ½ cup cold water into a 2-cup measuring cup; add enough ice cubes to measure 1¼ cups. Stir into gelatin until slightly thickened. Scoop out and discard any remaining ice cubes. Repeat, making strawberry gelatin.

5. In a small bowl, combine strawberries and 1 cup strawberry gelatin. In another bowl, combine blueberries and 1 cup blue gelatin. Refrigerate 20 minutes or just until soft-set. (Save remaining gelatin for another use.)
6. Stir gelatin mixtures. Slowly pour blueberry mixture into rectangle; spoon strawberry mixture into stripes.
7. In a large bowl, beat butter until fluffy; beat in confectioners' sugar and milk until smooth. Add marshmallow creme; beat well until light and fluffy. Spread 1 cup over sides and top edge of cake. Refrigerate remaining frosting 20 minutes.
8. Cut a small hole in the corner of a pastry bag; insert a large star tip. Fill the bag with remaining frosting. Pipe frosting in between rows of strawberry gelatin and around edges of cake. Refrigerate 1-2 hours or until gelatin is set.
1 PIECE: 438 cal., 18g fat (8g sat. fat), 81mg chol., 363mg sod., 67g carb. (51g sugars, 0 fiber), 4g pro.

FIRECRACKER FLOAT

Thanks to Pop Rocks candy, these frozen drinks will literally make your mouth tingle with great flavor!
—Taste of Home *Test Kitchen*

- -

Takes: 5 min. • **Makes:** 1 serving

- 3   scoops vanilla ice cream
- 1   envelope Pop Rocks candy, flavor of your choice
- 1   cup chilled lemon-lime soda

Place a scoop of ice cream in a tall glass; sprinkle with one-third of the candy. Repeat layers twice. Top with soda. Serve immediately.
1 SERVING: 530 cal., 22g fat (13g sat. fat), 87mg chol., 185mg sod., 82g carb. (68g sugars, 0 fiber), 7g pro.

READER REVIEW
"Super cute for Fourth of July! Made this recipe with my nephews expecting it to mainly appeal to their sugar-loving palates. But to my surprise, I really liked it too! Delicious and unexpected!"
—RUNNERGIRLMN, TASTEOFHOME.COM

ANGEL STRAWBERRY DESSERT

This is a wonderful treat when fresh strawberries are readily available. Every time I make this pretty dessert, someone asks for the recipe.
—*Theresa Mathis, Tucker, GA*

Prep: 30 min. + chilling
Makes: 16 servings

- 1½ cups sugar
- 5 Tbsp. cornstarch
- 1 pkg. (3 oz.) strawberry gelatin
- 2 cups water
- 2 lbs. fresh strawberries, divided
- 1 pkg. (8 oz.) cream cheese, softened
- 1 can (14 oz.) sweetened condensed milk
- 1 carton (12 oz.) frozen whipped topping, thawed (4½ cups)
- 1 prepared angel food cake (8 to 10 oz.), cut into 1-in. cubes

1. For glaze, in a large saucepan, combine sugar, cornstarch and gelatin; stir in the water until smooth. Cook and stir over medium-high heat until mixture begins to boil. Cook and stir until thickened, 1-2 minutes longer. Remove from heat; cool completely. Cut half the strawberries into quarters; fold into glaze.
2. In a small bowl, beat cream cheese until smooth. Beat in condensed milk until blended. Fold in whipped topping.
3. In a 4-qt. clear glass bowl, layer half the cake cubes, glaze and cream mixture. Repeat layers. Cut remaining strawberries in half and arrange over the top. Cover and refrigerate for at least 2 hours or overnight.

1 CUP: 344 cal., 11g fat (8g sat. fat), 24mg chol., 202mg sod., 57g carb. (43g sugars, 1g fiber), 5g pro.

ALL-AMERICAN BANANA SPLIT

In 1904, the first banana split recipe was made here in Latrobe, Pennsylvania, by David Strickler, an apprentice pharmacist at a local drug store. We still use his original formula when we make banana splits in our restaurants.
—*Melissa Blystone, Latrobe, PA*

Takes: 5 min. • **Makes:** 1 serving

- 1 medium banana, peeled and split lengthwise
- 1 scoop each vanilla, chocolate and strawberry ice cream
- 2 Tbsp. sliced fresh strawberries or 1 Tbsp. strawberry ice cream topping
- 2 Tbsp. pineapple chunks or 1 Tbsp. pineapple ice cream topping
- 2 Tbsp. whipped cream
- 1 Tbsp. chopped peanuts
- 1 Tbsp. chocolate syrup
- 2 maraschino cherries with stems

Place banana in a dessert dish; place scoops of ice cream between banana. Top with remaining ingredients. Serve immediately.
1 SERVING: 710 cal., 31g fat (17g sat. fat), 88mg chol., 184mg sod., 107g carb. (68g sugars, 6g fiber), 11g pro.

BANANA SPLIT TIPS

- **Can you serve a banana split in a different type of dish?** If you don't have a banana split dish at home, you're not alone! If you don't have a similar dish to use, you could simply slice up the banana even further so that the sundae will fit into a regular bowl.

- **How can you make a banana split your own?** While classic banana splits use scoops of chocolate, vanilla and strawberry, you can be as creative with the ice cream flavors as you'd like. Consider peanut butter, cookie dough and dulce de leche ice creams. For toppings, try salted caramel sauce, strawberry syrup, mini Oreo cookies, chopped peanut butter cups and raspberries.

CINNAMON STARS

These cookies are such a hit with my family. A few always seem to disappear before I can finish them! They're nice for any occasion.
—*Flo Burtnett, Gage, OK*

Prep: 25 min. + chilling
Bake: 10 min. + cooling
Makes: 2½ dozen

- 2 cups all-purpose flour
- 1 cup sugar
- 1 tsp. ground cinnamon
- ¾ tsp. baking powder
- ¼ tsp. salt
- ½ cup cold butter, cubed
- 1 large egg, room temperature, lightly beaten
- ¼ cup 2% milk

GLAZE/FILLING

- 2 cups confectioners' sugar
- ½ tsp. vanilla extract
- 2 to 3 Tbsp. 2% milk
  Colored sugar, optional
- ⅔ cup raspberry, strawberry or apricot jam

1. In a medium bowl, combine flour, sugar, cinnamon, baking powder and salt. Cut in butter until crumbly. Combine egg and milk; add to flour mixture and stir just until moistened. Cover and chill at least 1 hour.
2. On a lightly floured surface, roll dough to ⅛-in. thickness. With a 3-in. cookie cutter dipped in flour, cut out 60 cookies. Place on ungreased baking sheets. Bake at 375° for 7-9 minutes or until edges are lightly browned. Remove to a wire rack; cool completely.
3. For glaze, combine confectioners' sugar, vanilla extract and enough milk to achieve a spreading consistency. Spread on half of the cookies; sprinkle with colored sugar if desired. Let stand until set. Place 1 tsp. jam on the unglazed cookies and top each with a glazed cookie.
1 SANDWICH COOKIE: 137 cal., 3g fat (2g sat. fat), 15mg chol., 60mg sod., 26g carb. (19g sugars, 0 fiber), 1g pro.

WATERMELON BOMBE DESSERT

When cut, this sherbet dessert looks like actual watermelon slices—complete with seeds! It is fun to eat and refreshing too.
—*Renae Moncur, Burley, ID*

Prep: 20 min. + freezing
Makes: 8 servings

- About 1 pint lime sherbet
- About 1 pint pineapple sherbet
- About 1½ pints raspberry sherbet
- ¼ cup miniature semisweet chocolate chips

1. Line a 1½-qt. bowl with plastic wrap. Press a thin layer of lime sherbet around the inside of bowl. Freeze, uncovered, until firm. Spread a thin layer of pineapple sherbet evenly over lime sherbet layer. Freeze, uncovered, until firm. Pack raspberry sherbet in center of sherbet-lined bowl. Smooth the top to resemble a cut watermelon.
2. Cover and freeze until firm, about 8 hours. Just before serving, uncover bowl of molded sherbet. Place a serving plate on the bowl and invert. Remove bowl and peel off plastic wrap.
3. Cut the bombe into wedges; press a few chocolate chips into the raspberry section of each wedge to resemble watermelon seeds.

1 PIECE: 205 cal., 4g fat (2g sat. fat), 8mg chol., 60mg sod., 43g carb. (35g sugars, 0 fiber), 2g pro.

SAVE A STEP

You could fold the chocolate "seeds" into the raspberry sorbet before adding to the bombe and freezing it if desired. The frozen chips will be hard and cold to bite into, though, so definitely use miniature ones.

READER REVIEW
"This is so easy to make, delicious and refreshing. And it really does look like the picture!"
—LKERSEN, TASTEOFHOME.COM

Fall

Time to bring back yesteryear's Halloween staples: crisp caramel apples and crunchy popcorn balls. Cozy up to spices, pumpkin and maple too.

• •

EASY PUMPKIN PIE

Pumpkin pie does not have to be difficult to make. This recipe has a wonderful taste and will be a hit at your holiday meal.
—*Marty Rummel, Trout Lake, WA*

Prep: 10 min. • **Bake:** 50 min. + cooling
Makes: 8 servings

  3   large eggs
  1   cup canned pumpkin
  1   cup evaporated milk
  ½ cup sugar
  ¼ cup maple syrup
  1   tsp. ground cinnamon
  ½ tsp. salt
  ½ tsp. ground nutmeg
  ½ tsp. maple flavoring
  ½ tsp. vanilla extract
  1   frozen deep-dish pie crust (9 in.)
  1   sheet refrigerated pie crust, optional
      Whipped cream, optional

1. In a large bowl, beat the first 10 ingredients until smooth; pour into the pie crust. Cover edge loosely with foil.

2. Bake at 400° for 10 minutes. Reduce heat to 350°; bake 40-45 minutes longer or until a knife inserted in the center comes out clean. Remove foil. Cool on a wire rack.

3. If decorative cutouts are desired, roll pie crust to ⅛-in. thickness; cut out with 1-in. to 1½-in. leaf-shaped cookie cutters. With a sharp knife, score leaf veins on cutouts.

4. Place on an ungreased baking sheet. Bake at 400° for 6-8 minutes or until golden brown. Remove to a wire rack to cool. Arrange around edge of pie. Garnish with whipped cream if desired.

1 PIECE: 275 cal., 11g fat (5g sat. fat), 94mg chol., 306mg sod., 38g carb. (24g sugars, 1g fiber), 6g pro.

READER REVIEW

"I enjoyed this way more than traditional pumpkin pie as did my children. The maple syrup gave it a mildly sweeter taste. I will be using this recipe again. I did not put the extra crust shapes on top but topped it with whipped cream instead."
—PAJAMAANGEL, TASTEOFHOME.COM

TRADITIONAL
POPCORN BALLS

CHECK OUT
HOW EASY
THIS IS
Just hover your
camera here.

STICKY BUN ICE CREAM

This creamy homemade cinnamon ice cream has a rich caramel swirl and chunks of cinnamon buns. Serve the extra caramel sauce over this or other ice cream or pound cake.
—Taste of Home *Test Kitchen*

- -

Prep: 35 min. + chilling
Process: 20 min./batch + freezing
Makes: 2¼ qt.

- 1¾ cups whole milk
- ⅔ cup plus 2 cups sugar, divided
- 2 large eggs, beaten
- 3 cups heavy whipping cream, divided
- 2 tsp. ground cinnamon
- 1 tsp. vanilla extract
- 1 cup butter, cubed
- ½ cup water
- 1 Tbsp. corn syrup
- 2 baked cinnamon buns, cubed
- 9 Tbsp. chopped pecans, toasted

1. In a large heavy saucepan, heat milk and ⅔ cup sugar until bubbles form around side of pan. Whisk a small amount of hot mixture into eggs; return all to the pan, whisking constantly. Cook and stir over low heat until mixture reaches at least 160° and coats the back of a spoon.

2. Remove from the heat. Quickly transfer to a bowl; place in ice water and stir for 2 minutes. Stir in 2 cups cream, cinnamon and vanilla. Press waxed paper onto surface of custard. Refrigerate for several hours or overnight.

3. For caramel, combine the butter, water and corn syrup in a heavy saucepan. Cook and stir over medium-low heat until butter is melted. Add the remaining sugar; cook and stir until sugar is dissolved.

4. Bring to a boil over medium heat without stirring. Boil for 4 minutes without stirring. Continue to boil for 12-15 minutes, stirring constantly or until mixture is caramel-colored.

Remove from the heat. Carefully stir in remaining cream until smooth; set aside to cool.

5. Fill cylinder of an ice cream maker two-thirds full; freeze according to the manufacturer's directions. Refrigerate remaining mixture until ready to freeze.

6. In a large freezer container, layer a third of the ice cream, ½ cup caramel, ⅔ cup cinnamon buns and 3 Tbsp. pecans. Repeat two times. Swirl mixture; freeze until firm. Serve with remaining caramel.

½ CUP ICE CREAM WITH ABOUT 1 TBSP. SAUCE: 425 cal., 30g fat (17g sat. fat), 108mg chol., 160mg sod., 39g carb. (34g sugars, 1g fiber), 3g pro.

TRADITIONAL POPCORN BALLS

Sink your teeth into an old-fashioned popcorn ball and feel like a kid again. You'll find that one batch of this goes a long way.
—*Cathy Karges, Hazen, ND*

- -

Takes: 20 min. • **Makes:** 20 servings

- 7 qt. popped popcorn
- 1 cup sugar
- 1 cup light corn syrup
- ¼ cup water
- ¼ tsp. salt
- 3 Tbsp. butter
- 1 tsp. vanilla extract
  Food coloring, optional

1. Place popcorn in a large baking pan; keep warm in a 200° oven.

2. In a heavy saucepan, combine the sugar, corn syrup, water and salt. Cook over medium heat until a candy thermometer reads 235° (soft-ball stage).

3. Remove from the heat. Add butter, vanilla and, if desired, food coloring; stir until butter is melted. Immediately pour over the popcorn and stir until evenly coated.

4. When mixture is cool enough to handle, quickly shape into 3-in. balls, dipping hands in cold water as needed to prevent sticking.

1 POPCORN BALL: 177 cal., 6g fat (2g sat. fat), 5mg chol., 203mg sod., 31g carb. (18g sugars, 2g fiber), 1g pro.

POPCORN BALLS TIPS

- **Why won't my popcorn balls stick together?** First, the syrup must be brought to the proper temperature of 235°F, as the recipe indicates. The popcorn mixture must be kept warm so the syrup adheres well to it, so work quickly and confidently. If it gets too cool, put the mixture in a slow (barely warm) oven to gently warm it up.

- **What else can I add to popcorn balls?** Mix in crushed Oreo cookies and drizzle with white chocolate for a cookies-and-cream version. Or add chopped salted peanuts, candy corn, M&M's minis or other candies.

CARAMEL APPLES

Who doesn't love a good, gooey caramel apple? Make a double batch because these treats always go fast!
—*Karen Ann Bland, Gove, KS*

- -

Prep: 10 min. • **Cook:** 30 min.
Makes: 16 servings (8 apples)

1   cup butter
2   cups packed brown sugar
1   cup light corn syrup
1   can (14 oz.) sweetened
    condensed milk
1   tsp. vanilla extract
8   wooden sticks
8   medium tart apples
    Unsalted peanuts, chopped,
    optional

1. In a heavy 3-qt. saucepan, combine butter, brown sugar, corn syrup and milk; bring to a boil over medium-high heat. Cook and stir until mixture reaches 248° (firm-ball stage) on a candy thermometer, 30-40 minutes. Remove from the heat; stir in vanilla.
2. Insert wooden sticks into apples. Dip each apple into hot caramel mixture; turn to coat. Set on waxed paper to cool. If desired, roll the bottoms of the dipped apples into chopped peanuts.
½ APPLE: 388 cal., 14g fat (9g sat. fat), 39mg chol., 145mg sod., 68g carb. (65g sugars, 2g fiber), 2g pro.

MAKE IT YOUR OWN

- **Pick your own apple (variety).**
  Feel free to use whatever apple you prefer for eating. Granny Smiths are a traditional option if you want more tartness and a good crunch. We also love Gala apples for their sweet flavor.

- **Roll on the toppings**. You don't have to limit yourself to plain caramel! After dipping, while the caramel is still sticky, roll the apples in nuts, sprinkles or candies. You can also drizzle them with melted chocolate. If you like salty with your sweet, sprinkle a little sea salt on top when the caramel is just about set.

MAPLE NUT TRUFFLES

Let the kids help you roll these simple no-bake treats. They make wonderful gifts, and you only need five ingredients.
—*Rebekah Radewahn, Wauwatosa, WI*

Prep: 25 min. + chilling
Makes: 2½ dozen

- 1½ cups semisweet chocolate chips
- 4 oz. cream cheese, softened
- 1½ cups confectioners' sugar
- ¾ tsp. maple flavoring
- 1 cup chopped walnuts

1. In a small microwave-safe bowl, melt chocolate chips. Set aside to cool. In another bowl, beat cream cheese and confectioners' sugar until smooth. Add melted chocolate and maple flavoring; beat until well blended. Cover and refrigerate for 15 minutes or until firm enough to handle.

2. Shape into 1-in. balls; roll in the walnuts. Store in an airtight container in the refrigerator.

1 TRUFFLE: 103 cal., 6g fat (2g sat. fat), 4mg chol., 12mg sod., 12g carb. (10g sugars, 1g fiber), 2g pro.

Short & Sweet

PUMPKIN COOKIE POPS

These cookie pops are a great way to get in the spirit of Halloween. They're fun but not too spooky.
—*Taste of Home Test Kitchen*

Prep: 1 hour
Bake: 15 min./batch + standing
Makes: 2½ dozen

- ½ cup butter, softened
- ¾ cup packed brown sugar
- ½ cup sugar
- 1 large egg, room temperature
- 1 tsp. vanilla extract
- 1 cup canned pumpkin
- 2½ cups all-purpose flour
- 1 tsp. baking powder
- 1 tsp. baking soda
- 1 tsp. ground cinnamon
- 30 wooden pop sticks
- ⅓ cup green gumdrops, halved lengthwise

ICING

- 4 cups confectioners' sugar
- 3 Tbsp. meringue powder
- 5 Tbsp. water
    Green and orange paste or gel food coloring

1. In a large bowl, cream the butter and sugars until light and fluffy, 5-7 minutes. Beat in egg and vanilla. Beat in pumpkin. Combine the flour, baking powder, baking soda and cinnamon; gradually add to creamed mixture and mix well (dough will be soft).

2. Drop dough by 2 tablespoonfuls 2 in. apart onto greased or parchment-lined baking sheets. Insert sticks into dough. Insert a gumdrop piece into the top of each for the pumpkin stem.

3. Bake at 350° 14-16 minutes or until set and lightly browned around the edges. Remove to wire racks to cool.

4. For icing, in a large bowl, combine confectioners' sugar, meringue power and water until smooth. Remove ½ cup to another bowl; cover and set aside. Stir orange food coloring into remaining icing. Spread or pipe over cookies. Let stand for 30 minutes or until icing is set and dry.

5. Tint reserved icing with green food coloring; use colored icing to pipe leaves and vines.

1 COOKIE: 147 cal., 3g fat (2g sat. fat), 14mg chol., 88mg sod., 28g carb. (19g sugars, 1g fiber), 1g pro.

CHOCOLATE CANDY CORN CUPCAKES

My oldest son asks me to make these cupcakes every year for his class Halloween party. I always get lots of compliments about how tasty and cute these treats are.

—*Nicole Clayton, Prescott, AZ*

Prep: 25 min. • **Bake:** 20 min. + cooling
Makes: 2 dozen

- 1   pkg. fudge marble cake mix (regular size)
- 1   cup sour cream
- 2   large eggs
- ½   cup 2% milk
- ⅓   cup canola oil
     Orange paste food coloring
- 1   carton (8 oz.) frozen whipped topping, thawed
     Chocolate candy corn

1. Line 24 muffin cups with paper liners.

2. Reserve cocoa packet from cake mix. In a large bowl, combine cake mix, sour cream, eggs, milk and oil; beat on low speed for 30 seconds. Beat on medium for 2 minutes. Transfer half of the batter to a small bowl; tint with orange food coloring. To other half of batter, stir in contents of cocoa packet.

3. Divide chocolate batter among prepared cups. Carefully top with orange batter; do not swirl. Bake and cool as package directs.

4. To serve, top cupcakes with whipped topping and candy corn. Refrigerate leftovers.

1 CUPCAKE: 163 cal., 9g fat (4g sat. fat), 18mg chol., 113mg sod., 18g carb. (10g sugars, 1g fiber), 2g pro.

FOOTBALL CAKE POPS

My son loves football! For his eighth birthday, I made cake pops with a rich chocolate cake center and a yummy peanut butter coating. These are sure to be winners at parties, bake sales and sports-watching events.

—*Jenny Dubinsky, Inwood, WV*

Prep: 2 hours + chilling
Bake: 35 min. + cooling
Makes: 4 dozen cake pops

- 1   chocolate cake mix (regular size)
- 1   cup cream cheese frosting
- 1   cup dark chocolate chips
- 1   cup peanut butter chips
- 1   Tbsp. shortening
- 48 4-in. lollipop sticks
- ¼   cup white decorating icing

1. Bake cake according to package directions; cool completely. In a large bowl, break cake into fine crumbles. Add frosting and stir until fully incorporated, adding more frosting if needed, until mixture maintains its shape when squeezed together with palm of hand. Shape 1 Tbsp. into a ball, then mold into the shape of a football. Repeat with remaining mixture. Place on parchment-lined baking sheets; refrigerate until firm, about 30 minutes.

2. Meanwhile, place chocolate chips, peanut butter chips and shortening in a microwave-safe bowl. Microwave for 30 seconds and stir; repeat, stirring every 30 seconds until melted and smooth, adding more shortening if needed. Do not overheat.

3. Dip a lollipop stick into chocolate mixture; insert halfway through a football shape, taking care not to break through the other side. Return to baking sheet until set; repeat to form remaining cake pops. Coat each cake pop with the chocolate mixture, allowing excess to drip off; reheat and stir chocolate mixture as needed. Return cake pops to baking sheets, ensuring they do not touch one another. Allow chocolate coating to set until firm to the touch. To decorate, use icing to draw laces onto cake pops.

1 CAKE POP: 132 cal., 7g fat (3g sat. fat), 12mg chol., 96mg sod., 17g carb. (12g sugars, 1g fiber), 2g pro.

BEST CINNAMON ROLLS

Surprise a neighbor with a batch of oven-fresh cinnamon rolls slathered in cream cheese frosting. These breakfast treats make Christmas morning or any special occasion even more memorable.

—*Shenai Fisher, Topeka, KS*

- -

Prep: 40 min. + rising • **Bake:** 20 min.
Makes: 16 rolls

1	pkg. (¼ oz.) active dry yeast
1	cup warm 2% milk (110° to 115°)
½	cup sugar
⅓	cup butter, melted
2	large eggs, room temperature
1	tsp. salt
4	to 4½ cups all-purpose flour

FILLING
¾	cup packed brown sugar
2	Tbsp. ground cinnamon
¼	cup butter, melted, divided

FROSTING
½	cup butter, softened
¼	cup cream cheese, softened
½	tsp. vanilla extract
⅛	tsp. salt
1½	cups confectioners' sugar

1. Dissolve yeast in warm milk. In another bowl, combine sugar, butter, eggs, salt, yeast mixture and 2 cups flour; beat on medium speed until smooth. Stir in enough remaining flour to form a soft dough (dough will be sticky).

2. Turn dough onto a floured surface; knead 6-8 minutes or until smooth and elastic. Place in a greased bowl, turning once to grease the top. Cover and let rise in a warm place until doubled, about 1 hour.

3. Mix brown sugar and cinnamon. Punch down dough; divide in half. On a lightly floured surface, roll 1 portion into an 11x8-in. rectangle. Brush with 2 Tbsp. butter; sprinkle with half the brown sugar mixture to within ½ in. of edges. Roll up jelly-roll style, starting with a long side; pinch seam to seal.

Cut into 8 slices; place in a greased 13x9-in. pan, cut side down. Cover with a kitchen towel. Repeat with remaining dough and filling. Let rise in a warm place until doubled, about 1 hour. Preheat oven to 350°.

4. Bake 20-25 minutes or until golden brown. Cool on wire racks.

5. For frosting, beat butter, cream cheese, vanilla and salt until blended; gradually beat in confectioners' sugar. Spread over tops. Refrigerate leftover cinnamon rolls.

1 ROLL: 364 cal., 15g fat (9g sat. fat), 66mg chol., 323mg sod., 53g carb. (28g sugars, 1g fiber), 5g pro.

CINNAMON ROLL TIPS

- **How do you know when dough is kneaded enough?** You want to knead the dough until it is smooth and elastic. One trick to tell if your dough is done is to press it with your finger. If the indentation stays, the dough still needs more work. If it springs back to its original shape, your dough is ready to rest.

- **Why didn't my cinnamon rolls rise?** In general, sweet doughs take longer to rise because the liquid that feeds the yeast is absorbed by the sugar. To counteract this, be sure you allow sweet doughs, like cinnamon rolls, plenty of time to rise. Also, when kneading the dough, don't add too much flour. Doing so creates a tough, dry dough, which causes the yeast to not work properly.

- **Can I prep and freeze cinnamon rolls in advance?** Yes! To freeze unbaked rolls, cut as directed but don't allow to rise. Tightly cover and freeze in a single layer for up to 2 weeks. When ready to use, thaw in the fridge overnight. The next morning, bring the pan of rolls to room temperature and allow it to rise until doubled in size. Bake as directed.

GOURMET CARAMEL APPLES

These drizzled confections look fancy and taste over-the-top yummy. With peanut butter flavor and a salty burst, they'll be the treats you can't wait to make each year.
—Taste of Home *Test Kitchen*

Prep: 20 min. + standing
Makes: 8 servings

- 4   large tart apples
- 4   wooden pop sticks
- 1   cup milk chocolate chips
- 1   cup semisweet chocolate chips
- 4½ oz. white candy coating, coarsely chopped
- 1   tsp. shortening
- 1   pkg. (11 oz.) Kraft caramel bits
- 2   Tbsp. water
- 4   pretzel rods, coarsely crushed
- ½   cup Reese's Pieces

1. Line a baking sheet with waxed paper and grease the paper; set aside. Wash and thoroughly dry apples. Insert a pop stick into the top of each; set aside.

2. Place chocolate chips in separate microwave-safe bowls. Heat in a microwave until melted; stir until smooth. In another microwave-safe bowl, melt candy coating and shortening; stir until smooth.

3. Combine caramels and water in another microwave-safe bowl. Heat in a microwave until melted; stir until smooth. Dip apples into caramel; turn to coat. Immediately press pretzels and Reese's Pieces into sides of apples. Drizzle melted chocolate and candy coating over tops. Place on prepared pan; let stand until set.

½ APPLE: 589 cal., 26g fat (17g sat. fat), 5mg chol., 258mg sod., 93g carb. (78g sugars, 5g fiber), 5g pro.

PETER PETER PUMPKIN BARS

These wonderful bars will satisfy any sweet tooth. They have a delicious orange frosting and can be decorated with candy pumpkins.
—*Barb Schlafer, Appleton, WI*

Prep: 20 min. • **Bake:** 20 min. + cooling
Makes: 2 dozen

- ½   cup shortening
- 1   cup packed brown sugar
- 2   large eggs, room temperature
- ⅔   cup canned pumpkin
- 1   tsp. vanilla extract
- 1   cup all-purpose flour
- 1   tsp. ground cinnamon
- ½   tsp. baking powder
- ½   tsp. baking soda
- ¼   tsp. ground ginger
- ¼   tsp. ground nutmeg
- ½   cup chopped walnuts

ORANGE FROSTING
- 3   Tbsp. shortening
- 2¼ cups confectioners' sugar
- 3   Tbsp. orange juice
- 1   Tbsp. grated orange zest
    Optional: Orange and green frosting or candy pumpkins

1. In a large bowl, cream shortening and brown sugar until light and fluffy, 5-7 minutes. Add eggs, 1 at a time, beating well after each addition. Beat in pumpkin and vanilla. Combine the flour, cinnamon, baking powder, baking soda, ginger and nutmeg; add to the creamed mixture and mix well. Stir in walnuts.

2. Spread into a greased 13x9-in. baking dish. Bake at 350° until a toothpick inserted in center comes out clean, 20-25 minutes. Cool on a wire rack.

3. In a large bowl, beat the shortening, confectioners' sugar, orange juice and zest until blended. Frost bars; cut into squares. If desired, decorate bars with colored frosting or top with candy pumpkins.

1 BAR: 174 cal., 7g fat (2g sat. fat), 18mg chol., 44mg sod., 25g carb. (20g sugars, 1g fiber), 2g pro.

Winter

Vintage cookies, classic cakes and old-fashioned pastries make the most wonderful time of the year even better.

• •

HOLIDAY DANISH PUFFS

It's worth the extra effort to make this delightful candy cane-shaped dessert. Best of all, the recipe makes two pastries, so it's perfect for gift-giving.
—*Susan Garoutte, Georgetown, TX*

- -

Prep: 45 min. • **Bake:** 1 hour + cooling
Makes: 2 pastries (8 servings each)

  1   cup all-purpose flour
  ½   cup cold butter, cubed
  2   to 3 Tbsp. cold water
TOPPING
  1   cup water
  ½   cup butter, cubed
  ¼   tsp. salt
  1   cup all-purpose flour
  3   large eggs
  ½   tsp. almond extract
FROSTING
  1½   cups confectioners' sugar
  2   Tbsp. butter, softened
  2   Tbsp. water
  1½   tsp. vanilla extract
  ½   cup sliced almonds, toasted

1. Place flour in a small bowl; cut in butter until crumbly. Gradually add water, tossing with a fork until dough holds together when pressed. Divide dough in half. On a lightly floured surface, roll each into a 14x2½-in. rectangle. Transfer to an ungreased baking sheet; curve 1 end of each pastry to form tops of canes. Refrigerate while preparing topping.
2. Preheat oven to 350°. In a large saucepan, combine water, butter and salt; bring to a rolling boil. Add flour all at once and beat until blended. Cook over medium heat, stirring vigorously until mixture pulls away from side of pan and forms a ball. Remove from heat; let stand 5 minutes.
3. Add eggs, 1 at a time, beating well after each addition until smooth. Add extract; continue beating until mixture is smooth and shiny. Spread over pastry dough.
4. Bake 60-70 minutes or until puffed and golden brown. Cool on pans 10 minutes before removing to wire racks; cool completely.
5. In a small bowl, beat confectioners' sugar, butter, water and extract until smooth. Spread over pastries; sprinkle with almonds. Refrigerate leftovers.
NOTE: To toast nuts, bake in a shallow pan in a 350°; oven for 5-10 minutes or cook in a skillet over low heat until lightly browned, stirring occasionally.
1 PIECE: 247 cal., 15g fat (9g sat. fat), 69mg chol., 154mg sod., 24g carb. (11g sugars, 1g fiber), 4g pro.

EASY DOES IT
1. After shaping the dough into a 14x2½-in. rectangle, slightly curve the top to form a candy cane shape; place in the refrigerator.

2. Once you have prepared the almond-flavored topping on the stovetop, carefully spread the topping over the pastry. An offset spatula works great!

3. Bake as directed. The topping is similar to cream puff dough and will puff up dramatically in the oven. Cool completely before decorating.

SWEDISH SPICE CUTOUTS

My sister, Judith, brought this recipe with her when she came to the United States from Sweden in 1928.
—*Lilly Decker, Clancy, MT*

Prep: 25 min. + chilling
Bake: 10 min./batch + cooling
Makes: about 4 dozen

- 1 cup butter, softened
- 1¾ cups packed dark brown sugar
- 1 large egg, room temperature
- ¼ cup dark corn syrup
- ¼ cup molasses
- 4½ cups all-purpose flour
- 1¼ tsp. ground cinnamon
- 1 tsp. baking soda
- ¾ tsp. ground cloves
  Optional: Slivered almonds and frosting of choice

1. In a large bowl, cream butter and brown sugar until light and fluffy, 5-7 minutes. Beat in the egg, corn syrup and molasses. Combine the flour, cinnamon, baking soda and cloves; gradually add to creamed mixture and mix well. Cover and refrigerate for 4 hours or until easy to handle.
2. Preheat the oven to 375°. On a lightly floured surface, roll dough to ⅛-in. thickness. Cut with floured 4-in. cookie cutters. Place 1 in. apart on ungreased baking sheets. Top with almonds if desired or leave plain.
3. Bake at 375° for 8-10 minutes or until edges are lightly browned. Remove to wire racks to cool. Frost cookies if desired.

1 COOKIE: 119 cal., 4g fat (2g sat. fat), 14mg chol., 64mg sod., 19g carb. (10g sugars, 0 fiber), 1g pro.

CHOCOLATE RUM BALLS

Roll these truffle-like rum balls in crushed Oreos to get just the right amount of crunch. I've been known to freeze them for emergencies.
—*Dauna Harwood, Elkhart, IN*

Prep: 30 min. + chilling
Makes: about 3 dozen

- 1 tsp. instant coffee granules
- ¼ cup dark rum, warmed
- 4 oz. cream cheese, softened
- 1 cup confectioners' sugar
- 1 cup ground almonds
- 3 oz. unsweetened chocolate, melted
- 8 Oreo cookies, finely crushed

1. Dissolve coffee granules in warm rum. Beat the cream cheese, confectioners' sugar, almonds and rum mixture until blended. Stir in melted chocolate. Refrigerate until firm enough to roll, about 1 hour.
2. Shape mixture into 1-in. balls; roll in crushed cookies. Store rum balls in an airtight container in the refrigerator, separating layers with waxed paper.

1 RUM BALL: 70 cal., 4g fat (2g sat. fat), 3mg chol., 21mg sod., 7g carb. (5g sugars, 1g fiber), 1g pro.

TO MAKE AHEAD: Rum balls can be made 3 days in advance. Store in an airtight container in the refrigerator.

TIME-SAVING TIP

To save time and get great results, use your food processor to grind the almonds. After emptying the bowl, use the processor next to finely grind the Oreo cookies. No need to wash in between.

CHRISTMAS LIGHTS
COOKIES, PAGE 308

ALMOND
CUSTARD CAKE

ALMOND CUSTARD CAKE

This white cake pairs well with all sorts of frostings and fillings, but the chocolate frosting in this recipe is one of my favorites. Pressed for time? Add 1/2 tsp. of almond extract to a white cake mix instead.
—*Diane Shipley, Mentor, OH*

- -

Prep: 1 hour + chilling
Bake: 25 min. + cooling
Makes: 12 servings

CHOCOLATE FROSTING
- 1 cup (6 oz.) semisweet chocolate chips
- ½ cup half-and-half cream
- ¼ cup butter, cubed
- 2½ cups sifted confectioners' sugar

CAKE
- 4 large egg whites
- ½ cup shortening
- 1½ cups sugar, divided
- 1 tsp. vanilla extract
- 1 tsp. almond extract
- 2½ cups cake flour
- 3 tsp. baking powder
- 1 tsp. salt
- 1 cup plus 2 Tbsp. whole milk

CUSTARD
- ⅓ cup sugar
- 2 Tbsp. all-purpose flour
- ⅛ tsp. salt
- ¾ cup whole milk
- 1 large egg, lightly beaten
- ½ tsp. vanilla extract
- ¼ tsp. almond extract
- ½ cup chopped almonds, toasted

OPTIONAL DECORATIONS
-     Christmas Lights Cookies (recipe on page 308) or decorated cookies of your choice
-     Green frosting

1. For frosting, in a small saucepan, heat chocolate chips, half-and-half cream and butter over medium-low heat, stirring until blended. Transfer to a large bowl; gradually beat in the confectioners' sugar until smooth. Cool to room temperature, stirring occasionally. Transfer to a covered container; refrigerate until cold or overnight.

2. For cake, place egg whites in a large bowl; let stand at room temperature 30 minutes. Preheat oven to 375°. Line bottoms of 2 greased 9-in. round baking pans with parchment; grease paper.

3. In a large bowl, cream shortening and 1 cup sugar until light and fluffy, 5-7 minutes. Beat in the extracts. In another bowl, whisk cake flour, baking powder and salt; add to creamed mixture alternately with milk, beating well after each addition.

4. With clean beaters, beat egg whites on medium speed until soft peaks form. Gradually add remaining sugar, 1 Tbsp. at a time, beating on high after each addition until sugar is dissolved. Continue beating until stiff glossy peaks form. Fold into batter.

5. Transfer batter to prepared pans. Bake 25-30 minutes or until a toothpick inserted in center comes out clean. Cool cakes in pans 10 minutes before removing to wire racks; remove paper. Cool completely.

6. For custard, in a small heavy saucepan, mix sugar, all-purpose flour and salt. Whisk in milk. Cook and stir over medium heat until thickened and bubbly. Reduce heat to low; cook and stir 2 minutes longer. Remove from the heat.

7. In a small bowl, whisk a small amount of hot mixture into egg; return all to pan, whisking constantly. Bring to a gentle boil; cook and stir 2 minutes. Remove from heat. Cool 15 minutes, stirring occasionally. Transfer to a small bowl; stir in extracts and almonds. Press plastic wrap onto surface of custard. Refrigerate until cold.

8. To assemble cake, in a large bowl, beat cold frosting until fluffy and spreadable. Cut a small hole in the tip of a pastry bag; fill bag with ⅓ cup frosting.

9. Place 1 cake layer on a serving plate. Pipe a border of frosting along edge of cake. Fill center with custard. Top with remaining cake layer. Frost top and side with remaining frosting. If desired, decorate with cookies and pipe with green frosting. Refrigerate until serving.

NOTE: To toast nuts, bake in a shallow pan in a 350°; oven for 5-10 minutes or cook in a skillet over low heat until lightly browned, stirring occasionally.

1 PIECE: 580 cal., 22g fat (9g sat. fat), 36mg chol., 395mg sod., 91g carb., 2g fiber, 8g pro.

TO FROST CAKE WITH WHITE FROSTING: Prepare chocolate frosting as directed, substituting 1 cup white baking chips for semisweet chocolate chips and increasing confectioners' sugar to 3½ cups.

PEANUT BUTTER CHOCOLATE MELTAWAYS

Short & Sweet

People are amazed how easy it is to make these impressive-looking chocolate peanut butter cup candies. The recipe makes a big batch for you to share.
—*Darcie Vezzi, MacDonald, PA*

Prep: 20 min. + chilling
Makes: about 4 dozen

1 pkg. (10 to 13 oz.) white baking chips
1 cup semisweet chocolate chips
1 cup creamy peanut butter
2 Tbsp. shortening

1. In a microwave-safe bowl, combine all ingredients. Cover and microwave on high for 1½ minutes; stir. Microwave, uncovered, on high 30 seconds longer; stir until smooth.
2. Pour into miniature muffin liners. Place on a baking sheet; refrigerate until set. Store in the refrigerator.
NOTE: Reduced-fat or generic brands of peanut butter are not recommended for this recipe.
1 CANDY: 85 cal., 6g fat (3g sat. fat), 1mg chol., 31mg sod., 7g carb. (5g sugars, 0 fiber), 2g pro.

READER REVIEW
"This is my no-fail treat for bake sales!"
—AKMOMOF6, TASTEOFHOME.COM

CHRISTMAS LIGHTS COOKIES

What better way to brighten chilly winter days than with light-shaped cookies? My classic dough recipe has been a holiday tradition in our family for years.
—*Carolyn Moseley, Dayton, OH*

Prep: 45 min. + chilling
Bake: 10 min./batch + cooling
Makes: 1½ dozen

½ cup butter, softened
½ cup sugar
1 large egg, room temperature
¾ tsp. vanilla extract
¼ tsp. almond extract
1¾ cups all-purpose flour
½ tsp. ground cinnamon
¼ tsp. salt
¼ tsp. baking powder

FROSTING
5 cups confectioners' sugar
1 Tbsp. light corn syrup
¾ tsp. vanilla extract
5 to 6 Tbsp. water
   Red, blue, green, yellow and gray paste food coloring
   Assorted colored sugar, optional

1. In a large bowl, cream butter and sugar until light and fluffy, 5-7 minutes. Beat in egg and extracts. In another bowl, whisk flour, cinnamon, salt and baking powder; gradually beat into creamed mixture. Shape into a disk; wrap and refrigerate 1 hour or until firm enough to roll.
2. Preheat oven to 350°. On a lightly floured surface, roll dough to ⅛-in. thickness. Cut with a floured 4-in. Christmas light-shaped cookie cutter. Place 1 in. apart on ungreased baking sheets. Bake 9-11 minutes or until light brown. Remove from pans to wire racks to cool completely.
3. In a small bowl, beat confectioners' sugar, corn syrup, vanilla and enough water to reach desired consistency. Reserve ⅔ cup frosting for bottom of cookies and reflections. Divide remaining frosting between 4 bowls. Tint 1 red, 1 blue, 1 green and 1 yellow. Frost tops of cookies. If desired, sprinkle with colored sugar. Tint half of the reserved frosting gray; frost bottom of cookies. With remaining white frosting and a #5 round tip, pipe on the reflections. Let stand until completely set.
TO MAKE AHEAD: Dough can be made 2 days in advance. Wrap and store in an airtight container in the refrigerator.
FREEZE OPTION: Freeze undecorated cookies in freezer containers. To use, thaw in covered containers and decorate as desired.
1 COOKIE: 250 cal., 6g fat (3g sat. fat), 24mg chol., 86mg sod., 49g carb. (39g sugars, 0 fiber), 2g pro.

WATCH US
DECORATE
THE
CHRISTMAS
LIGHTS
Just hover your
camera here.

CHOCOLATE YULE LOG

For many years, this impressive rolled cake has been a favorite Christmas dessert for our family— everyone just loves it! I'm also asked to bring it to our annual church Christmas function.
—*Bernadette Colvin, Tomball, TX*

Prep: 50 min. • **Bake:** 10 min. + cooling
Makes: 12 servings

- 4 large eggs, separated
- ⅔ cup sugar, divided
- ½ cup all-purpose flour
- 2 Tbsp. baking cocoa
- 1 tsp. baking powder
- ¼ tsp. salt

FILLING
- 1 cup heavy whipping cream
- 2 Tbsp. sugar
- ¼ tsp. almond extract

FROSTING
- ½ cup butter, softened
- 2 cups confectioners' sugar
- 2 oz. unsweetened chocolate, melted
- 2 Tbsp. 2% milk
- 2 tsp. vanilla extract

1. Place the egg whites in large bowl; let stand at room temperature for 30 minutes. Line a greased 15x10x1-in. baking pan with parchment; grease the paper and set aside.

2. Preheat oven to 375°. In a large bowl, beat egg yolks on high speed for 5 minutes or until thick and lemon-colored. Gradually beat in ⅓ cup sugar. Sift flour, baking cocoa, baking powder and salt together twice; gradually add to yolk mixture and mix well (batter will be very thick).

3. With clean beaters, beat egg whites on medium speed until soft peaks form. Gradually beat in remaining sugar, 1 Tbsp. at a time, on high until stiff peaks form. Gradually fold into batter. Spread evenly into prepared pan.

4. Bake until cake springs back when lightly touched, 10-12 minutes. Cool for 5 minutes. Turn cake onto a kitchen towel dusted with cocoa powder. Gently peel off parchment. Roll up cake in towel, jelly-roll style, starting with a short side; cool completely on a wire rack.

5. Meanwhile, for the filling, beat cream in a large bowl until soft peaks form. Gradually add sugar and almond extract, beating until stiff peaks form. Unroll cake; spread filling to within 1 in. of edges. Roll up again.

6. In a large bowl, cream butter and confectioners' sugar until light and fluffy, 3-4 minutes. Beat in chocolate, milk and vanilla until smooth. Frost the cake, using a metal spatula to create a bark-like effect.

1 PIECE: 245 cal., 14g fat (8g sat. fat), 89mg chol., 143mg sod., 29g carb. (24g sugars, 1g fiber), 3g pro.

CHOCOLATE YULE LOG TIPS

- **How do you roll a Yule log without breaking it?** The most important thing you can do to prevent breakage is to avoid overbaking the cake. This can make it dry and crumbly. Since this cake is tender and can tear easily, work slowly when spreading the filling and rolling the cake in a clean towel. Cool the rolled cake seam side down to prevent it from unrolling.

- **How can you make the frosting and decorations look realistic on a chocolate Yule log?** Make it look like your Yule log has bark by dragging a small palette knife and/or a fork lengthwise through the frosting. There's no need for straight lines, because wavy lines make it look more realistic. You can decorate your chocolate Yule log with cinnamon sticks, fresh rosemary sprigs, cinnamon candies or even meringue mushrooms to give it a woodland look. Take it over the top by dusting the entire log with a light snowfall of confectioners' sugar!

- **How do I make the candied cranberry garnish?** Heat 3 Tbsp. light corn syrup in microwave until warm; gently toss with 1 cup fresh or frozen cranberries, allowing excess syrup to drip off. Toss berries in ⅓ cup sugar to coat. Place on waxed paper; let stand until set, about 1 hour.

NO-CHURN EGGNOG ICE CREAM

As a fanatical lover of all things eggnog, I adore this soft-serve eggnog ice cream. Served with gingerbread or holiday cookies, it's bound to find a place in your heart too.
—Colleen Delawder, Herndon, VA

Prep: 10 min. + freezing
Makes: 8 servings

- 2 cups eggnog
- 1 cup heavy whipping cream
- ½ cup sugar
- ¼ cup spiced rum
- ½ tsp. ground cinnamon
- ½ tsp. ground nutmeg

Place all ingredients in a blender; process until thickened, 1-2 minutes. Transfer to freezer containers, allowing headspace for expansion. Freeze until firm, several hours or overnight.
½ CUP: 222 cal., 14g fat (9g sat. fat), 71mg chol., 43mg sod., 19g carb. (19g sugars, 0 fiber), 4g pro.

EGGNOG ICE CREAM TIPS

- **How long does eggnog ice cream last?** Ice cream's flavor and texture can degrade in your freezer over time, so it's best to eat it within 1 month. We guarantee this eggnog ice cream will not last that long, though! Store your ice cream in a shallow, airtight, lidded container, preferably made of glass, metal or freezer-safe plastic. In a pinch, loaf pans or pie plates work quite well—just make sure all of your ice cream will fit in the container and that you can keep it tightly covered to prevent freezer burn.

- **What can you mix into eggnog ice cream?** Once your ice cream has frozen to a point where it can be softly stirred, crumble up Biscoff cookies or amaretti and swirl the crumbs into the ice cream for an extra bit of flavor and texture. For a real holiday treat, add crumbled bits of gingerbread!

GINGERBREAD SANDWICH TREES

Fun and festive, these cookie sandwich trees will be a huge hit with kids of all ages.
—Steve Foy, Kirkwood, MO

Prep: 25 min. + chilling
Bake: 10 min./batch + cooling
Makes: about 2 dozen

- ¾ cup butter, softened
- 1 cup packed brown sugar
- 1 large egg, room temperature
- ¾ cup molasses
- 4 cups all-purpose flour
- 3 tsp. pumpkin pie spice
- 1½ tsp. baking soda
- 1¼ tsp. ground ginger
- ¼ tsp. salt
  M&M's minis
- ¾ cup vanilla or chocolate frosting
  Green food coloring, optional

1. Cream butter and brown sugar until light and fluffy, 5-7 minutes. Beat in egg and molasses. In another bowl, whisk flour, pie spice, baking soda, ginger and salt; gradually beat into the creamed mixture. Refrigerate, covered, until easy to handle, about 2 hours.
2. Preheat oven to 325°. On a lightly floured surface, roll dough to ⅛-in. thickness. Cut with a floured 3-in. tree-shaped cookie cutter. Place 2 in. apart on ungreased baking sheets. Gently press M&M's into half of the cookies. Bake until edges are firm, 8-10 minutes. Remove to wire racks to cool completely.
3. If using vanilla frosting, tint with green food coloring if desired. Spread frosting over bottoms of plain cookies; cover with decorated cookies. Store in an airtight container.
1 SANDWICH COOKIE: 230 cal., 7g fat (4g sat. fat), 23mg chol., 176mg sod., 38g carb. (21g sugars, 1g fiber), 3g pro.

DECORATED SPRITZ

A touch of almond extract gives these spritz cookies wonderful flavor. For Christmas, you could tint half of the dough with red food coloring and the other half with green.

—*Irmgard Sinn, Sherwood Park, AB*

- -

Prep: 20 min.
Bake: 15 min./batch + cooling
Makes: 4 dozen

1	cup butter, softened
⅔	cup sugar
1	large egg, room temperature
½	tsp. almond extract
½	tsp. vanilla extract
2¼	cups all-purpose flour
1	tsp. baking powder
	Prepared frosting, assorted sprinkles and decorating sugars

1. In a large bowl, cream butter and sugar until light and fluffy, 5-7 minutes. Beat in egg and extracts. Combine the flour and baking powder; gradually add to the creamed mixture.

2. Using a cookie press fitted with the disk of your choice, press dough 1 in. apart onto ungreased baking sheets. Bake at 350° until the edges are firm and lightly browned, 12-13 minutes. Remove to wire racks to cool. Frost and decorate as desired.

1 COOKIE: 68 cal., 4g fat (2g sat. fat), 14mg chol., 42mg sod., 7g carb. (3g sugars, 0 fiber), 1g pro.

READER REVIEW

"This is nearly the same as the spritz cookie recipe that's been used in my family for 50 years. The only differences: I use three egg yolks instead of one whole egg, and no baking powder. The egg yolks make the cookies extra tender. In my family, it's not Christmastime until the spritz cookies get made. I always make them green and use my Christmas tree disk for the cookie press. I carefully pack them in tins and send to my three brothers who live across the country ... just like our mom used to do for them once they moved away from home."

—MEHRESMA, TASTEOFHOME.COM

General Index

Alphabetical Index